PUTTING SYSTEMS TO WORK

PUTTING SYSTEMS TO WORK

Derek K. Hitchins
Royal Military College of Science
Cranfield at Shrivenham, UK

JOHN WILEY & SONS
Chichester • New York • Brisbane • Toronto • Singapore

Copyright © 1992 by John Wiley & Sons Ltd,
Baffins Lane, Chichester,
West Sussex PO19 1UD, England

Other Wiley Editorial Offices

John Wiley & Sons, Inc., 605 Third Avenue,
New York, NY 10158-0012, USA

Jacaranda Wiley Ltd, G.P.O. Box 859, Brisbane,
Queensland 4001, Australia

John Wiley & Sons (Canada) Ltd, 22 Worcester Road,
Rexdale, Ontario M9W 1L1, Canada

John Wiley & Sons (SEA) Pte Ltd, 37 Jalan Pemimpin #05-04,
Block B, Union Industrial Building, Singapore 2057

Library of Congress Cataloging-in-Publication Data

Hitchins, Derek.
    Putting systems to work / Derek Hitchins.
        p.   cm.
    Includes bibliographical references and index.
    ISBN 0-471-93426-7
    1. System design.   2. Systems engineering.   I. Title.
QA76.9.S88H58   1992
003—dc20   91–42834
                                                    CIP

British Library Cataloguing in Publication Data

A catalogue record for this book is available from the British Library

ISBN 0-471-93426-7

Printed and bound in Great Britain by Biddles Ltd, Guildford and King's Lynn

To my beloved wife,
without whom ...
very little.

Contents

Part B—System Building Blocks

Part C—System Synthesis

Part D—Future Vision?

About the Book

We humans have a habit of classifying things, of putting them into separate pigeonholes—so much so that at times we cannot see the essential similarity between them. We produce great volumes about the differences between things, losing sight of their essential sameness. Consider animals. How many have dual brains, single hearts, twin kidneys, four limbs each with five digits, one liver, and so on? If, instead of searching for differences, we looked for similarities, might we see something rather interesting? Why five digits? Why not four or six? Why two kidneys, but only one liver? How was this common pattern derived, and why has it proved so successful?

This is not a book about animals or plants or anything in particular. It is more a book about everything in general—a book about systems, what they are, how we can view them and, above all, how we can make systems ideas useful to us in everyday life. It is also very much my own. I have admired many other systems thinkers, but all too often their work has left me lacking a clear mental image and a set of basic system principles which I can put to useful work.

I have seen students grappling with "soft" and "hard" systems philosophies and being greatly confused in the process. They have difficulty in grasping the concept of an *open* system—a difficulty shared by many scientists and engineers. Yet virtually all real systems are open, that is, they receive inflows and pass outflows continually. "You are what you eat" says the dietitian. How true; we humans are open systems with every single part of us absorbed and constructed from ingested substance. But families, schools, universities, businesses, plants, governments, ecologies—all are open systems. Even a mechanical clock is an open system—who winds it, who reads the time? Schools and universities, open systems though they may be, teach mainly closed systems philosophies

Classical science and engineering concentrate on closed systems. Physics and the second law of thermodynamics would have us believe that entropy, the degree of disorder, is increasing with time in a closed system. But if the systems we see and interact with daily are open systems, that knowledge is not very useful. Could this be why classical science and engineering are out of step with the times? Certainly as our social fabric becomes more sophisticated and interwoven, the general level of satisfaction with technological solutions to social problems receives less approbation. Nuclear energy, genetic engineering, stock market instability—the contribution of science and technology can be questioned. But perhaps the greatest question hangs over our environment, now and in the future. Industry with its engineering-fuelled revolution is continuing to foul our biosphere. We may introduce new philosophies like "cost-effectiveness" or "just-in-time" or even "quality chains", but they overlook the effects of their aggregation. For example, if a variety of industries in an area are all operating cost-effectively, is the overall economy cost-effective? Will the local environment continue to support those industries?

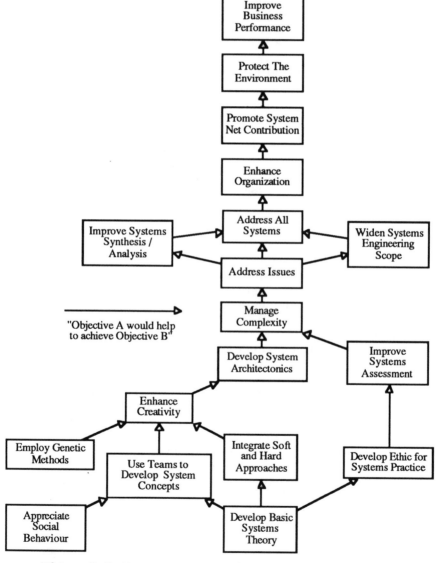

Figure 1. Putting systems to work—the topics and objectives

In developing the ideas for this book, then, I perceived the need for an ethic, presently difficult to see in operation anywhere, which would promote harmonious living, prosperous business, etc., but which would simultaneously preserve the environment.

The objectives of the book are shown Figure 1 which, since it is a book about systems, has been organized systematically into a so-called intent structure. Pervasive objectives are at the bottom of the diagram, while superior objectives (those to which all the others contribute) are at the top. This type of structure is often used in the development of mission statements for organizations, so I suppose my mission statement is:—

"To develop a sound systems ethic and systems methods that will improve the performance of systems, organizations and businesses while preserving the environment."

Figure 2, intended as a guide or route map, shows the parts and chapters in the book and their inter-relationships. There are four distinct but inter-related parts, progressing from basic systems notions and principles, through the establishment of some building blocks, through to full systems synthesis. Here, classical systems engineering is addressed, as a basis for comparison with, and foundation for, a New Systems Engineering. Finally, I unashamedly indulge myself with speculation about the way in which some aspects of system design might be undertaken in the future.

In some cases, the objectives from Figure 1 map into Figure 2 directly; the objective "enhance creativity" maps to Chapter 9, "Creativity", at least in part. For other objectives, the mapping is less simple and there are no chapters which correspond to the objectives "protect the environment" and "improve business performance", since both of these are hoped-for outcomes.

Running as a theme throughout the book is the notion of traversing systematically from soft, unstructured ideas to firmer concepts and eventually to hard, specific system solutions to needs. This so-called "bridging" from soft to hard is at variance with many current practices, where the vogue is to polarize toward one or other mode of thinking. To me such polarization is counter-productive; "soft" and "hard" exist on a continuum in the same sense as do "vague" and "precise", and system practitioners should be able, and should be encouraged, to operate wherever the need arises along that continuum, but would generally move from the higher to the lower entropy, since reducing entropy or disorder has surely to be the common theme of all systems practice.

You need no special skills to understand this book, although a science and/or engineering background may help. You do need an open and curious mind. It has been developed from work in industry and from undergraduate and postgraduate lectures and projects, but experienced systems practitioners with no formal qualifications should find it useful.

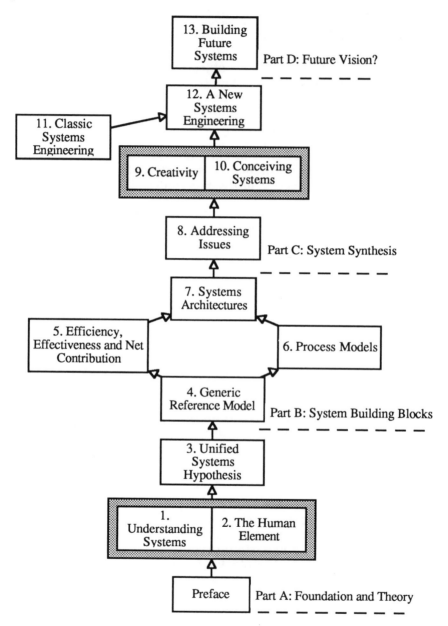

Figure 2. Putting Systems to Work—parts, chapters and relationships. The so-called "intent structure" of this diagram will be used throughout the book and is explained in Chapter 9

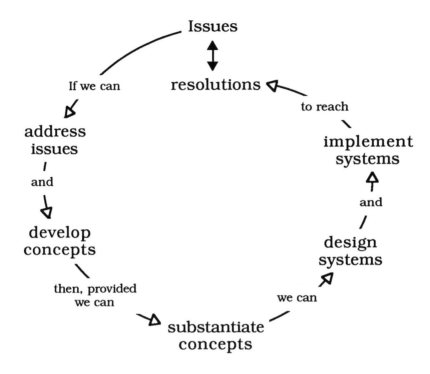

Figure 3. Bridging from soft to hard. The objective is to move from vague, unstructured issues progressively towards solutions to those issues. Progress requires understanding, the development of robust solution concepts and the implementation of those solutions to resolve the original issue, hopefully in a way that avoids creating more problems in the process

I hope you enjoy the book; it is intended to be read, but above all to be used. Use it to address problems and issues, to derive solutions or perhaps even to understand why solutions are not always practicable in the real world.

Derek Hitchins

Part A

Foundation and Theory

Outputs

Basis for Issue, Concept Development
and New Systems Engineering Methods

Universal, Scale
-independant
USH Principles of
Interacting Systems

Complementary
Systems

3. Unified
Systems
Hypothesis

Systems
Science

1.
Understanding
Systems

2. The Human
Element

Inductive
Reasoning

Systems
Philosophy

Contemporary
Systems
Thinking

Decision
Research

Social
Psychology

Inputs

Chapter 1
Understanding Systems

Wisdom is the principal thing; therefore get wisdom:
and with all thy wisdom, get understanding...
Proverbs, 4:7

AN INTRODUCTION TO SYSTEMS

If, like me, you have spent most of your time in engineering, operations, maintenance, marketing or management, you may not have noticed the systems revolution. Names like Bertalanffy, Ackoff and Boulding probably mean nothing to you. This introduction presents a brief overview of systems principles and of the main thrusts in developing systems concepts.

Where to start? First, let's delve into a few general ideas. For instance, if we are about to think about them—systems, that is—what are they?

- Complex whole, set of connected things or parts; organized body of material or immaterial things
- Group of bodies moving about one another in space under some dynamic law, such as gravitation
- Set of organs or parts in animal body of same or similar structure, or subserving the same function; animal body as a whole
- Department of knowledge or belief considered as an organized whole—comprehensive body of doctrines, beliefs, theories, practices, etc, forming particular philosophy, religion, form of government, etc.
- Orderly arrangement or method

Or so the dictionary says. Now, if you find those definitions a little all-embracing, so you should. "System" is a broad concept—so broad, perhaps, that it might seem impossible to find common ground between the various definitions. And then there are the spin-off words:

- Systematic—methodical, arranged, conducted according to system or organized plan

- Systemic—of, affecting a whole system, of the system or body as a whole

All these definitions, not surprisingly, give rise to a variety of viewpoints, or *Weltanschauungen*—world views in English. If we can look at a system from different viewpoints, perhaps we can see different features and gain a better understanding. Consider a football match:

- A team contest
- An entertainment
- A means of making money
- A means of losing money
- A meeting place for rival gangs to work-out
- A means of employing policemen
- A means of training policemen in crowd control

The bullets represent different *Weltanshauungen*—the development of different viewpoints when exploring a problem situation is a keystone of modern systems thinking.

So, when did this quiet systems revolution take place? Recently, is the best answer, and mostly this century, with the pace accelerating during and after World War II. It is a young discipline, concerned with a different way of thinking about the world. In particular, it is concerned with wholes—holistic. Much of the more recent work has been directed toward organization and the understanding/management of complexity. The systems discipline is a natural successor to conventional disciplines—physics, engineering, management, biology, etc.—by the process of abstraction and the identification of isomorphisms. To use the jargon, it is a meta-discipline, sitting "above" conventional disciplines, seeking to provide an umbrella over them, and to establish a comprehensive and universal set of principles.

Peter Checkland (1981) of Lancaster University, who has had a significant impact on systems thinking in the UK in particular, gives an excellent discourse on the evolving systems movement, (and I have no intention of trying to compete with his masterly work). Many people have been influential in this developing shift in perception. Chief among them must be the following, whose views have been selected and paraphrased for relevance to the themes of this book:

- *C. West Churchman* observed, *inter alia*, that the systems debate is concerned with the values of those who wish to intervene in human systems by means of science or planning, or some other method.

> ...individual human values....cannot be represented ....by any kind of explicit assumption-making method...because the real values of a person (cannot)...be determined by any kind of "investigation" by either scientist planner, or anyone else. Churchman, 1968

- *T. S. Kuhn* is attributed with originating the term "paradigm shift". This most influential of thinkers addressed the concept of a body of knowledge, which makes experiments meaningful. He studied the history of science and proposed that science made advances discontinuously, with periodic changes of viewpoint among the body of scientists as a whole. Between such shifts, scientists conducted experiments which were largely concerned with filling-in the detail of the viewpoint. As time passed, inconsistencies between the commonly-held viewpoint and the evidence accumulated until the difference between the two was sufficient to trigger a change, which then seemed to occur rapidly

- *Karl R. Popper* addressed, amongst many other matters, the logic of the way in which scientific progress is made, for example proof by deduction as opposed to proof by induction. If some situations or problems deny the opportunity for classical scientific controlled experimentation, then progress has to be made by some other means. (Such situations include not only complex human issues, but astrophysical problems, too.) Popper used the example of the black swan to illustrate the limitations of proof by induction. Proof that all swans are white could be undertaken by progressively searching the world and finding more and more swans to be white—which theory would be confounded by eventually finding black swans in Australia. Theorists could then either accept the theory to be wrong or *might* be motivated to re-categorize 'swan' as white by definition ...

  Popper addresses the *principle of falsifiability*, in which theories could be viewed according to whether they could be determined to be true or false. A theory which enables prediction, also lends itself to being proved false if that prediction is incorrect.

- *Sir Geoffrey Vickers* presented the view that, in well-defined habitats, densities and mutual relationships of inhabitants tend toward a stable form, owing to three basic factors :

  (1) Amount of energy generated by the system

  (2) Volume of information on which the system relies

  (3) Needs which members of the system must satisfy.

In Western societies many of these constancies are disappearing, affecting system stability, while the institutions which cause disturbance and instability are unlikely to provide solutions.

Hence, political dialogue is essential among the mediators of change:

> " The responsibilities for policy making....must be more clearly identified by our culture and ....institutions if our policy making is to ensure our 'balancing', let alone the most modest ' optimising'."

> Vickers, 1983,The Art of Judgement: A Study of Policy Making

GESTALT AND GESTALTEN

Gestalt is a German word without a clear English equivalent; the best translation lies somewhere between "pattern" and "configuration".   The Gestalt movement started early in the twentieth century (Rock and Palmer, 1990); Gestalt psychology was launched in 1912 by Wertheimer who published a paper on the visual illusion of movement formed by presenting a series of still pictures. The central tenet of Gestalt psychology was that the whole was greater than the sum of the parts; what people perceived was not simply a sum or sequence of sensations, but a whole entity, of which the sensations were part but which alone did not explain the whole. Gestalt theory was holistic; it embraced the concept of emergent properties (q.v.). Koehler, a Gestaltist, held that many physical systems, which he dubbed *Gestalten*, evolved towards a state of equilibrium (Koehler, 1970).   Soap bubbles evolved towards a spherical shape, for example, because that shape was a minimum energy configuration.   The human brain was considered to be another example of *Gestalten.*

Gestalt has left a legacy, often overlooked, but nonetheless deeply embedded in today's systems thinking.   Contemporary systems engineering, for example, seems in practice to owe more to Gestalt than to operations research, since ideas of holism and emergence are firmly embedded whereas mathematical optimization might be pushed by academics but finds little consonance with systems engineers.

HARD AND SOFT, OPEN AND CLOSED

Systems practitioners presently fall into several camps, chief among which are management science, operations research and systems engineering. Different kinds of system are considered and, since some are intractable, the different camps have followed different routes.   There seem to be two fundamental schisms in thinking: the hard/soft and the open/closed.

Hard systems viewpoints are basically those held by designers and engineers who are trying to create systems to meet an understood need in an effective and economic manner. Those in the soft camp caricature the approach as "head-down", concerned with optimization, obsessed with quantitative metrics and highly pragmatic. So much so, in fact, that the term 'systems thinking' has been purloined by the soft camp as though they alone thought! The soft camp use the term "engineer's philosophy", not too endearingly, to describe the hard approach, in which the requirement is stated by a customer and the engineer satisfies the requirement without question. A fairer description follows:

> A certain objective is given; to find ways and means for its realization requires the system specialist (or team of specialists) to consider alternative solutions and to choose those offering optimization at maximum efficiency and minimum cost in a tremendously complex network of interactions. *von Bertalanffy*, 1973

Soft systems viewpoints are those held by behavioural, management, social anthropology, social psychology and other science students concerned with observing the living world, and in particular the human world. Human activity systems (HASs) are "messy", in that they do not exhibit a clear need or purpose—if they can be said to exhibit purpose at all. Indeed, so complex is the real world of people that the idea of driving towards optimal solutions may be a non-starter—perhaps we should see if we can simply understand and concern ourselves with improving the situation. Peter Checkland put it like this:

> Hard systems thinkers view systems like a bag of marbles; you can put your hand in the bag, remove a marble, examine it, replace it and all is well. Soft systems thinkers view systems like a privet hedge; if you try to pull out a branch, you will strip off its leaves and twigs, damage the hedge in the process, and it is not replaceable.

In the light of such thoughts, some questions emerge:

- Can the scientific method cope with the complexities associated with human activity (social) systems ?
- Can we produce hypotheses commensurate with the complexity of the system ?
- Can experiments be carried out which do not disturb the fabric they seek to study ?
- Can we manage complexity by reducing a complex whole into understandable, manageable parts ?
- Can we study parts of society separately and join the parts together meaningfully ?

Kenneth Boulding (1956), one of the founding fathers of General Systems Theory, developed a system classification as shown in

Table 1.1 According to Kast and Rosenzweig (1972), the first three levels in the hierarchy can be classified as physical or mechanical systems, i.e. hard, and are the province of of the physical sciences, such as physics and astronomy. The fourth, fifth and sixth levels are concerned with biological systems and are the province of biologists, botanists and zoologists. The last three levels are the concern of the social sciences and of the arts, humanities and religion. So, as we ascend the hierarchy we seem to becoming progressively "softer". Where do "open" and "closed" come in? Boulding's classification[1] suggests that closed may be taken as the first three levels, the remainder being open. A closed system is one which receives no external inputs and gives no outputs externally either. One might describe a mechanical clock as a closed system and, to our knowledge, the universe is a closed system.

Table 1.1 Boulding's classification of systems

LEVEL	CHARACTERISTICS	EXAMPLE
1. Structures	Static	Bridges
2. Clock works	Predetermined motion	Solar system
3. Controls	Closed loop control	Thermostat
4. Open	Self-maintaining	Biological cells
5. Lower organisms	Growth, reproduction	Plants
6. Animals	Brain, learning	Birds
7. Man	Knowledge, symbolism	Humans
8. Social	Communication, value	Families
9. Transcendental	Unknowables	God

On the other hand, a biological cell is an open system, in that it receives nutrient and energy through the cell wall and disposes of waste and enzymes, etc., outwards, organizing and maintaining itself in the process. As such, its size and constituents need not be constant, it may vary in internal energy and—most particularly—it may reduce its entropy. Closed systems are obliged to observe the second law of thermodynamics; open systems invoke a revision of that law. Similarly, closed systems generally employ feedback to stabilize themselves, whereas open systems need not. An open system without feedback may be thought of simplistically as a bath with the taps running and the plug left out—the level in the bath is set by the difference between inflow and outflow rates. With the taps left full on, a fixed level in the bath would arise only if the outflow increased as the water level rose.

---

[1] It is noteworthy that each proponent of a viewpoint about systems seems intent on capturing the high ground for his own view. So, human systems are "above" biological, which are "above" hard.

It is widely proposed and accepted that living systems are open, as are human activity systems, organizations, companies, ecologies, etc. Indeed, the clock, our archetypal closed system, requires external energy to maintain operation, and is part of a system for recording and presenting the passage of time to humans, who put the energy in and take the information out—so is a clock *really* a closed system? In general, it would seem to be prudent to start by assuming that all systems-to-be-understood are open until proven otherwise. Systems may be considered in principle by: rate of change, purpose or connectivity.

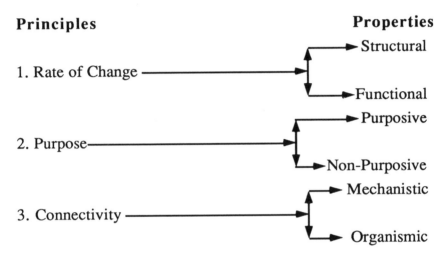

Figure 1.1 Jordan's taxonomy

Jordan's (1968) taxonomy of systems adopts a different perspective, as shown by Figure1.1. These considerations lead to categorization of the system in question as structural, if the rate of change is slow, or functional if fast. Similarly, systems are purposive or non-purposive, where purposive is the attribution of purpose by an observer outside the system. Finally, a system is mechanistic or organismic. If mechanistic, then the parts of the system are not strongly interdependent, while organismic means that such interdependence is strong. This last criterion is, perhaps, a little difficult to understand. Checkland (1981) gives the example of a bubble as organismic, since to remove part of it would destroy the whole. A pile of rubble, on the other hand, would be mechanistic since to remove one part would not necessarily affect the whole.

Checkland (1981) also categorizes systems, as shown in Figure 1.2. Within this categorization, the seeming absence of a socio-technical system is notable. For example, is an information system any one of the categories, or is it a combination of, say, designed-physical systems and human activity systems?

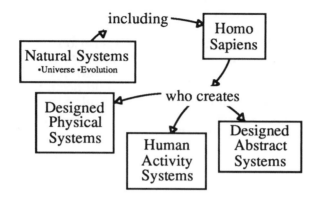

Figure 1.2 Checkland's categorization of systems

EMERGENCE AND HIERARCHY

Explanations of these system fundamentals are as follows:

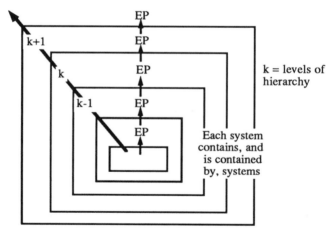

Figure 1.3 Emergence and hierarchy

- Emergence, emergent properties—the principle that whole
  entities exhibit properties which are meaningful only when
  attributed to the whole, not to its parts, e.g. the picture emerging
  from a completed jigsaw, the self-awareness of a brain. Every
  system exhibits emergent properties which derive from its
  component activities and structure, but cannot be reduced to
  them. The concept of emergence is fundamental to systems
  thinking, analysis and synthesis (q.v.).

- Hierarchy - the principle according to which entities meaningfully treated as wholes are built up of smaller entities which themselves are wholes, and so on. In a hierarchy, emergent properties denote levels

The concept of emergence is truly fundamental, and is of great importance in systems engineering. for example, it is quite reasonable to define the primary task of systems engineering as:

"To identify, realize and maintain the requisite emergent properties of a system to meet customers' and end-users' needs."

CYBERNETICS

Figure 1.4 presents the so-called cybernetic model:

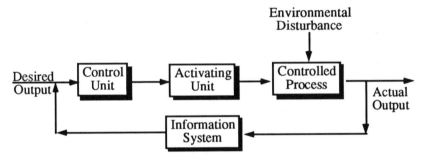

- CU compares Actual with Desired Output
- AU receives signals from CU - responds by making changes in CP
- CP - that which is being controlled
- IS - measures actual output, relays information to CU

Figure 1.4 The cybernetic model

The model is used in a wide sphere of activities, soft and hard. Definitions of cybernetics include:

... the science of effective communication in man and machine".
Norbert Wiener
... cybernetics is the science of effective organization. Stafford Beer

The characteristics associated with cybernetic systems include :

- Complex
- Dynamic

- Probabilistic
- Integrated
- Open

Stafford Beer (1985) has taken the cybernetic model as the basis for his "viable systems model", an interesting view of organizations, which employs W Ross Ashby's (1956) important "law of requisite variety" as its cornerstone. This law may be stated as follows:

> *Given a system with a regulatory process R, intended to maintain a goal state G, but affected by a disturbance D: the goal state G can only be maintained if the regulator R has sufficient variety and channel capacity to counter the variety in D*

Many people subscribe to the cybernetic model as the basis for all conscious or unconscious controlled action, stability, etc. As we have already seen, stability need not depend on feedback in open systems—although it is commonly found so to do.

Some important cybernetic principles are proposed as follows :

- Complex systems organize themselves
- Complex systems have basins of stability separated by thresholds of instability
- Outputs that are important to a system will have feedback loops

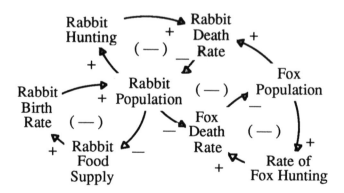

Figure 1.5 Cybernetic loop generation

Figure 1.5 represents a complex system of interactions between rabbits, foxes, fox-hunting and rabbit food supplies. Such a system, comprising at least four negative feedback loops as shown, will tend towards a stable configuration. It evidently does organize itself after a fashion and outputs do seem to have feedback, although whether on the basis of "being important to a system" or not is a moot point. Such complex systems can prove dynamically stable, oscillating to a regular pattern.

MACHINE AGE VERSUS SYSTEMS AGE

Most scientists and engineers are raised on the concept of reductionism as fundamental. These are based on Descartes' principles of 1637:

- Accept only that which is clear and distinct as true
- Divide each difficulty into as many parts as possible
- Start with the simplest elements and move by an orderly procedure to the more complex
- Make complete enumerations and reviews to make certain that nothing was omitted

Systems thinking has been directed along the reductionist path since that time, which Russell Ackoff (1981) refers to as the Machine Age. Now, he states, we are in the Systems Age, which needs to take a different approach.

Table 1.2 Machine-age thinking versus system-age thinking

MACHINE AGE	SYSTEMS AGE
Procedure:	Procedure:
1. Decompose that which is to be explained (decomposition)	1. Identify a containing system of which the thing to be explained is part
2. Explain the the behaviour or properties of the contained parts separately	2. Explain the behaviour or properties of the containing whole
3. Aggregate these explanations into an explanation of the whole (synthesis)	3. The explain the behaviour of the thing to be explained in terms of its *role(s)* and *function(s)* within its containing whole.

For example, a machine age thinker faced with the need to explain a company would begin by considering its department and divisions, would describe what each of them does and then would explain how they worked together to operate as a company. A systems age thinker would start by identifying a system containing the company, say the industrial system, and would then define the functions or objectives of the industrial system with reference to an even wider social system that contains it. Finally, he would explain the company in terms of its rôles and functions in the industrial system. Evidently, analysis (reduction) and synthesis both have their place.

MACHINE-AGE ANALYSIS	SYSTEMS AGE SYNTHESIS
Analysis focuses on structure; it reveals how things work	Synthesis focuses on function; it reveals why things operate as they do
Analysis yields *knowledge*	Synthesis yields *understanding*
Analysis enables description	Synthesis enables explanation
Analysis looks *into* things	Synthesis looks *out* of things

Table 1.3 Machine-age analysis versus system-age synthesis

In systems design, parts identified by analysis of the function(s) to be performed by the whole are not put together like unchangeable pieces of a jigsaw puzzle; they are designed to fit each other so as to work together harmoniously as well as efficiently and effectively. Ackoff (1981)

PRESENT LIMITATIONS IN SYSTEMS ENGINEERING METHODS

Systems engineering method is perhaps best exemplified by the work of Gwilym M. Jenkins (1972). He considered that systems engineering was concerned with the optimal use of resources of all kinds. The major resources were the four Ms:

• Men   • Machines • Materials   • Money

Systems engineering was, moreover, a multi-disciplinary approach, becoming progressively more essential to accommodate increasing complexity in engineering systems.
He described 4 phases in the systems engineering approach:

1. Systems analysis
2. Systems design
3. Implementation
4. Operation

Each phase was progressively broken-down into further set of activities, making systems engineering "an orderly and well-disciplined way of getting things done". Jenkins thus presented the systems engineering approach as logical, rational but not seemingly based on any science in the way that other branches of engineering were, such as mechanical or electrical engineering.   Instead of theory, there has arisen a "theology" of systems engineering.

The Systems Engineering Theology

There is within the minds of most practitioners a wide acceptance of the meaning of "the systems approach". In broad terms, there is a kernel "top down" approach to system design, which supposedly pursues the following path:

A Start at the highest abstract level of system requirement description
B Functionally decompose the requirement
C Map the decomposed functions to the elements of a physical architecture
D Develop, and progressively integrate the physical elements into a system

Hall (1962;1989) provides a more detailed, classical view of the steps in systems engineering. Unfortunately, there is no generally accepted way to achieve the first three steps, although many systems engineers have patent methods of their own; it is perhaps for this reason that some observers regard systems engineering more as an arcane art-form than a science-based engineering discipline.

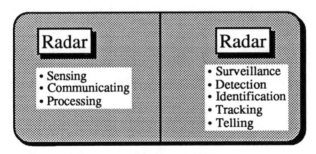

Figure 1.6 The notion of function. The decomposition at left is physical, not functional. The functional breakdown at right is concerned with purpose, and each element cannot be wholly attributed to any one part of the radar

A function is activity, or set of activities, performed by a system. Beyond that simple statement, there is no consensus on the meaning of "function" in the systems approach. Many experienced systems engineers cannot establish the range of functions in, say, a radar system. The usual first decomposition is into sensors, communications, processing and display.   Unfortunately, that turns out to be most unhelpful since these so-called functions apply to almost every system of significance and hence the division offers no insight into a particular system.

The point can best be understood by attempting to functionally decompose a human being. To start at sensors (all five), nerves and brain is not really helpful: not only is it true for all animals (and therefore offers no discrimination or differentiation), but the decomposition misses out the interesting parts of the human design. Functions, then, are best considered as activities performed by the system as a whole which, although supported by parts within the system, cannot be wholly attributed to any one of those parts. If this definition is redolent of that for emergent properties, then all to the good: it seems most appropriate that both function and emergent property should share common roots.

Similarly, functional-to-physical mapping is obscure in practice, with most practitioners unwilling to be drawn on their methods, which are often therefore declared to be "obvious". These methods generally recognize the complexity of interfaces between groups of functions and attempt to group functions so as to reduce the residual interface complexity between the resulting groups. The methods tend to be difficult to justify under pressure, the more so since they are generally based on an uncertain definition of functions to be grouped.

Part of the systems engineering theology includes the development of design options, their modelling and subsequent tradeoff to select the most cost-effective solution. Choosing the appropriate range of design options from which to trade is, at the best, a crude art. Modelling of systems is becoming increasingly expensive, although there is a growing tendency to prototype information systems. Trading between options often employs dubious weighting-and-scoring techniques. And there is, surprisingly, no agreed way of defining what the term "cost-effective" means.

All in all, it has to be said that the theology on which systems engineering is supposed to be based has some dubious foundations. Systems engineering survives, even thrives, despite this lack of scientific underpinning, principally because it is a theology, a way of approaching problems that is axiomatically sound. It must be better to approach a problem top-down, to view the whole system rather than simply its parts, to proceed from function or purpose toward realization, and so on.

Software Engineering Threats to Systems Creativity

There is a risk, currently significant and increasing rapidly, that the application of requirements capture tools to higher levels of system design will erode creativity at those levels. The tools are seductively simple to use, being generally graphically based, but it is broadly their task to decompose established design concepts into their component parts, ensuring consistency and completeness in the process. The present tendency to use these tools to formulate the design concepts themselves, and particularly those of the higher, parent system rather than the computer-dominated sub-system, is not encouraging.

Examples of this problem area are security-sensitive in some instances. One recent paper on the application of Yourdon (Real Time), as defined by Ward and Mellor (one of the many software requirements analysis tools), concerned a complex but un-named modern defence platform. The tool had been used to perform a functional decomposition of the complete platform requirement, after a period of knowledge elicitation. The result was incomprehensible to users and to peer group designers and was not followed up by functional-to-physical mapping. This last point arose for several reasons. First, the time taken to perform the analysis had exceeded expectation; second, the team could find no way to integrate the decomposed functions; third, not surprisingly, the customer was becoming nervous about both cost and the validity of the approach

"Off-the-Shelf" Syndrome

Before moving on to softer issues, it is worthwhile to consider perhaps the biggest element which militates against top-down design in industry. Companies which design, develop and manufacture components and systems, invest intellectual effort as well as money in the process. Faced with the requirement for a new system, the pressure to simply adapt their available, "off-the-shelf" system to a new requirement is almost irresistible

Unfortunately, there is ample evidence to show that complex systems rarely repeat themselves and that the off-the-shelf solution is an illusion. That this must be so, can be seen by considering just one aspect, the timescale of contemporary projects. An off-the-shelf solution must have been designed several years before to be on the shelf now. With the pace of technological development so high, the off-the-shelf solution is out of date. Perhaps it is for this reason that more developed countries attempt to unload their present solutions on to third world countries. Third world countries are no longer naive, however, and are often smarting from having been "sold a pup" in the past. The true ethic of the systems engineer has always been to do the best by his customer. Current claims being made for "total quality management" and similar vogue concepts look suspiciously like the standards which were applied assiduously in the past by systems engineers

ENQUIRING SYSTEMS

Since the end of the nineteen seventies the systems science community has seen an upsurge of the so-called "soft" systems approach as opposed to "hard" methods which, according to Checkland (1981), are characterized by assumptions that "problems can be formulated as making a choice between alternative means of achieving a known end". It is not the purpose of this chapter to provide an authoritative assessment of these methods, but some are of considerable interest, particularly in the field of management, and their broad approach may offer succour to systems engineers who, as has been demonstrated, are moving steadily into less firm territory in an attempt to solve mounting human difficulties being experienced by the users of their technological solutions to problems. These problems include the understanding of the requirement, an area where soft methods promise capability.

SSM and Peter Checkland

The doyen of the soft academics in the UK is undoubtedly Professor Peter Checkland from Lancaster University who produced his seminal book *Systems Thinking, Systems Practice* in 1981. Checkland's Soft Systems Methodology, see Checkland (1972, 1981), conceives of hierarchies of systems including natural systems whose origin is in the origin of the universe, designed physical systems which man has made, ranging "from hammers via tram cars to space rockets", designed abstract systems such as mathematics, poetry, books and human activity systems. Brian Wilson (Wilson,1984) describes human activity systems as "undertaking purposeful activity such as man-machine systems, industrial activity, political systems, etc."

Both Checkland and Wilson follow a classically simple route in exploring their problem domains. In essence, they appreciate a real problem situation, develop a variety of viewpoints concerning the real problem situation, form idealized conceptual models of the problem situation, compare characteristic features of the idealized model with the real world, and hence identify any feasible and desirable change. "rich pictures" (often hand-drawn stick figures and cartoons) are drawn to express the problem situation. "Cloud" diagrams are used in conceptual models to illustrate messy systems with indistinct boundaries. By choosing a variety of viewpoints they hope to bring robustness to the process and avoid the pitfalls of pre-conceptions. (I hope that this precis of their approach is not so brief as to misrepresent it).

While SSM is clearly a method, with procedure and a degree of formality, it seems to lack a theory. On the other hand, for the right practitioner, it works and it is seductively simple in concept. For industry, there are some difficulties; the systems thinking phase may result in work which it would be imprudent to show directly to some pragmatic industrial leaders for fear of ridicule—quite unwarranted though that might be. On the other hand, it does incorporate a formal systems model, a generalized view of any human activity system, which is perhaps under-rated. The elements of the formal systems model require that a system has the following characteristics:

- Purpose or mission
- Measurable performance
- A decision-making process
- Components which are themselves systems
- Components which mutually interact
- A boundary
- Resources
- Continuity
- Exists in a wider system and/or environment with which it interacts

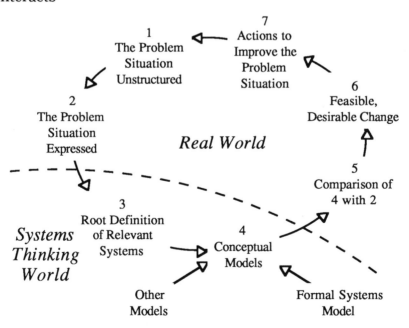

Figure 1.7 Checkland's soft systems methodology (simplified)

Ross Janes

Ross Janes, in the Department of Systems Science at City University, London, adopts the facilitator role. Janes favours "interpretive structural modelling", a very powerful method for developing structure within a set of situation objectives, aims or factors by successive pair-wise comparison. The potential combinatorial explosion implicit in large-scale problems is contained using processor based tools to eliminate redundant comparisons and to manipulate and draw the resulting hierarchical networks. Janes's approach is exciting for two reasons:

- It is a group exercise, in which participation by the owners of the problem is of necessity involved, with Janes acting as an expert facilitator but, in principle, introducing no problem-related expertise which he might possess. Under his guidance, the group generates ideas about, and develops its own understanding of, the issues it faces. Members prioritize and rank the issues. And in the process of participation, both a group consensus and a group identity emerge. It is this last, more than any other aspect, which seems to be the benefit of the Janes approach

- The process reveals emergent properties in the problem which are not necessarily visible in the individual factors which are generated under Janes' guidance by the participating group. The structuring and grouping of the issue factors reveals architecture.

Colin Eden

Colin Eden, Strathclyde University, has developed a comprehensive capability over a number of years for helping organizations to manage the complexity of their organizations and management. One of his many techniques is sometimes referred to as "cognitive mapping". The example of cognitive mapping below is mine, not his, and refers to an engineering organization in the defence industry which was going through a period of soul-searching some years ago.

As the cognitive map shows, some of the concerns are sources of arrows, while others are sinks, in the sense that all (or most) of the associated arrows point towards them. Sinks are the outcomes, the symptoms if you will, of the malaise rather than the underlying causes, represented by the sources. So, in Figure 1.8, "high average age" is an underlying cause, while "low morale", and "need clear long-term plan" are symptoms. (These factors are the same as those used in Chapter 8.2, where the analysis is taken further.) Colin Eden accommodates rather more complex problems than that expressed above, of course, with the numbers of entities considered running into several hundreds.

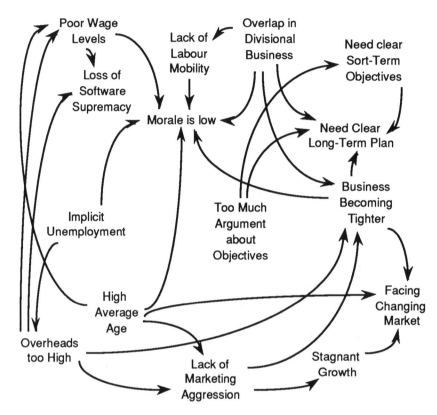

Figure 1.8 Company self appraisal—A cognitive mapping

Decision-Based Approaches

John Friend, of the Institute for Operational Research and the Tavistock Research Institute, presents yet another soft approach to managing complexity, see Figure 1.9. Complexity, he states, is not systemic, so it is better approached from a decision perspective than from a systems perspective. He draws together concepts, approaches and methods from both OR and from social science into a framework which, as the figure shows, operates in one of four modes—shaping, choosing, comparing and designing. His ideas are particularly appealing because they show an orderly progression toward a decision. Typical applications of his methods have been: county council planning; LPG storage and distribution for the Dutch government; pollution control on the Rhine; and community health services.

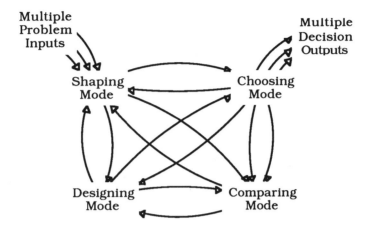

Figure 1.9 Handling Complex Environments

System Dynamics

Last in the brief series of soft method overviews is System Dynamics—see Roberts (1983), Forrester (1961), Coyle (1977) and Lammers (1987)—a technique viewed with the gravest suspicion in some industrial circles, owing to its potentially imprecise approach to modelling—although it is that very imprecision which makes systems dynamics potentially useful for addressing softer issues. In use, the formulation of so-called "influence diagrams"—see Figure 1.10, which is self-explanatory—precedes any numerical modelling, and it is my view, based on evidence that will be presented in subsequent chapters, that influence diagrams have much to offer in the development of system design concept formulation. Experience to date suggests that System Dynamics may be an effective approach to the thorny issue of bounding systems—if indeed there is a real need to bound systems at all—see Chapter 12.   N.B. The formation of cybernetic loops, shown earlier, was an influence diagram.

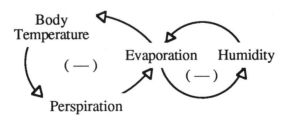

Figure 1.10 Simple influence diagram showing body temperature regulation in a closed environment

CHAOS

Relatively recent upon the systems scene, and presenting significant problems to soft and hard systems practitioner alike, is deterministic chaos, the phenomenon in which seemingly well-understood systems develop irregular behaviour. Readers will be familiar with the executive toy-pendulum suspended over four magnets, such that the path pursued by the pendulum is quite erratic. This is at odds with the deterministic view that, since knowing, as we do with great precision, the laws governing magnetic and gravitational attraction, it should be quite practical to calculate the pendulum's path.

Similarly, in pool or snooker, consider the ability to perform a "plant", in which the cue ball strikes an object ball which then strikes another object/target ball which then enters the pocket. If two or more object balls are set up in the chain and are separated from each other by a few centimetres, it becomes impossible for even the expert to sink the target ball reliably. (In many senses, this is not dissimilar to a project comprising serial activities, the output of each forming the input to the following.)

Chaotic behaviour arises in systems whose time history has a sensitive dependence on initial conditions (Lorenz's "butterfly effect"). Non-linearity is a necessary but insufficient condition. Deterministic chaos is *not* the result of random or noise inputs. Forced pendulums, fibrillating hearts, turbulent fluids, lasers, non-linear optical devices, biological population models, chemical reactions—all exhibit deterministic chaos.

In addition to sensitivity to starting conditions, chaotic systems display broad Fourier spectra when pumped by singular frequencies, increasing complexity of regular motion when some experimental parameter is changed (e.g. period doubling) and non-periodic bursts of irregular motion interspersed by periods of regular motion.

The study of chaotic systems has resulted in useful concepts to aid our understanding of complex dynamical systems, and in our ability to predict within bounds the dynamical evolution of chaotic systems. It has also—or perhaps *should* have also—shaken the faith of those who believe in the neat predictability of their ordered world. The vast majority of real world systems are non-linear and present at least some of the conditions necessary to permit or promote deterministic chaos.

CHAOS AND SELF-ORGANIZED CRITICALITY

Chaos is thought to arise where non-linear processes are repeated many times. For example, in recursive form, the logistic equation is:

$$X_{n+1} = (k_1.X_n + k_2.X_n^2).\delta t + X_n \qquad\qquad (1.1)$$

This well known equation produces the familiar S-shaped, sigmoid, or logistic curve which is used to describe all manner of things from the growth of bacteria in a Petri dish, to the growths of economies, populations, health, etc. If X is replaced by a complex variable Z and the equation recursed many times, the result is chaotic behaviour quite unlike the seemingly highly predictable S-curve. The conclusion drawn by analysts is that many of our systems may be far from predictable and that seemingly very simple systems may harbour the seeds of chaotic behaviour.

A recent theory by Bak and Chen(1991) concerns self-organized criticality. Whereas uncertainty in fully chaotic systems grows exponentially, for other systems uncertainty grows as a power law—these are said to be "weakly chaotic". Bak and Chen's theory applies to composite systems containing millions of elements interacting over short range. Earthquakes, resulting from shifts in the earth's crust, fit the bill. So, too, may economies, wars, evolution and many, many more. Noise in resistors and other electronic components fits the pattern, too; there are many more small noise peaks than large ones. In electronics, this phenomenon is known as $1/f$ noise, indicating the inverse relationship of peak amplitude to frequency. Quite unlike random events, such patterns indicate that current events are dependent on an accumulation of past events.

The archetypal system displaying self-organized criticality concerns a pile of sand on to which is dropped more sand, grain at a time. The pile is formed on a small, circular, horizontal plate. At first, the pile just builds until a critical stage is reached. At this point, sand may slip. Some slips consist of a few grains. Occasionally, slips involve many grains. After each slip, the pile grows again. Sometimes the pile grows beyond the critical point—it goes super-critical—and a slip will occur to restore it towards the critical point. This model is very interesting for several reasons:

- A graph of the size of slip (measured, say, in grains of sand) against the frequency with which that size occurs, forms a power curve.

- The phenomenon is long-term stable—once a critical condition has been reached, all slips tend to restore towards the critical point.

The theory of self-organized criticality is a holistic theory; it is not dependent on the scaling-up of physical laws regarding the behaviour of two or three sand particles. Chaos and catastrophe theories are similarly holistic.

Lewis F. Richardson, a British meteorologist, collected data from 1820 to the second world war (Richardson, 1960). In particular, he observed a relationship between the number of wars in which a given number of people were killed and the frequency of such wars. He found, not surprisingly perhaps, that the the more frequent wars incurred less casualties and vice versa. Figure 1.11 shows my graph

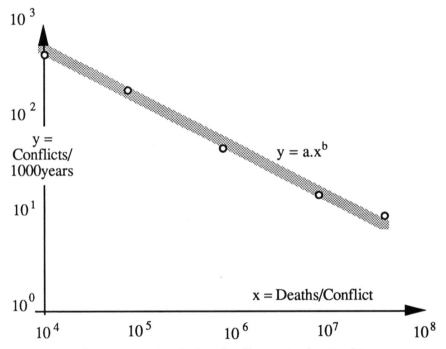

Figure 1.11 Conflict and self-organized criticality

of the number of deaths per war against the frequency of such wars, both scales being logarithmic. Data from Richardsons work are shown as small circles against a power law curve fit (a straight line on a log-log graph.) The fit is remarkable, with a high negative correlation coefficient. Attempts to fit the data to an exponential curve were much less successful.

What can we deduce from this closeness of fit? If Bak and Chen's theory of self-organized criticality holds, the implication is that conflict is an instance of weak chaos. Perhaps, like earthquakes, thermal noise, or the pile of sand, there is continual friction between groups of humans which releases occasionally in conflict of uncertain size. Were this to be so, it suggests ways in which such conflict could be reduced: minimize the degree of contact; "smooth the edges" between conflicting groups in some way; "lubricate"; or perhaps bind between groups in some way so that the rubbing and friction cannot arise in the first instance.

CONCLUSION

This chapter has provided a brief overview of some of the more recent "systems" developments, looking at the soft and the hard with, hopefully, some even-handedness, and providing a backcloth against which further investigation by the reader can be undertaken. Strong and weak chaotic behaviours have been introduced to avoid any impression of certain predictability in the behaviour of systems, be they seemingly simple or complex.

Chapter 2
The Human Element in Systems

*There is but one law for all, namely that law
which governs all Laws ... the Law of
Humanity, Justice and Equity—the Law of
Nature, and of Nations.*
Edmund Burke, 1729-1797

HUMAN 'DESIGN'

Man is not really the best at anything, physically—not the fastest, strongest, or most agile. We pride ourselves on being the most intelligent without any proof. But we probably do excel in one particular—our "design" does seem to be a master of compromise; we do seem to be delightfully designed in such a way that the individual may be capable, but the group is more capable. We are thus essentially social animals and our design evolved to capitalize on this social capability, with brain-sensor-motor-social skills second to none.

There are many more examples of this seeming compromise in design; one more that is worthy of particular mention is the human throat. Man is the only simian unable to breathe while swallowing; this has arisen because our throats are adapted for speech. The price is death for those who choke to death, but the advantage to the species conferred by speech far outweighs the price.

The internal human 'design' exhibits splendid features too: a dual-redundant brain within a hardened cranial protector, with each half adapted to different purposes but operating in partnership with the other; heart, spleen and liver protected by flexible ribs which double as a means of protecting and inflating the lungs; dual-redundant kidneys; armoured yet flexible spinal covering for the main communications artery; and so on. None of the internal organs is optimized in its own right; instead, each contributes to the effective overall operation of the human—surely an object lesson for all would-be designers.

Small wonder that our man-made systems present us with problems; we attempt to design them to be optimum in their own right, when we, their users, are not optimum in our own right. It is noticeable that the man-made systems with which man has the greatest affinity are individual, one-on-one, from the club and hammer, screwdriver and pen, to the personal computer, typewriter, word processor, graffiti spray-can, personal communicator, etc. When we attempt to construct *social* man-made systems by connecting geographically dispersed elements, we experience difficulty not with the technology but with the human-to-human and the human-to-machine interactions. In essence, we build rigid, non-adaptive systems which fail to evolve with changing environment while adaptation in humans is a *sine qua non*.

Table 2.1 Compromise in human "design". Human "design", which is not really design but the outcome of evolution by natural selection, may be viewed as a masterpiece of compromise, with each limitation in our individual capabilities contributing to group performance, so that the group survives and flourishes

FEATURE	COMPROMISE	LOSE	GAIN
Bipedalism	Reduced running speed, Manoeuvrability	Survival (flight); energy; olfactory tracking	Free hands, early warning from raised sensors, better inter-group communications
10—15 year nurture	Limited pre-birth imprint; infant helplessness	Group mobility; survival (flight)	Adaptability; flexibility, social cohesion
Hardening	Limited cranial, thoracic and spinal protection	Survival (fight)	Mobility; survival (flight)
Distributed processing (spinal reflex)	Some processing occurs outside of the brain	Central control	Speed of response
Weight/size/ volume	Not the largest/ fastest/ strongest of animals	Individual survival (fight)	Larger group size; greater group survival
Small eyes	Limited night vision	Ability to operate at night	Simpler, more survivable sensors by day
Eyes and ears	Co-located and passive	Direct range information	Ease of correlation; avoidance of detection
Cone of foveal resolution	Narrow cone supported by aural and peripheral flicker vision cues	Wide field of view	Faster processing; speed of response

By the same token, those systems with which we interact most effectively are "transparent" to use, i.e. they do not impede, add to, or subtract from, our human interactions. The telephone is a good example, but the videophone, used now in security systems, will be an even better one when it comes into more general use.

Left Brain-Right Brain

Roger Sperry, the Caltech psychobiologist earned a Nobel Prize in 1981 for unravelling the respective roles and functions of the two hemispheres of the human brain. For most right-handed people, broadly the left hemisphere, which controls the right side of the body, is responsible for language and logic; the right hemisphere, which controls the left half of the body, deals with creative, intuitive non-verbal factors, emotions and spatial cognitive relationships. The two halves communicate via the corpus callosum, a bundle of fibres carrying signals in both directions. Sperry worked with epileptics, whose corpora callosa had been surgically cut, and from their behaviour deduced the respective half-brain functions.

Until recently, the division of functions seemed clear; some 95% of right-handers and 67% of left-handers have the left-brain specialized for language. New evidence (Jones and Wilson, 1987) suggests that the right brain may handle some important speech functions, including recognizing narrative and humour, interpreting tone of voice, forming metaphors. Whereas it was felt that the left brain was dominant during waking, with the right brain emerging into semi-consciousness during dreaming sleep, now it is suggested that each hemisphere has a specialty which leads as needed when awake.

In general, the right brain is seen as creative and general, trying solution after solution until one fits, while the left brain is the specialist, working logically and methodically. There are structural differences in the two hemispheres to support this notion: right brain has longer fibres reaching into many brain areas, while left brain has shorter fibres, addressing local areas. Unfamiliar faces are recognized by the right hemisphere, familiar faces with the left. It seems that even dreams can be seen in a different light: dreams may be an evolved response to aid survival, by enabling the dreamer to go over, or practise, responses to threatening or disturbing events which have occurred in the past.

Understanding how the brain functions is essential if we are to appreciate how we make decisions, how we learn, how we become expert, how our creativity arises, how that creativity might be stifled or encouraged, how our emotions and motivations arise, and many, many other things.

HUMAN PREDICTABILITY

In a short chapter it is not possible to cover human behaviour to any sensible degree. Nonetheless it is possible to raise some issues and to discuss some points of interest. For example, some observers view humans as too complex and too variable to be predictable to any useful degree. This is, predominantly, a "soft" viewpoint and is generally uppermost in most present-day analyses

On the other hand, some view the human as an adjunct to the system—the human will learn to respond to, and interact with, the technology, the situation and the environment. This is, predominantly, a "hard" viewpoint and, as has just been discussed, this does not match up with the facts. True, some humans will show amazing ability to come to grips with machine operation, but the combination of man and machine is then limited because the human energy is directed towards mastery of the machine instead of towards achieving their supposed common goal. We may reasonably conclude that neither viewpoint fits the observed facts.

In the spirit of this book, let us consider the multitude of human behavioural aspects that offer some pattern, rather than those that divide.

Social psychologists and social anthropologists study the behaviour of individuals in society, and seem to have developed highly fruitful avenues of research into the behaviour of humans in social groups, e.g. management, organization, etc.

There are features of human social behaviour which encourage the notion that we might be able to understand and predict human behaviour, at least to some degree. Consider the following list:

- *Motivation*—inclinations to conform to social norms (achievement motivation and compliance motivation). Humans are motivated to conform either to achieve social goals (which may, or may not be considered "social", e.g. vandalism) or to comply with group behaviour patterns.
- *Dominance/submission* —tendency to lead or be led
- *Territorial imperative*—strong sense of territory ownership and *territorial marking*—visible signs/ symbols of ownership. Territorial imperative and territorial marking are commonplace. Bigger desks, larger offices, executive toys, carpets, company cars, hostility to other managers at the same hierarchy level, insistence on pursuing an irrational decision, all are examples. Placing a desk opposite the entrance, with the occupant facing the door and with his back to the wall or window is classic territorial behaviour. Open plan offices are divided with panels, ostensibly for sound-proofing, but they serve as boundary markers, too.
- *Personal space*—egocentred space, physical and emotional
- *Family loyalties*—Unquestioning adherence to relationship
- *Tribal loyalties*—Unquestioning adherence to relationship. Tribal loyalty is a very strong influence. To see it at its most naked, observe regiments or squadrons in the forces at a dining-in night, a school reunion, or team supporters during a sporting event.
- *Dyadic reciprocity*—interactions between individuals. Dyadic reciprocity is particularly noteworthy, with humans adapting their behaviour on a one-to-one basis as they communicate. So, we find we have different stored behaviour patterns, learned from childhood, such that we communicate quite differently when interacting with spouses, bosses, subordinates, tradesmen working on our houses. We are born with this ability, being able to attract our mothers or to indicate sufficiency, from the first moments of seeking the nipple. So well developed is our dyadic reciprocity, that we are almost universally unaware of it in everyday action.

- *Natural pre-disposition*—inherited tendency to respond
- *Cultural pre-disposition*—learned tendency to respond
- *Group polarisation*—tendency for group discussions /decisions to move to the extremes

On the other hand, psychologists have developed a range of behavioural categorizations that suggest that, although we may analyse, we may have difficulty comprehending. Such Freudian terms as the following are in vogue, see Jones and Wilson (1987):

- Repression
- Regression
- Projection
- Denial
- Reactive formulation (in which the individuals convince themselves that the opposite of the truth exists, and then replays their their revised versions continually
- Reversal
- Isolation
- Sublimation
- Displacement (in which emotion/behaviour is transferred from one object to another)
- Intellectualization
- Etc.

These terms, many of which are familiar in everyday life, may encourage the notion either that humans are too complex to understand/predict or, on the contrary, that a better understanding would enable such prediction.

PERSONALITY

The study of personality, particularly by Carl Jung, has led to significant understanding of different types of people. Jung originated the terms *introvert* and *extrovert* but recognized that these two categories failed to explain the perceived richness of behavioural variety in people. Jung sub-divided introverts and extroverts according to the relative dominance of four psychological functions: sensation; thinking; feeling; intuition.

Subsequent research suggests that most people lie somewhere between the sixteen type extremes and, indeed, that any given individual may change his personality both on a short-term and a long-term basis.

E. Spranger emphasized the "dominant value direction" of personality and postulated six ideal types, corresponding to six major values:

Theoretical	Economic	Aesthetic
Social	Political	Religious

Both Jung's and Spranger's work has been developed by others into methods for revealing a subject's personality by rating them under the respective headings. Jung's work was developed, for example, into the Myers-Briggs Type Indicator (Briggs, 1990).

SOCIAL INTERACTIONS

We employ 4 types of interpersonal communications (Tajfel and Fraser, 1978):

1 *The verbal system.* Expletives and phonemes that make up speech
2 *The intonation system.* Systematic use of different pitches, stresses and junctures e.g. "help? " and "help!"
3 *Paralinguistics.* Additional vocalisations, shared by members of a cultural group, and used communicatively, e.g. "Um", "ah", tone of voice, pauses, extremes of intensity, pitch, drawl, laughing, crying, etc.
4 *Kinesics.* Body and facial movement, including eyebrow position, eye contact, body shift to punctuate discussion, etc., often grouped as body language.

These four methods of communication are used within a framework which manages our interactions with each other:

- *Interaction regulation*—assumption of alternative participation, relative contributions according to relative status, social setting—eye contact to initiate, then intermittent eye contact interspersed with listener "nods", etc.
- *Interpersonal communication*
  - Social and personal identities (accent, dress, hair style, social class, education, etc.)
  - Temporary states and current attitudes (angry, anxious, hostile, responsive, distaste, etc.);
  - Social relationship (smiling, bodily contact, method of address)

- *Representational communication*—the meaning of what is said, but more than semantics, . e.g. "dinner" as a mid-day or evening meal reveals class origins.

Evidently, our means of communication are highly complex, adaptable, variable and sophisticated, with protocols for communication style, interaction management, selection of communication medium, etc., all in operation at once

MAKING DECISIONS

Decision-making is something at which we humans excel—we do it all the time, so it should be simple for us to understand the processes—right? Wrong. It seems that we have great difficulty in understanding ourselves and in particular, how we *really* make decisions. Moreover, we have a penchant, even a fundamental need, to make decisions, when logic might tell us that decisions are being made on uncertain information and in a climate where predicting the future is not possible/practicable.

There is a view, for instance, that better decisions will be made if more, good information is available to the decision-maker. But what is a better decision? What is good information?.

In a dynamic situation, change is the order of the day. any reasonable information system will be expected to report upon this change, and moreover the interaction between the many systems interlaced in many modern systems suggests that interaction complexity will be high too. Change makes data more volatile, i.e. of shorter validity. It also makes more data queue, increasing delays within the information system. Systems interaction compl-exity prejudices predictability. These factors combine to reduce the quality of a decision, since the decision-maker will face large amounts of increasingly dated information, reducing the probability of a correct decision. In any event, with so many factors changing in an unpredictable situation, it may be impossible to determine the correctness or otherwise of a decision, since cause and effect may be impossible to unravel.

The decision-maker himself may not be entirely without fault, either. Psychologists recognize "cognitive bias" as a feature of many decision makers. Who could fail to recognize the following, from an incomplete list:

- Adjustment and anchoring. Decision-maker selects a norm and fits other data to it improperly
- Data saturation. Reaches premature decisions on too small a sample and then ignoring further data

- Self-fulfilling prophecy. Values certain outcomes and acquires and analyses only data that supports that outcome
- Attribution error. Associates success with inherent personal ability and failure with bad luck. "When *you* are wrong, you screwed up, when *I'm* wrong it was just bad luck"
- Gambler's fallacy. Assumes the occurrence of one set of events enhances the probability of an event that has not yet occurred. 'I have smoked for 10 years without getting cancer—clearly I am immune, so I can go on smoking'. (This type of thinking is apparently behind much of the counter-intuitive results of advertising the dangers of drug-taking and AIDS.)
- Order effects. Order of information presentation affects retention and weighting. This phenomenon is used by presenters to influence those to whom they are presenting and by organizers of beauty contests, who present their selections in revers order
- Panic. Under stress, facing many options which cannot be evaluated, either selects at random or fails to act at all

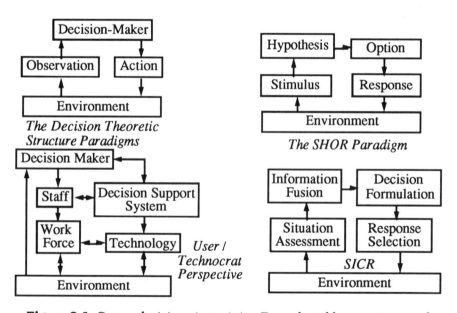

Figure 2.1 Group decision viewpoints. Reproduced by permission of AFCEA International Press

Decision makers also exhibit group phenomena, the best known being "risky shift". There is evidence to show that a group of people, isolated from outside influence and under pressure to make a decision, will polarize . Such polarization results in an extreme decision , where 'extreme may mean either very conservative or very risky—hence risky shift . President Kennedy and the Bay of Pigs is sometimes put forward as the archetypal risky shift decision. Social psychologists recognize a deep, underlying behaviour pattern in these group effects, but are not agreed as to their substance.

Figure 2.1 shows four of the many different viewpoints of group decision taking—see Mayk and Rubin (1988) for a most comprehensive coverage. The simplest, at the top, are the Decision Theoretic Structure and the SHOR (or SHORe) paradigm (Wohl 1981). They are interesting in what they do *not* say. No mention is made of single or group activity. Little mention is made of the actual decision-making process—the SHOR paradigm does introduce the notion of choosing in some way between options, a theme which will recur below.

At bottom left is the User/Technocrat Perspective, which views the scene in physical blocks, thereby generating a model which relates to that which is visible, but in the process creating artificial barriers to function and the smooth flow of serial activity. For example, the idea of group decision formulation is more difficult to see in this perspective. That deficiency is amended at bottom right, where the process of decision taking is enhanced into four discrete steps.

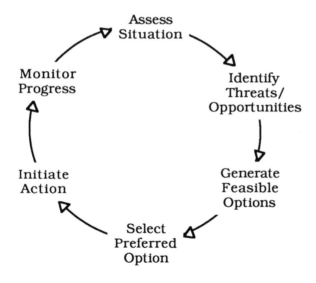

Figure 2.2 Decision circle

Figure 2.2 shows my approach to the paradigm game—the decision circle, which represents decisions as a cyclic process. This concept is very general-purpose: it applies equally to a committee, a boardroom, and so on. But what does it *not* say?

No mention is made of "how". How do we identify threats, options, constraints? How do we select the preferred option? And so on. Nonetheless, it is a useful kernel on which to build a management decision-taking process; each activity can be made the focus of another cyclic process, producing seven meshed wheels and providing the basis for formal group actions.

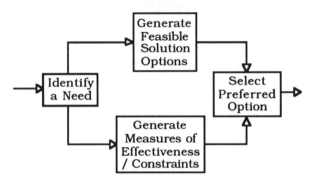

Figure 2.3 Archetypal decision model

But how do we actually *make* decisions? For many years it had been thought that we followed a standard rote, suggested by some of the paradigms above. Figure 2.3 shows the widely-accepted model. Essentially the model suggests that we review all options at once, using a means of trading-off between them against the measures of effectiveness, so identifying the option which is best overall. This, then, is an optimizing model. But is it how we actually go about things?

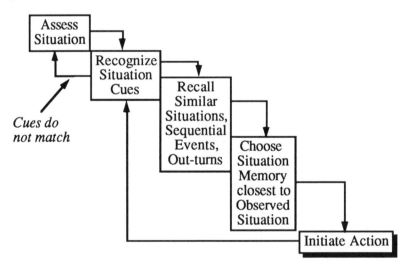

Figure 2.4 A satisficing decision model

Well, sometimes. Work done initially by Simon (1955) and latterly by Klein (1989) suggests that we may, on occasions 'satisfice' make choices which are "good enough". There is a suggestion that humans evolved as satisficers; it is, after all, pragmatic and fast, and much more likely to result in survival than a careful planning mode when chased by a predator or fighting in battle.

The waterfall diagram, Figure 2.4, starts in the top left-hand corner, where a situation is assessed and certain cues are observed. If the decision-maker is an expert, and particularly if he or she is under time pressure, then they are most likely to fall back on experience of similar situations and to choose a course of action based on that which has worked in the past. This mode of decision-making is fast and carries a degree of assurance with it, being based on experience.

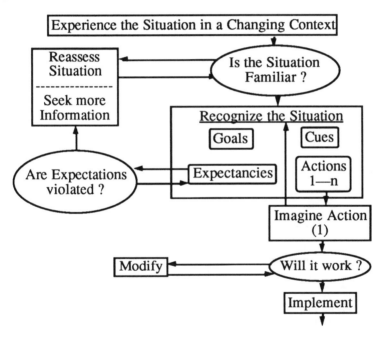

Figure 2.5 Klein's model of recognition-primed decision-making. Reproduced by permission of Dr Klein and Klein Associates Inc

When faced with a situation, and under time pressure, the expert decision maker examines the situation to see if it is familiar. He or she may flip mentally through a series of mental situation models, stopping at the first that apparently fits the observed facts—satisficing. The expert will then consider the sequence of actions drawn from the familiar model, imagining the present situation at a series of future stages. If the imagined scenes offer an apparent solution, they will initiate action and will watch for the expected events and occurrences predicted from their imagined progress. Should the situation expectancies not occur to order, they will assume that the original selection was incorrect and start again to select a new mental situation model from their experience bank.

Klein calls these Recognition-Primed Decisions (RPDs). RPD is fast and effective. He further found in his research, contrary to expectations, that experts were willing to substitute alternative courses of action when cues indicated that their expectations from the prior course were violated.

The Klein model of decision-making is quite different from the classic idea that all options are reviewed in parallel; instead, it seems, experts satisfice rather than optimize and achieve fast, reliable performance in the process. Perhaps this is why carefully worked-up plans, based on sound analysis by subordinates, are frequently cast aside with barely a glance by an experienced leader who uses his experience and satisfices, Klein style. If so, the notion has significant implications for the way in which we design decision support systems for expert users—the normal case.

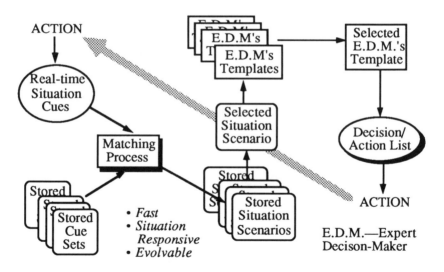

Figure 2.6 Recognition-primed decision making—
technological support

Figure 2.6 shows one scheme in which technology might be brought to bear in decision support for making RPDs. Real-world cues are matched against sets of cues stored in advance by the Expert Decision Maker (EDM). Each set of cues corresponds to a stored situation scenario, which is the EDM's view of what the cue-set represents. Corresponding to each scenario is an EDM's template, showing the decisions he would make and the outcomes expected as the situation unfolds. The selected template results in a set of decisions which should result in the appropriate cues being received either in confirmation of the original selection, or in its contravention. In the latter case, the system will seek a further scenario.

Such a system could be developed on-line with an EDM at the helm, so to speak, and the cues/scenarios/templates/action lists being progressively refined. The potential for such an approach seems good in high-pressure, reactive situations.

Table 2.2 summarises recent research by Cohen (1988) which suggest that all is not as we might think with our current advocacy for fused data presentations.

Table 2.2 Dynamic fused-data display anomaly.

User Viewpoint	Analyst Viewpoint
• Pilot, uncertain about presence of an enemy surface-to-air missile installation on his planned path • Pilot seeks to develop a single, concrete, "worst-case" scenario	• Analyst, whose goal is to help the pilot • Analyst seeks to develop a system that mathematically aggregates the possibilities—average of probabilities, weighted according to probable outcome. Display corresponds to no actual outcome, e.g. "expected danger" contours

RESEARCH FINDING (COHEN)

• Research shows that pilots prefer a single-possibility outcome e.g. worst case. Pilots adopt a sophisticated, active process of problem solving underlying selection and rejection of single-possibility presentations. Research further suggests that pilot's approach is powerful, and approaches theoretical best.

• *What price knowledge based devices which present time-constrained users with views incompatible with their mental models ?*

DECISION CENTRES

Consider Figure 2.7 which shows the bridge of some hypothetical craft. It exhibits classic features. The captain sits centre-stage, looking down from a height advantage over the operators who have little initiative in his presence; they look outwards and respond to orders. Science and communications officers sit behind the captain, acting as eyes and ears on the unseen world. All three are capable of swivelling their seats to enter into a conference, and in so doing they become 'un-plugged' from their technology, typically to discuss something unusual. They too can look down over the operators to observe the same scene as the captain. The engineer is sidelined at an intermediate level, of limited value unless something goes wrong.

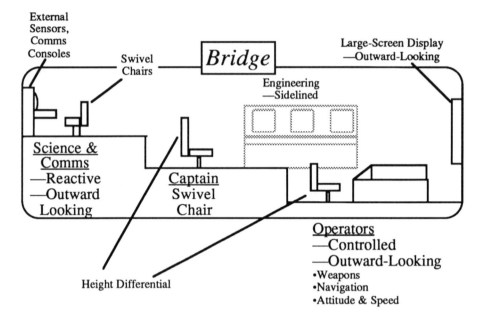

Figure 2.7 The psychology of the bridge

These features are evident in many socio-technical systems. Air-traffic management sees controllers largely glued to their screens, remotely supervised. Boardrooms, on the other hand, have seen little technology as the decision-making is generally of a less predictable nature.

HUMAN-ANALOGOUS SYSTEMS

The Heuristic, Intelligent, Threat-Assessment System (HITAS)

Consider a new design where the need is for a small, agile planetary explorer which can operate on or above the surface in very low orbit. Crew workload dictates a two-man crew; an electronic crew member is required as a substitute for the second man to detect, locate and respond to obstacles and threats.

One approach is to design the explorer along lines analogous to the human central nervous system. The design needs the following capabilities:

- Non-imaging sensors
- Thermal imager
- Radar
- Multi-sensor correlation
- Hazard sensor
- Ranking
- Response

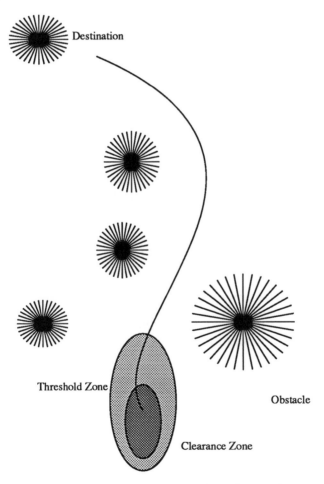

Figure 2.8   Heuristic for obstacle avoidance
               while goal-seeking

The non-imaging sensors give very low directivity but wide scan, and are used as peripheral vision sensors to direct the infra-red and radar which equate to foveal vision in their resolution. Thermal imager and radar give scene interpretation on their own, but their outputs are correlated to give a combined scene which is set against stored multisensor models representing the known obstacles and threats.

Recognized obstacles/threats are ranked using a 3—D cognitive map, with the explorer at one focus of an ovoid, or solid ellipse—see Figure 2.8—the major axis of which extended in front of the craft by an amount related to explorer speed; the faster the explorer, the longer the ovoid. Around recognized obstacles/threats are generated, in the systems processors, spheres of danger corresponding to the ranges of the recognized obstacles/threats. The volume of the solid intersection between these threat spheres and the zone of safety set by the ovoid represents the degree of risk facing the explorer. Threats are ranked according to degree of risk and imminence.

The various degrees of risk are used via an autopilot to steer the vehicle by the minimum risk path via the obstacles in precisely the same way that pedestrians avoid each other when hurrying along a busy street—a model based on research work into human cognition done at Newcastle University.

HITAS has to "learn" about obstacles and threats. The basic idea is to present the sensors first with a series of physical models, suitably scaled, so that the processors can learn what an obstacle or threat looks like. Next, the same process is repeated against real targets. HITAS could gather intelligence by recording real threats that do not fit its models and a degree of latitude can be provided in the design such that HITAS can modify the parameters which form the basis of its threat models. Hence, the system is heuristic, and intelligent, using that last term in a limited sense that it is able to learn from its environment and to modify its behaviour sensibly according to that learning.

A list of the analogous, human-like features embedded in the HITAS design concept include:

- Peripheral flicker vision
- Foveal vision
- Heterogeneous remote sensors
- Sensor correlation
- Image learning
- Image recognition
- Cognitive mapping
- Route finding
- Reflex
- Learning

- Adaptive behaviour
- Judgement/prioritization

Function-Mapped Systems

The system of Figure 2.9 connects a number of discrete workstations via a Cambridge Ring or similar. Each workstation corresponds to an operational group. There are stations for intelligence, communications, operations, engineering, plans & resources and, of course, the commander. Each workstation supports a set of terminals working through it, so that a section of staff can simultaneously contribute to the task in hand; these supporters could, but normally would not, communicate over the Cambridge Ring—each section is clan-based, in the human societal sense.

A strict code of data ownership is necessary. So, the intelligence desk officer is responsible for all intelligence data; others might read it, only he can authorize its update. This approach maintains territorial imperatives and pecking orders.

Each centre communicates with other centres via bridges between the rings. Intelligence communicates with intelligence, operations with operations, engineering with engineering, and so on, so maintaining clan protocols. Communications are responsible for establishing and maintaining external links, managing message traffic, handling sensitive messages, etc., and not for the network *per se*.

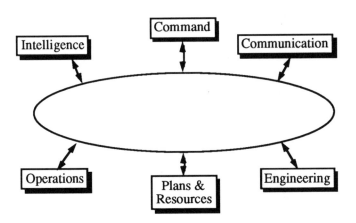

Figure 2.9 User-mapped technology

Subordinate formations also stick to the clan code. A logistic depot, for example, communicates stock levels exclusively to the plans & resources officer, who then authorizes the data for dissemination. This also maintains essential pecking orders.

Each workstation is "stand-alone" presenting a clear, physical, territorial boundary. The separation between the purposes and activities of different workstations is also instantly understood; it maps directly on to military organizations. The physical design of each workstation employs a low desk, with inset graphics display screens and controls, so operators—generally senior personnel in this configuration, i.e. clan leaders—can literally sit in a circle, as in the diagram, facing inwards and backed by their supporting sections. These could be visible or concealed, able in either case to communicate verbally and through the various section terminals. The commander's desk is similar to the others except that it may be a little higher and have a larger graphic screen, consistent with his position of dominance.

Such systems approaches recognize the tribal nature of human interactions and seek to build on it, rather than to submerge it—generally, an unsuccessful enterprise.

DESIGN ANALOGUES

Figure 2.10 shows at left the concept of the Pain-Gate Theory, proposed by Professor Patrick Wall at London University. The theory proposes that pain signals pass through gates which can be switched off, either by a signal from the brain showing lack of interest or locally because of an excessive number of pain stimuli arising from one part of the body. The theory explains why swimmers can have a leg bitten of by a shark and feel no pain until later, why sprinters can have a spike pass through the foot and continue running, why people may be shot and stabbed without realizing it and so on. Basically, under fight or flight conditions, the brain switches its attention away from pain sensing to more pressing matters of survival.

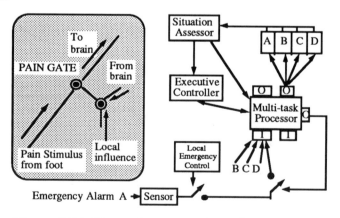

Figure 2.10 Human/security system design analogue

At the right is a computer system designed by analogy to the pain gate. It is like no computer system in use. We would conventionally bring all remote signals into the processor and scan them periodically—in this design, the signals may not reach the processor. Why is Nature different? It is difficult to be certain, but Nature's approach minimizes input/output, reduces the risk of cross-talk between the connectors running to the central processor, and minimizes the processing load during emergencies—perhaps we still have something to learn?

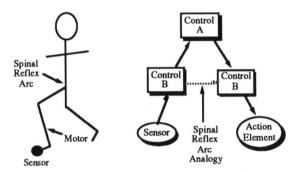

Figure 2.11 Spinal-arc reflex analogy

When we step on a thorn, the pain signal passes to the brain up the sensor system and we take action to remove our foot through our motor system—or do we? The round trip time, sensor, to motor, is more than 200-300 milliseconds for most people, by which time the thorn would be well and truly embedded in the foot. In addition to the conscious mechanism described we, along with other animals, have a spinal arc reflex, a crossover from sensor to motor at the base of the spine, which transfers the pain signal rapidly, lifting the foot before our conscious effort can be applied. Such short cuts are essential in vital, fast response systems, as indicated at the right of Figure 2.11. So, an air defence system must have delegated power to defend against aggressors without continual reference to higher authority, which reference would be too slow to permit effective defence.

CONCLUSION

- Our systems and designs are inevitably anthropomorphic in some degree
- Since the human body and human social groups are so well developed, we can and should learn from them

- It seems likely that human behaviour is reasonably predictable, given an understanding of situation, environment, culture and pre-cursor events
- Given the likelihood of behavioral-predictability, we can design systems that accommodate, even respond to, human behaviour, rather than suffer from apparent "human irrationality"
- Human decision-making is more complex and effective than might be thought, to the extent that some approaches to knowledge engineering, particularly the use of fused-data presentations and the presumption of optimizing rather than satisficing, may be seriously counter-productive.

ASSIGNMENT

- Design a commodities dealing room in which the ten dealers have to communicate directly with each other, and yet have to refer continuously to their data displays. The commodities are grains and sugars, which are loosely related in that bulk grain and sugar movements can alternatively use the same transporters, a factor of interest to the dealers who must not only sell and buy, but guarantee delivery, too.
- Design a floorplan which distributes the occupants of the dealing room so as to encourage useful communication, permit sensible supervision and create an effective, competitive yet friendly environment. Allow space for relaxation and private working. Consider the use of the walls and ceiling for hanging or suspending displays
- Show each person, their work space and facilities, orientation and connectivities
- Justify your design

Chapter 3
A Unified Systems Hypothesis

Observe How System into System Runs,
What Other Planets Circle Other Suns
Alexander Pope 1688—1744

INTRODUCTION

At the time of writing, science is steadily losing the esteem with which it was formerly regarded by the general public—see Vickers (1981). Scientific method applied to social issues such as nuclear energy and genetic engineering and to complex socio-technical facilities such as information, economic and stockmarket systems, has often fallen far short of the mark as seen from the public's viewpoint. This is leading in turn to a disaffection with science, a feeling that it is inappropriate for complex social and moral issues. The classic scientific method, which has contributed so much to man's progress, is itself seen as inappropriate to issues with significant moral or ethical content. Scientists and engineers must address this loss of confidence by developing new methods appropriate to the wider world into which they are being drawn. The Unified Systems Hypothesis (USH) is presented in this wider context.

Some forty years ago there was a hope that the science of systems would offer a way forward. This hope was engendered in General Systems Theory (GST).

General Systems Theory

GST, however, originated by von Bertalanffy (1950) and others, has not fulfilled its promise of a single approach to all systems. The social, behavioural and management sciences are still essentially separated from the traditional, harder sciences such as physics and chemistry. It is in the social and management sciences in particular that advances in methods have been made, but often without the mathematical rigour seen as fundamental by the physical sciences. Independent schools have grown up, the so-called "hard" and "soft" advocates corresponding broadly to the physical/mathematical and to the social and management schools respectively. Von Bertalanffy did highlight the vital "open system" concept, and in so doing presented a new and exciting perspective on systems, which has subsequently influenced the softer sciences particularly to consider the whole, as well as the parts, of systems.

Addressing Complex Issues

The softer sciences have gained some success in their approach to the delicate subject of addressing issues, using so-called soft methods, organization development interventions and so on. They seek often to understand complex situations and perhaps to improve situations, rather than to proffer optimal solutions—the goal of the so-called hard systems practitioners. Soft methods are often procedural, frequently interactive, encouraging commitment through participation, developing consensus rather than solving problems. Soft and hard systems methods alike lack a theoretical base, so that the undoubted reasonableness of their several approaches is more in the nature of a theology than a science. This is particularly so of systems engineering

Systems Engineering

Systems engineering has made some advances since the introduction of GST galvanized systems theorists in the nineteen-fifties and -sixties, but not many, and few seemingly related to the theory. Indeed, it is hard to find a theory of systems engineering, although there is plenty of empirical, ad hoc method and, of course, it has some roots in operations research with its optimization ethic. Human factors or human engineering, ergonomics, anthropometrics, etc. have crept into the systems engineering scene, but there still exists something of a gulf between the human factors specialist, focused on the human in his working environment and relating to machinery, and the engineers who design that machinery. They lack a common language; the human factors specialist finds it difficult to be precise in engineering terms about matters of engineering concern, while the design engineer might like nothing better than a transfer function describing a human that he could plug into his calculations.

Systems engineers exist in, and are concerned with the creation of, socio-technical systems—that is, systems which are social as well as technical, as for example in the case of an information system where the technology and the human users/operators are interacting parts of the same overall system. Current approaches to systems engineering, while paying lip service to being open, tend to treat design as concerned with "closed systems", or systems which exist in isolation from inflows and outflows of energy, materials and information. To be sure, systems engineers create interfaces to other systems, but they generally enquire little about activities beyond the interface—it is not, after all, their concern. Or is it? If von

Bertalanffy is correct, then the principles he expounded concerning open systems should have relevance to today's complex systems engineering projects, be they hard or soft, closed or open.

Introducing USH

If systems engineering is concerned with socio-technical systems, and if there is a split between the social and the technical in terms of practice and theory, then it is to be expected that the systems created by systems engineers may be less than satisfactory. So it turns out. While there have been many spectacular successes, engineered systems are increasingly failing to live up to their promise as they become more complex. By comparison with their human counterpart, they are inflexible, non-adaptable and difficult to operate and to understand. The Unified Systems Hypothesis (USH) presented in this chapter is intended to bridge that gap by introducing a view of systems and a set of systems principles that are common to all systems. It is for others to judge the success of the USH, but it seeks to pave the way to greater harmony between man and his systems and, perhaps, offer both the softer and harder sciences a new perspective on their domains of interest and practice.

The notion of a single set of principles which apply to any system, whatever might be its classification, size or substance/non-substance, is challenging in the extreme. Such a set of principles must be:

- Universal
- Scale-independent
- Understandable
- Useful

There are few examples to follow. In physics, for example, models tend to be scale-particular; gas models are either macroscopic, giving rise to Boyle's and Charles's Laws, or microscopic/atomic/subatomic, leading to kinetic gas theory. That such differing viewpoints give consistent results is encouraging, but not the stuff of universal principles.

A visitor from space would see networks rather than systems:

- The Great Wall of China
- Rivers
- Roads
- Power Grids
- Reservoirs

In this perspective of networks lies the foundation of USH—it looks at systems from the viewpoint of their interactions, inter-connections and relationships, rather than from within any one system. In so doing, USH implicitly assumes that all systems of in-terest are essentially open, that is there is a flow into, out from, and between systems. This 'looking-between the systems' is not new, but seems to have been less favoured than the 'let's look inside the sys-tem' approach.

Consider the range of typical networks: radio and TV, newspapers, rivers, canals, sewers, gas pipes, timekeeping, postal deliveries, veins and arteries, arterial roads, railways, undersea oil pipes, electronic circuit boards, house wiring, computers, bus services, corridors, stairs and lifts, mines, spies, contacts, banks, informers, tasks, power grids, trees and roots, management, chain stores, burrows, suppliers, cracks, teaching, food chains, forces, telephones, carrier pigeons. The list is endless. Many of the above might be thought of as systems and so they are at one level of hierarchy. A chainstore is clearly a system, but it is also part of a retailing network which interconnects manufacturers and consumers.

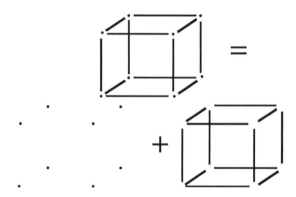

Figure 3.1 Links versus entities

Is this network viewpoint tenable? Consider Figure 3.1. The cube is made up of dots at each corner and links. Presenting the corner entities is insufficient to tell the whole story, since their inter-relationship is uncertain—they could be connected through the cube centre, for instance. Similarly, presenting the links only, while locating the entities, fails to describe them. Interestingly, as the simple diagram shows, a more coherent picture, in terms of the degree of order of the structure, might be said to emerge from the links alone than from the corner entities alone. This is particularly interesting. since it is more common practice to concentrate on the corner entities—the systems—than on their inter-relationships.

Entropy

Interest in order is interest in reduced entropy—the degree of disorder. Entropy can be defined in many ways—at least fifteen have been catalogued. Consider a box inside which two gases are present. It would be normal for these gases to be so mixed that, at any time, a sample of the mixture taken anywhere in the box would contain approximately the same proportion of molecules of each gas. The mixture is disordered. It might be possible to separate the gases such that each occupied one half of the box; this would require work to be done, and the result would be a reduction in the disorder. Entropy and work or energy are clearly related, but for our purposes consider now an area of virgin land.

Social Entropy

Human occupants enter the land, somewhat haphazardly. They associate into, say. three or four villages. The 'coming together' into villages represents a reduction in overall disorder, when compared with the previous meanderings. The three villages independently set up organizational structures: they elect leaders and allocate tasks to individuals, they till the land and raise cattle, seeking to create order. Entropy seems to be reducing again. Now, some of the villagers set out to explore, find the other villages and move home. In the process of leaving their villages and exploring, disorder increases. As they settle into their new homes and, perhaps, bring new organizational ideas and structures to bear, entropy again reduces. There seems to be a pattern in open systems, with entropy first increasing and then reducing, to be followed by another increase and then a further reduction. This notion will recur throughout the book.

In the same vein, it is possible to consider systems as, by their nature, reductions in entropy—at least within the boundary of the system. Similarly, connections between systems, bringing order and structure, must reduce configuration entropy, although entropy may well have increased during the creation of the links. At a fundamental level, it seems likely that the common thread binding all systems ideas together is the desire to perceive order, to reduce entropy either in fact, or in perception. It also seems likely that energy promotes variety and differentiation within interacting systems, as evidenced in many walks from Nature's variety (which is greater in warmer climes) to that of motor vehicle makes and models, religions, educational courses, fighter aircraft, and many, many more, all of which increase with social affluence/energy. Hence we see energy promoting entropy and systems forming to reduce it—hence, perhaps, the continual variation in entropy.

USH SYSTEM IMAGES

A General System View

Sachs (1976) asks "given an entity about which we know nothing, what should we presuppose about its nature in the process of conducting an enquiry?". He argues that the best strategy "to conduct the enquiry is to examine the entity under consideration simultaneously with its parts and a larger whole in which it is embedded, and never to assume that all its relevant properties may be obtained analytically from its properties already known". In other words, it is most prudent to assume that any entity under investigation is a system, is open and is inductive (as opposed to deductive). This is sound advice for all systems analysts, and has been observed throughout in the USH, particularly in forming the following systems images, which all apply simultaneously to any system. None of these images is an any way particularly new, or startling, but they have been selected to illustrate particular viewpoints as a basis for later analysis

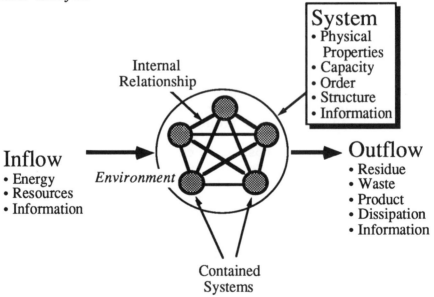

Figure 3.2 A general view of any system

The first image, Figure 3.2, is of a system receiving inflows, passing outflows and containing related and intra-connected systems. The inflows generally comprise energy, matter and information. The outflows are similar in substance but attract different titles. The system exhibits physical properties, it has order, structure or hierarchy, and it has capacity, intrinsic or explicit, to store/process energy, matter and/or information. Environment pervades and impinges upon the system and its contained systems. Evidently, this system image is of an open system, connected to other systems not shown.

Systems Hierarchy

The second image, Figure 3.3, presents a three-level systems hierarchy in which a "system-in-focus", that in which an observer has immediate interest, both contains systems (sub-systems) and is itself contained in a containing system along with other sibling systems. These siblings are related/interconnected to the system-in-focus; its contained systems are intra-connected. Environment pervades the containing system, but need not be homogeneous. Environment exists within the system-in-focus, but need not be identical with that outside in the containing system. Boundaries, shown as hard edges, may in fact be soft and fuzzy.

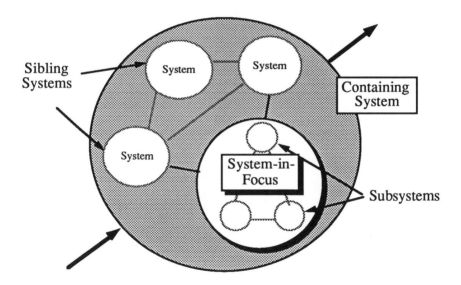

Figure 3.3 Systems hierarchy

Interacting Systems

The third image, Figure 3.4, combines the first two into a networked set of contained systems with mutual interflows, such that the outflows from some form the inflows to others. One system's residue becomes another's resource; one system's dissipation becomes another's energy source. Information is, unlike energy and material, exchanged without significant loss to the supplier. The interacting systems exist within a container which also receives, dissipates and exchanges, so providing hierarchical consistency.

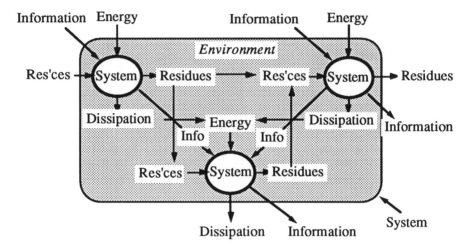

Figure 3.4 Recursive, networked systems

Simultaneous Multiple Containment

The fourth image presents a different thought: that a system may be simultaneously contained within more than one container, as a

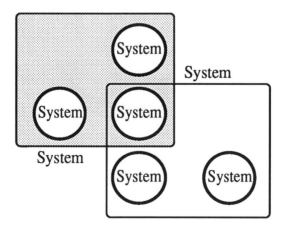

Figure 3.5 Multiple containment

bus-driver is simultaneously within a transportation system, a family system and a social system with his passengers. The potential complexity engendered by this image is staggering; if each system at each level of hierarchy can be simultaneously in a variety of containers then the resulting n-dimensional weave could be beyond untangling.

Cohesion and Dispersion

For a system to continue as an aggregation, it follows that there must be some cohesive influence attracting the contained systems, one to another. That each system does not collapse to a point suggests that there must be counteracting influences tending to disperse the contained systems. Cohesive and dispersive influences must balance for a system to persist. Such balance could be static or dynamic (oscillatory) Since systems wax and wane, it must be possible for the balance to be changed in either or both directions. The fifth image presents system inflows and outflows as the mediators of change in this weakening or strengthening of binding influences.

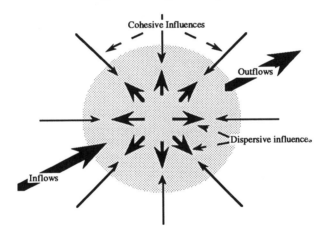

Figure 3.6 Cohesive and Dispersive Influences

USH DEFINITIONS OF SYSTEM, ENVIRONMENT AND EQUILIBRIUM

System

Within a Unified Systems Hypothesis, the definition of "system" is of particular interest, since there have been many definitions. Sachs (1976) suggested that "a system is a set of related entities, re-

ferred to as constituents of the system". Jordan (1960) produced
some 15 definitions, before contending that a thing is called a system when we wish to express the fact that the thing is perceived as
consisting of a set of elements or parts that are interconnected with
each other by discriminable, distinguishable principle. Hall (1962)
defined "system" as "a set of objects with relationships between the
objects and between their attributes".

Most satisfyingly, from my perspective, Russell Ackoff (1981) defined as follows. "A system is a set of two or more elements that satisfies the following three conditions: (1) The behaviour of each element has an effect on the whole (2) The behaviour of the elements
and their effects on the whole are interdependent and (3) However
subgroups of the elements are formed, each has an effect on the
whole and none has an independent effect.

Most commentaries agree that there are concepts both of parts,
and of relationships between those parts, in the notion of system. I
would contend that it is the *orderliness* of the systems concept
which is appealing, in that it reveals pattern in complexity or from
obscurity. Degree of orderliness is not evident in the plethora of definitions of system as a dominant feature. The following definition,
used as a basis within the Unified Systems Hypothesis, is intended
to be sufficiently vague to capture all kinds of systems, yet
sufficiently explicit to be useful:

> *A system is a collection of interrelated entities such that both the
> collection and the inter-relationships together reduce local entropy.*

In this definition, the relationships receive a degree of prominence
equal to that of the entities, because the pattern or network of relationships reduces uncertainty just as much as the collecting of entities. The notion of local entropy has been addressed above, and
simply suggest that the system may have bounds beyond which its
influence does not reduce disorder. The definition covers all kinds
of systems, human activity, man-made, natural, etc., and is compatible with open as well as closed classifications. It is also compatible
with systems as intellectual constructs—perceptions of the world,
theologies, paradigms and transcendental systems. This is not to
suggest a relational structural approach: Angyal (1941) suggested
that "systems cannot be deduced from relations, while the deduction
of relations from systems still remains a possibility". Since systems could be related in many ways, a particular pattern of relationships carries information, reduces uncertainty—the definition
seeks *parity* for structure with entity, but not *precedence*.

Environment

"Environment" is a strange concept to define. It seems often to be
thought of as a vague "soup" or medium in which systems exist.

Kremyanskiy (1960) had a clear view of environment. "The external environment penetrates the entire living whole of ... a group and turns in part into its internal environment ... ". Hall (1962), however, stated: "For a given system, the environment is the set of all objects outside the system: (1) a change in whose attributes affect the system and (2) whose attributes are changed by the behaviour of the system." Sachs (1976) avowed that "the environment of an entity is the collection of its envelopes relative to all its relevant properties. The entity itself is sometimes excluded by convention from the environment". The notion of envelope is one of co-production, in which the response of an entity to a stimulus is defined, not by the stimulus alone, but by other factors impinging on the entity at the same time. Ackoff and Emery (1972) hold similar views about environment and co-production. In Sachs's view, the environment was itself a system.

Von Bertalanffy (1950), with his seminal open systems formulation, had little to offer on environment, causing Emery and Trist (1965) to introduce the notion of "causal texture of organizational environments". In their view, "while Von Bertalanffy's formulation enables the exchange processes between the organism, or organization, and elements in its environment to be dealt with in a new perspective, it does not deal with all those processes in the environment itself, which are among the determining conditions of the exchanges".

Overall, it has to be said that the handling of environment seems to be either vague or inconsistent. And yet it is an essential feature from the most abstract of system levels down to the air we breathe and the situations in which we live. I therefore propose a seemingly new definition, designed as with "system" to be both vague, yet precise:

> *Environment is that which mediates the interchanges between systems. Total environment is the sum of all such mediations*

How does this definition work? Consider any two systems. Identify the exchanges between them. Identify that which mediates the interchanges; that is environment. For example, that which mediates the interchange between economic systems is money, barter and trade—we often speak of a "favourable trading environment". Consider a suburban dormitory system and a city business. That which mediates the interchange of people is the commuting facilities—we often refer to the travelling environment. Plants and animals exchange CO_2 and O_2 using the atmosphere and the biosphere as mediator. In physics, forces are mediated by the exchange of particles. Heat being conducted along a metal rod is mediated by conduction electrons. Environment is that which mediates the multitude of interchanges between us and the surrounding features when we are living, walking in the town and country, etc.

So the consistency with general understanding of the term arises. Kremyanskiy's "pervasive soup" can be seen as the sum of all the discrete one-to-one mediations going on at any time, some of which are interesting, others less so. And here is the value of the new definition. It enables identification of the environment of particular interest, part by part, so that we may be precise about those parts of the environment in which we have an interest, but may be vague about the other parts.

We humans tend to organize our environment into transport systems, communication systems, infrastructure systems and so on. This presents no problems within USH, since it is merely a hierarchy shift. It is, however, convenient to retain the notion of environment as mediating interchange between systems—it is a useful model.

Equilibrium

As with environment, so the notion of "equilibrium" has been disturbed by systems thinking. Koehler (1938) held the view that equilibrium was essentially associated with a low state of energy, as for a marble running to the lowest level in a saucer, while for many organisms what was frequently referred to as equilibrium corresponded instead to a heightened energy state. Koehler referred to such phenomena as stationary processes, and his distinction is still valid. Nonetheless, the term "equilibrium" is in general use and needs to be addressed.

As Figure 3.7 shows, candle flame length is stabilized without feedback when the rate of flow up the wick equals the rate of flow leaving the flame. Similarly, the capacitor voltage is stabilized without feedback—a current source, having infinite output impedance cannot experience feedback in the illustrated circuit—when the rate of current flowing in from the source equals the rate of current leaving via the resistor. Both the flame and the capacitor represent stable open systems; in neither case is equilibrium reached under some minimum energy condition.

Figure 3.8 shows two models of an open system (using the STELLA® notation), graphed alongside their dynamic responses to a constant inflow. The outflow is the same in each case in that it is proportional to the contemporary level, but in System B the outflow has been delayed—delay is not shown. System A behaves just like the candle flame—it grows rapidly, but growth rate levels off and it reaches a steady state. System B on the other hand oscillates and the oscillations will either diminish or increase in amplitude according to the amount of the delay. Boulding's classification of systems (1956) places such open or self-regulating systems at hierarchy level 4, the level of the cell in biology, with the first three levels (static structures, simple dynamic systems, control mechanisms) being closed in relation to their environment. And yet, as the Figure 3.8 illustrates, the model could be a representation of a simple physical system such as a bath or an electronic capacitor in parallel with a load resistor, charging from a constant current source. There seems to be some discrepancy with Boulding's system classification, which is particularly interesting because it is often used as the basis for discriminating between living and non-living entities—see Kast and Rosenzweig (1972).

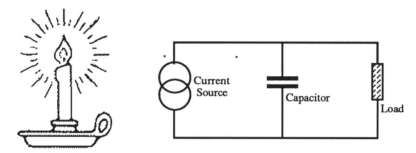

Increasing flame stabilized by maximum flow rate in wick.

Capacitor voltage stabilized by increasing current in load

Figure 3.7 Open system stability at high levels of energy

Evidently there can arise a static or dynamic balance between inflows to, and outflows from, an open system such that it reaches a stationary or stable condition. I do not believe it necessary, as did Koehler, to give this a title other than equilibrium since there is clearly a parity in operation, albeit not induced by feedback. The essential point that Koehler makes concerning energy wells is, however, important in open systems; the test for equilibrium cannot be one of minimum energy. Instead, I propose the following definition for all system:

Interacting systems can be said to be in equilibrium when their environment is stable, statically or dynamically

This definition of equilibrium employs the USH definition of environment, above. It should, to satisfy the objectives of USH, address all systems satisfactorily, including physical systems. The marble at the bottom of the saucer is subject to forces, mediated by their respective molecular structures. There is no movement and no friction. If the marble is displaced, it will roll back and forth under unbalanced forces, settling eventually at the bottom of the saucer again. While rolling, the frictional force is mediated by the adhesive forces between marble and saucer, and between marble and air, which are constantly changing until the marble is once again stationary.

The marble example shows a difference between the form of the usual definition of physical stability, based on a balance of forces, and the new definition. The balance of forces paradigm is prescriptive—if a suitable force is applied, it will result in equilibrium. The USH definition is descriptive—if the environment is stable, then it may be deduced that interacting systems are in equilibrium. In USH, stable environment is the litmus test of equilibrium.

USH PRINCIPLES

We are now in a position to identify some simple systems principles which are induced from observation, accepting Popper's (1968) admonition on the limited value of induction, but nonetheless presenting the principles in Popper's (1972) spirit of openness as the

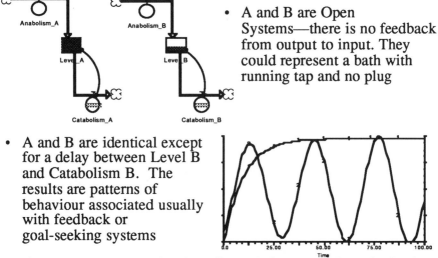

- A and B are Open Systems—there is no feedback from output to input. They could represent a bath with running tap and no plug

- A and B are identical except for a delay between Level B and Catabolism B. The results are patterns of behaviour associated usually with feedback or goal-seeking systems

Figure 3.8 Exponential and oscillatory behaviour without feedback

basis for progress. Later, predictions will be made from the principles which satisfy Popper's dictate of falsifiability, such that there is a potential for the principles to be refuted.

The Principle of Reactions

Le Chatelier's Principle is a general principle of interacting forces in classical science. "If a set of forces is in equilibrium and a new force is introduced then, in so far as they are able, the existing forces will rearrange themselves so as to oppose the new force." In Figure

3.9, the three forces at the left are in equilibrium. At the right, a fourth force is introduced and the original three readjust to a new point of equilibrium for all four. The example is of forces in a single plane, but the concept is seen so often in everyday life that a wider interpretation seems eminently reasonable.

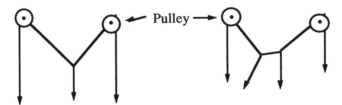

Figure 3.9 Forces in Equilibrium

The Principle of Reactions flows simply from the images and definitions above, and are as follows:

> *If a set of interacting systems is at equilibrium and, either a new system is introduced to the set, or one of the systems or interconnections undergoes change then, in so far as they are able, the other systems will rearrange themselves so as to oppose the change*

The principle is unexceptional for physical systems, to the point that it may seem axiomatic; it was expounded by Le Chatelier (1850-1936) in 1888 in that context. It is not so for all systems, however. The contention of USH is that the principle applies equally to interactions between economic, political, ecological, biological, stellar, particle or any other aggregations which satisfy the definition, *system*.

An example of interacting systems seeking a new equilibrium can be found in urban commuting systems. Raising rail fares sharply to increase revenue in a supposed inelastic market can result in short-term advantage, to be replaced by long-term loss as commuters switch to other forms of transport and companies opt out of the expense of urban operations.

A "hard" example might be the hydraulic brakes on a car. The driver depresses the brake pedal, increasing hydraulic pressure through the hydraulic fluid, as the various brake pistons progressively experience resistance from the brake pads and shoes contacting the braking surfaces. Pressure equalization will result in each of the brakes receiving an equal thrust and resisting the pressure equally in an equilibrium of balanced forces.

The principle does not indicate the *manner* of movement. There is certainly nothing in the principle to suggest that movement should be linear. According to the systems and to their interactions, movement could be slow, fast, even explosive, as suggested by catastrophe, chaos and self-organized criticality theories (*qv*).

These theories would seem to interface with the Principle of Reactions.

The Principle of System Cohesion

The Principle of System Cohesion derives simply from the fifth image, Figure 3.6 above, and may seem axiomatic, particularly for physical systems:

> *A system's form is maintained by a balance, static or dynamic, between cohesive and dispersive influences. The form of an interacting set of systems is similarly maintained*

The Earth is held in its orbit around the Sun by a balance between gravitational and centripetal forces; that orbit will change as the Sun's mass decreases through its emission as radiation and the solar wind. For physical systems, the dispersive and cohesive influences are generally evident.

Since the USH is intended to apply to all systems, this principle must apply not only to such physical systems, but also—for example—to social systems such as families or ethnic groups. It is, perhaps, an unusual thought to consider that the influences which bind a stable family together equate to the influences which tend to disperse them. The notions are appealing, however, in that they stimulate thoughts as to what those influences might be and how change might be associated with external influences permeating the family group.

An example from the world of bees is relevant. As hives get bigger, the pheromone emitted by the dominant queen which assures bees that all is well with the world has to spread further and each bee receives less in consequence, until the level per bee falls below a threshold. At this point bees swarm to find a new hive. The cohesive influence is carried by the pheromone. The dispersive influence is unclear, but may be an evolved response to anticipate reduction in food due to concentrated local foraging. Perhaps the example of the bees gives a clue about limits to growth, evident in organisms, structures, societies and organizations which exhibit tendencies to divide beyond a certain size, measured either dimensionally or in numbers in the system.

The Principle of Cohesion is relevant to socially developed transcendental systems too: the Ten Commandments from the Old Testament of the Bible are a classic example of a set of rules by which people can live together without mutual interference, a dispersive influence. And Jesus Christ developed the most effective rule "do unto others as you would have them do unto you" which, if observed by all, would virtually eliminate all socially dispersive influences. (From a systems viewpoint, Christ's "rule" is pure simplicity, since it turns everyone's dispersive tendencies against themselves, promoting only the mutually self-rewarding (q.v.) influences between people in their place—in systems terms, a masterstroke). Buddhism may be similarly viewed in systems terms as reducing dispersive tendencies while at the same time preserving natural variety—truly the original "green" philosophy.

The Principle of Adaptation

The Principle of System Cohesion generates other images. In particular, a set of open, interacting systems in a changing environment will endure only if they can adapt to that environment. Hence the mean rate of adaptation must exceed the mean rate of change of environment.

> *For continued system cohesion, the mean rate of system adaptation must equal or exceed the mean rate of change of environment*

This notion is developed in Chapter 12.

The Principle of Connected Variety

The Principle of Connected Variety is concerned with stability[2] of interacting systems. The third image above showed a small set of three interacting systems. As the number of interacting systems increases, and as their mutual interconnections increase both in number and in the variety of energy, matter and information exchanged, they develop a closer and more cross-coupled weave in which it is increasingly likely that system outflows will match other system inflows[3], leading to a stable environment. These considerations lead to the Principle of Connected Variety:

> *Interacting systems stability increases with variety, and with the degree of connectivity of that variety within the environment*

Evidently, there are shades of Ashby's (1956) law of requisite variety in this principle, but it is not intended as a cybernetic statement. Instead, the image evoked by the principle is one of

---

[2] Stability is not always a desirable state. A set of stable interacting systems may be resistant to change. While such resistance may be admirable in the biosphere, it may be less so in, say, business or politics, where controlled change may be the objective.

[3] Implicit in the definitions of interactions is the sense of flow and interchange. Relationships and connections which disconnect, which bar interchange and flow, require to be reformulated before applying the Principle of Connected Variety

"complementary systems", sets of open systems whose outflows and inflows are mutually satisfying. The balance between floral and faunal CO_2 and O_2 exchanges was mentioned in the discussion of environment above, and is an ideal example of complementary systems; the balance depends upon variety and connectivity, and is evidenced by a stable environment.

The value of this concept may be considerable; it may even provide a new ethic for systems engineering, where concentration on local optimization could be overtaken by the concept of complementary systems (q.v.).

The Principle of Limited Variety

The Principle of Limited Variety is stated as follows:

Variety in interacting systems is limited by the available space and the minimum degree of differentiation

The principle is axiomatic once "space" and "minimum differentiation" have been established. To explain, consider a guitar string. It can vibrate in a variety of modes limited by the need for nodes at bridge and stop. This maximum set of modes is the available space; the minimum differentiation is set by the need for each mode to comprise waves in integer half-wavelengths only. Consider religions. There are only so many religions in the world. The principle suggests that this arises because religions, to be different, must have a minimum significant differentiation; in this case, the available space is set by Man's intellectual view of religion. The variety of basic ethnic types is similarly limited by our perception of differentiation. Consider lastly differentiation. Kast and Rosenzweig (1972) observe that open systems tend towards greater differentiation and states of higher order (reduced entropy). Odum (1971) showed that specialization increases as the environment becomes more benign. In such benign environments, the "space" for increased specializations increases; what constitutes a specialization is determined by the minimum differentiation required for one role to be considered discrete from another. The process of differentiation seems to be associated with the degree of energy 'pumping' the network of interacting systems. Differentiation is observed in such diverse spheres as makes and models of cars (greater in richer markets), predators (fewer and each more omnivorous in colder, tundra climates), professions (more in richer conurbations).

The Principle of Preferred Patterns

As the weave of interactions between systems becomes more complex, it is increasingly likely that feedback loops will arise, some perhaps acting through many successive systems and exchanges. The prospect increases of non-linear interacting system behaviour. The occurrence of positive feedback loops is to be expected, if only because of resulting delays and phase changes, and leads to the Principle of Preferred Patterns:

The probability that interacting systems will adopt locally-stable configurations increases both with the variety of systems and with their connectivity.

Locally-stable, interacting systems abound. Cities, computer giants, international conglomerates, thunderclouds and tornadoes, molecular microclusters, ecological niches, bat and moth sonars, bureaucracies—all are instances of positive feedback, or mutual causality as Maruyama (1968) described it, leading to stable configurations. The general expectation of positive feedback is that it will produce some form of regenerative runaway. That need not be the case when such positive feedback exists within a web of essentially-negative feedback loops. Instead, multiple points of stability can occur.

A simple physical example of positive feedback is presented by the standard physics demonstration using soap bubbles or balloons: see Figure 3.10. The demonstration shows that the smaller bubble inflates the larger, contrary to expectations. Pressure in each bubble is inversely proportional to radius: the smaller bubble therefore exerts the greater pressure and, as air flows from smaller to larger, the situation is reinforced. This is regeneration. The process proceeds until the smaller bubble ceases to be a sphere and becomes a curved film over the end of the tube, of radius equal to that of the larger bubble. This is a point of stability. Had the smaller bubble been, instead, slightly larger at the start, or had the diameter of one outlet been different from the other, then different stabilities would have arisen. The characteristics of the process are that regeneration tends to cause a very rapid—sometimes even explosive—move towards a new point of stability.

Duncan and Rouvray (1989) discovered that small aggregates of atoms form a discrete phase of matter, and that they aggregate in particularly stable configurations. Such cluster species are referred to as "magic numbers" by analogy with the quantum model of atomic nuclei in which certain combinations of protons and neutrons are allowed and others are not.

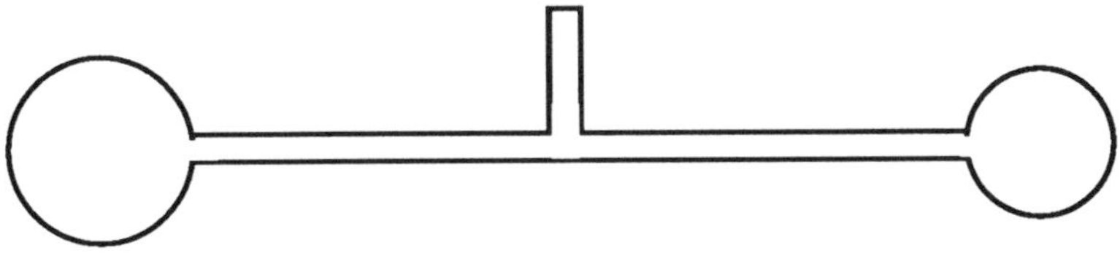

Figure 3.10 The Soap-Bubble Experiment

A new economic theory by Arthur (1990) suggests that the long-held view of supply and demand as a moderating, or essentially negative feedback system, is untenable, particularly where modern high-technology products are concerned, and that positive feedback could provide a much more convincing argument to explain the dominance of, particularly, organizations which entered into a new, high-tech field early in its development.

There are many, many more examples from many diverse spheres of the development of preferred patterns, sufficient for the principle to be established by induction and to be mathematically modelled.

The Principle of Cyclic Progression

The last of the USH principles addresses a phenomenon which we all recognize, that systems do not last for ever. Civilizations may be considered as systems and as H. G. Wells (1922) noted, they come and go, as follows: neolithic civilization; Sumeria; Egypt; Babylon and Assyria; the primitive Aryans; the early Jews; the Greeks; Alexandria; the Romans; Carthage; China; the Barbarians; the Byzantine and Sassanid Empires; the Arab Nations; the Mongols; the Americans; the Industrial Revolution; and so on up to the present. Such thoughts lead directly to the Principle of Cyclic Progression, expressed in words and graphically as shown in Figure 8.11.

The principle does not imply that the *same* systems emerge. Clearly with civilizations, that is not so. Emerging systems may occupy the same "space" however, whatever that term implies in particular situations. Variety is generated in the space by influx from surroundings, or by mutation of systems (Maruyama,1968), or both. A recent investigation into recurrent fires in Yellowstone National Park was undertaken by Romme and Despain (1989). The subject of interest was the relatively rare occurrence of major fires, although minor fires, initiated by dry weather and natural or man-made sources, occurred frequently. Between the early 1700s to the summer of 1988, there were major fires in 1690-1709, 1730-1749, 1850-1869 and 1988.

The suggested reason for the rarity was connected with ecological succession. Each major fire created space in the locale. A few species were adapted to survive fire, and these grew. The space encouraged the generation of species variety, some from deep root varieties and some imported from surrounding areas by wind and animal. The varied flora encouraged varied fauna. The faster-growing tree species overtook the original, slower-growing survivors to form dense stands, intercepting the sun, and reducing the ground-level vegetation. Original survivors died out, to be replaced by second generation varieties, letting in some sunlight and stimulating the growth of vegetation on the forest floor. Finally, matured trees died, small trees and dead branches accumulated, leaving the forest fully supplied with fuel for the next fire to become a major catastrophe, and so starting the cycle again.

The weight of evidence suggests that there may indeed be a repeating pattern in systems where variety, the mediator of stability, is suppressed by dominance, which in turn leads to vulnerability through inability to change. Dominance denotes substantial imbalance in favour of one system at a given hierarchy level.

A simple mechanical analogy might be that of plucking a guitar

Interconnected systems driven by an external energy source will tend to a cyclic progression in which system variety is generated, dominance emerges to suppress the variety, the dominant mode decays or collapses, and survivors emerge to regenerate variety.

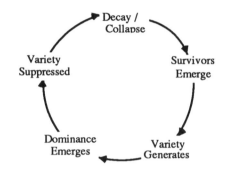

Figure 8.11 Cyclic progression

string off-centre, so as to create a wealth of harmonics. Gradually the overtones subside, leaving the dominant fundamental which decays in its turn. If the finger is moved along the fretboard while the harmonics are present, any may be picked out. If only the fundamental is left, moving along the fretboard will suppress the vibration. Response to change is better where the variety exists. More generally, the Principle is an expression of the cyclic rise and fall of entropy introduced at the beginning of the chapter.

USH PRINCIPLES AS A SET

The Basis for Systems Practice

As Figure 3.12 illustrates, there are three areas towards which the USH may contribute. At present, each of these areas is treated somewhat differently:

- Addressing issues. There appears to be no real theory for addressing issues, although there are many methods, some quite successful. As usual, such ad hoc methods, while pragmatic, may fall short of providing an ideal solution

- Developing systems concepts. At present, system concepts are not always rigourously developed, the procedure being to go directly from a solution-transparent requirement into design. There appears to be a gap in the process, prior to formulating a firm requirement, in which creative, innovative concepts are developed, explored and assessed. In industry, for example, marketing staff quite often return from a visit to a customer having agreed with him the broad outline or architecture of a system, thereby setting in concrete one of the most important and difficult aspects of design without realizing the significance of their actions. There seems to be, moreover, no established theory for the development of traceable, supportable concepts

- Systems engineering itself is short on theory, as has been discussed

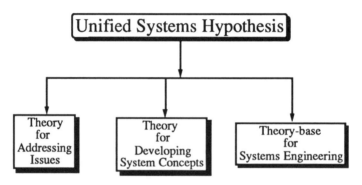

Figure 3.12 The purpose and application of USH

USH PRINCIPLES AS ONE

Each of the seven principles has been presented independently. It is evident, however, that they address complementary aspects of interacting systems:

- The *Principle of Reactions* addresses the tendency to react to change and towards equilibrium
- The *Principle of Cohesion* addresses the changing form of an interacting system and limits to growth
- The *Principle of Adaptation* addresses the ability of a system to endure in a changing environment
- The *Principle of Connected Variety* addresses the basis of stability between interacting systems

- The *Principle of Limited Variety* addresses the limits to differentiation in interacting systems, and hence the limits to stability
- The *Principle of Preferred Patterns* addresses the emergence of dominance
- The *Principle of Cyclic Progression* examines life cycle

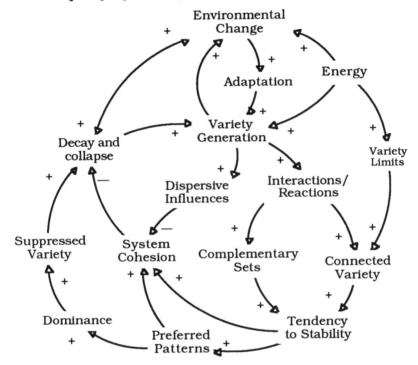

Figure 3.13 The USH principles as one

The principles fit together into an interesting and useful Causal Loop Model (CLM), shown in Figure 3.13. The CLM (like an influence diagram but with cause and effect in place of influence in each arrow) shows the interactions between the USH principles, the environment and the external energy source necessary to drive continual change. Environmental change drives adaptation (or extinction), which leads to the generation of variety. From variety stem more interacting systems, encouraging the occurrence of more complementary sets and more connected variety, always supposing there is sufficient energy entering the set to generate differentiation/variety. The connected variety and cmplementary sets encourage stability of the open systems, leading to preferred patterns engendered by positive feedback and overall system cohesion. Cohesion is prejudiced by the generation of variety, which generates dispersive influences too. Preferred patterns may, in the fullness of time, lead to dominance within the interacting systems which, should it suppress variety will lead to eventual decay and collapse. System cohesion counteracts that tendency, of course. Decay and collapse makes way for the generation of fresh variety and the cycle continues as long as the energy source persists and the environment changes; this change is unstoppable once started, since all the systems interact with the environment and each changing system changes the environment for the others.

One last point about the USH principles: there is nothing to suggest that the system interactions should in any way be linear or continuous.   The tendency to stability and the formation of preferred patterns certainly need not be linear—indeed they could be explosive, catastrophic or chaotic.   Rather than invalidating the model, it lends strength to it, suggesting that there may be a key here to understanding the behaviour of interacting systems at a heretofore unprecedented level.

Predictions

The previous section suggested the value to be gained by considering engineering projects as open, interacting systems. All systems engineering activities are *de facto* open systems both as human activity systems, and in the tasks undertaken. Systems engineering is perhaps the archetypal socio-technical system (Emery and Trist, 1960), since it not only is an open system of men, money, machines, and materials (Jenkins,1972), but it seeks—or rather, should seek— to create open systems as its *raison d'être*.

Predictions will be made on a broader front, in keeping with the principle of Popper's black swan—Popper (1972)— since to choose particular examples proves nothing, being inductive. Instead, a broad prediction will be more falsifiable—and it is to be remembered that the USH seeks to address all classifications of systems.

Finally, the principles are *themselves* the predictions—they propose what should occur to any system under conditions stated in the principles.

CONCLUSION

USH brings together views and concepts from a wide variety of systems thinkers, old and new, and presents a set of system images, definitions and principles which are intended to provide a common basis for the perception, understanding, analysis, design and creation of all systems. This is a bold aim and it is difficult to prove—or disprove—many of the contentions presented. But then, it is a hypothesis and not a theory. USH will have value if it provides an evolving basis for all systems practitioners to work together, soft with hard, open with closed, so that we may jointly improve our practices.

At the beginning of this chapter, the following four features were presented as valuable for any USH. It should be:

- Universal
- Scale-independent
- Understandable
- Useful

USH has been presented by induction, not by deduction, and is open to criticism on that score. I hope that, along with the criticism, there will be an attempt to prove or disprove the principles since they can provide useful insights into so many issues and problems. In any event, the USH principles will be used throughout this book as the basis for all, or nearly all, that follows. I hope that the reader will find that, at least, the last two bullets above have been satisfied.

ASSIGNMENT
THE DOMINO EXERCISE

Using only the USH principles:

Characterize and explain the systems behaviour of the Warsaw Pact/COMECON countries of Eastern Europe, initially under Soviet management. Identify the USH Principles at work in the creation and maintenance of system cohesion during the twentieth century. Explain why the system eventually dispersed, suggesting why the collapse occurred in domino fashion. Characterize and explain occurrences in the Soviet Union and—using USH principles—predict the likely outcomes within Europe as a whole, taking the EC, the Western European Union and NATO into account.

Part B
System Building Blocks

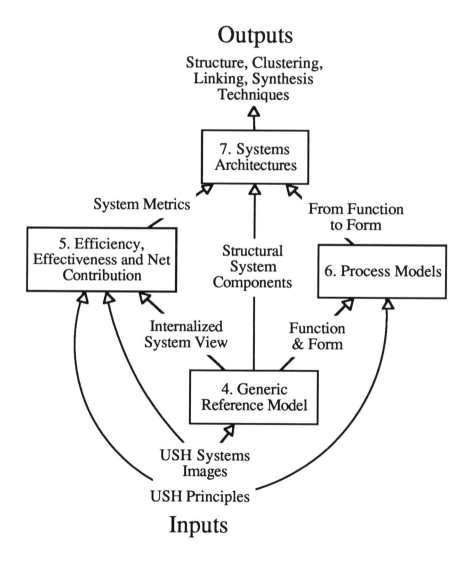

Outputs

Structure, Clustering,
Linking, Synthesis
Techniques

7. Systems
Architectures

System Metrics

From Function
to Form

5. Efficiency,
Effectiveness and Net
Contribution

Structural
System
Components

6. Process Models

Internalized
System View

Function
& Form

4. Generic
Reference Model

USH Systems
Images

USH Principles

Inputs

Chapter 4
The Generic Reference Model (GRM)

Rules and models destroy genius and art.
William Hazlitt 1778-1830

INTRODUCTION

The Generic Reference Model (GRM) is intended as a reference for any system such that features in the system can be seen against corresponding elements in the model. In this way, the GRM can be used to guide system design, to check design for completeness, to help in the diagnosis of system deficiency and to evaluate systems.

The model uses the USH images from Chapter 3, and comprises two parts : the Generic Reference (Function) Model, and the Generic Reference (Form) Model. The first, as the name implies, is concerned with what the system *does*, the second with what the system *is*. Both models present an *internalized* view of a system. This is because the GRM is concerned with the design of a system which is generally undertaken from an internalized viewpoint (but see Chapter 12), yet which seeks to establish requisite emergent properties—the externalized view of a system. How the two viewpoints are to be reconciled will be discussed later.

Neither model is prescriptive; instead, each seeks to identify the necessary and sufficient (N&S) sets of descriptive information which together make up a full, or closed, system description. Nor are the models analytical in the sense of, say, Beer's Viable Systems Model (Beer, 1984)

THE GR (FUNCTION) MODEL

The GR (Function) Model concerns itself with the internal functions or activities of a system. Functions are shown under three headings: "mission", "viability" and "resource management". They form an N&S set for system functions; mission describes system purpose, viability establishes the system to pursue that purpose, and resources are used both in the pursuit of mission and in the maintenance of viability. Given all three, there exists a closed set of features assuring continued pursuit of mission—although not necessarily achievement of that mission, since obstacles may deny completion.

Together, mission, viability and resource management are referred to as the management set. The term does not necessarily presume sentient behaviour from the system, although many systems may be consciously managed. The Sun, for example, may be thought of as "managing" its hydrogen resource in its process of nucleosynthesis. The interior of the Sun is structured and organized into three concentric convection zones, allowing material carrying matter and heat energy to pass radially to and from the hot interior. That this organization occurred naturally does not invalidate it from being described as resource management.

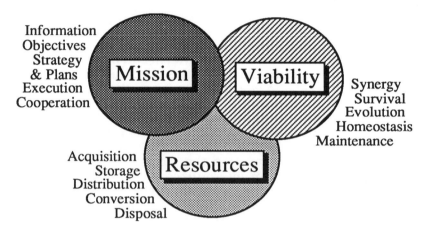

Figure 4.1 The Generic Reference (Function) Model

Mission, viability and resource management, each a member of an N&S set, can be elaborated into further N&S sets, as presented in following paragraphs.

Mission Management

Purposeful or purposive[1] systems pursue a mission. A mission may be some grand design, such as propagation of the species, or something rather simpler like looking for food, igniting petrol vapour in an internal combustion engine or resolving a dispute.

A mission, as shown in Figure 4.1, is comprised of parts:

------

[1] A purposeful system exhibits its own will. A purposive system may have purpose ascribed to it by an external viewer. A cardio vascular system is purposive; it serves the purpose of maintaining life. An aircraft is purposive, while its pilot is purposeful. Pilot and aircraft together become a purposeful system as long as the aircraft performs to the will of its pilot.

- Collecting or receiving information, either via information channels or sensors
- Setting objectives, consciously or unconsciously, achieving all of which will achieve the mission
- Formulating a strategy and a plan, again consciously or unconsciously, for the achievement of the mission
- Executing the plan
- Co-operating, if appropriate, with others in the environment

There is nothing more that the undertaking of a mission can entail, since all phases have been addressed (if, as is assumed, execution includes any recovery to post-mission location). A lowly worm, intent on making its hermaphroditic contribution to posterity by finding and reproducing with a like worm, goes through all the phases. Placing Neil Armstrong on the Moon likewise went through all phases.

Viability Management

A viable system is one which is able to maintain its separate existence within the environment. It can draw upon energy and resources from that environment, with which it can maintain itself. A non-viable system will not persist. A system may be non-viable because its contained systems do not operate correctly, due to failure, damage or being presented with an unsuitable environment. And a system must exhibit internal control, conscious or unconscious, over its parts if they are to operate as one—that is, to be a system. From these considerations emerge the N&S set for viability management as follows, and as shown in Figure 4.1:

- Synergy is co-operation between the parts; it generally requires co-ordination between subsystems, implying inter-communication and sufficient variety in that communication to effect control. (Synergy should not be confused with co-operation under the mission heading; this latter refers to co-operation with external siblings.) Feedback will often feature in control, but is not fundamental. Some sub-systems carry a plan and some kind of clock, so that co-ordination can be achieved without communication, by acting according to plan at appropriate times
- Survival features are invariably to be found in systems. These may may take many forms, from concealment, deception, evasion and camouflage through self-defence to damage-tolerance and protective devices. Security may be a survival feature in HASs

- Evolutionary capability must exist in a viable system in some degree if it is to adapt to changing environment and threat. In Nature, evolution may be Darwinian, i.e. only perceptible through generation-to-generation changes, or social through adaptive behaviour as in higher animals. In man-made systems, reserves may be built-in to allow some evolution, as in the practice of designing systems with spare capacity or power to accommodate the unknown

- Contained systems must continue to operate; homeostasis is the maintenance of suitable operating conditions for all contained systems. In animals, homeostasis is concerned with temperature, fluids, ion balance, blood-sugar and so on. In most cases it is autonomic, but not always—temperature regulation in so-called cold-blooded animals may be a conscious response, causing them to move into the sun to warm up or the shade/water to cool down. In a company, the routine administration corresponds to homeostasis in part. Organizing staff into shifts, covering for absentees, maintaining communications channels, providing heating, lighting and ventilation and many more, all seek to maintain the *status quo.*

- Maintenance is essential to remove and replace failed parts of the system

Resources Management

Resources are required by a system, essentially for two purposes : pursuit of mission and maintenance of viability. It would not be inappropriate to incorporate resource management within either of the other two members of the management set, but it is considered simpler and "cleaner" to treat it as a separate element. Resource management can be considered as follows:

- Resource acquisition, the achievement of resource inflows to the system

- Storage of resources once acquired, either explicitly in storage media, or intrinsically in the structure, links and organization of the system

- Distribution of resources to the points of need

- Conversion of resources which require it, either for transport or utilization reasons, as in animals which store fat so that it can be converted to energy when required

- Disposal of resources or waste. Strangely, perhaps, a company's products comes under this heading. The residue from all the materials and energy which have been put into a production system result *inter alia* in product, as shown in figure 4.1, along with dissipation, waste and information.

THE GR (FORM) MODEL

The Generic Reference (Function) Model concerned itself with describing what a system *does*. This section presents a descriptive model of what a system *is*. The GR (Form) Model is presented as follows:

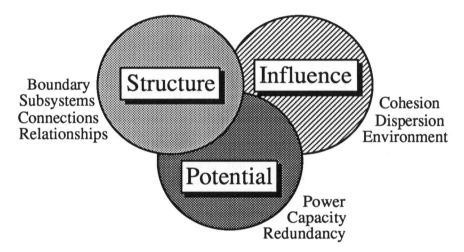

Boundary
Subsystems
Connections
Relationships

Cohesion
Dispersion
Environment

Power
Capacity
Redundancy

Figure 4.2 The Generic Reference (Form) Model

The GR (Form) Model is also N&S or closed, in the sense of describing form. Structure describes the evident features of a system, Influence identifies those features which hold that structure together and in balance (be that balance dynamic or static), while Potential describes those features held in the structural web which enable the system, which characterize it as big or small, powerful or weak, sluggish or agile, and so on. As with the GR (Function) Model, the GR (Form) Model concerns itself exclusively with an *internalized* view of systems

Structure

From the foregoing statement and figures it is evident that all systems have some form, to the extent at least of containing (sub-) systems which are intra-connected and of having interconnections with other sibling systems. These statements clearly imply that a boundary must be considered, within which a particular system exists. For some systems, interconnection may be less apparent than relationship; some entities may be part of the same system because of their relationship, while actual connectivity may be less apparent. Connectivity implies relationship; relationship need not imply connectivity. Relationship may refer to position, affinity, hierarchy, rapport, affiliation, etc, none of which entirely amounts to connectivity in the sense of enabling flow or the application of force or influence.

Influence

To describe what a system *is* needs more than the somewhat static description offered by the structural elements above, however. The components or members of a system aggregate under some influence. For the solar system, it is gravity that attracts. For an ecology, it may be food and water. For an ethnic group, it might be the familiarity of culture and the feeling of security afforded by community—and so on. Whatever the system, there must be an attractive or aggregating influence.

By the same token, there must be a dispersive influence to counteract the aggregating influence, or else the system would collapse to a point. For the solar system it is centripetal force and for the Sun itself it is the continuing expansion of substance due to the nuclear synthesis generating heat in the core; both counteract gravity. For the ecology, it may be competition for space and habitat in which to hunt, graze and/or breed. For the ethnic group, it may be the need for personal and family space, together with the attractions of life, culture, work and play in the world beyond their bounded culture with which they come into contact every day.

Environment is the medium in which the cohesive and dispersive influences operate upon the structure. For the solar system, environment is the near-vacuum of space, the solar wind, cosmic dust, magnetic and electric fields, etc. For an ecology, it is the biosphere with all that the term implies. For an ethnic group it is the surroundings, buildings, ambience, media, transport and other features which we normally think of as urban environment, but it may include economic, political, religious, geographic and technological factors too, where these permeate the system of interest.

Potential

Potential describes what a system might be able to achieve in principle on the basis of its internal features. For the solar system, it might be reduced to Einstein's energy-mass equivalence equation, since this describes the potential energy to be had by converting all the solar mass to energy. Happily, this conversion is gradual. Of much more importance in describing the Sun or any other system is its power, or the *rate* at which it is potentially able to expend energy or do work. So, for the Sun as a viable system it is more useful to describe it in terms of its surface temperature, or the amount of energy radiated per unit time, since both of these allow us to rank it against other stars and to calculate its effects on the Earth and the other planets. Its mass and volume are important in the sense that they indicate for how long the Sun can continue to radiate energy. In this context, mass and volume indirectly describe capacity in Figure 4.2, since they dictate the limits of the power source.

Similar concepts apply in the description of all systems. An ecology can be usefully thought of as means of converting solar energy into other forms of energy; we can describe the efficiency with which it undertakes such conversion, for example.[2] Describing an ethnic group by its power may seem fanciful and it would surely make little sense in the simple terms used above. However, if we were to compare two dissimilar groups, we might well be struck with differences in their respective energies, degrees of social activity and so on. On reflection, it does not seem to be stretching the point of a descriptive model too far to use the term power here too, as the rate of generating energy within the ethnic societal group.

Power as a term in the GR (Form) Model should not be thought of as an emergent property of the system; it is very much intended as an internal view, indicating potential which may not be achievable. This internalized view is consistent with that of internal energy[3] in physics, referring to the summed particle kinetic energy in substances.

Once power is accepted as a descriptor, capacity is then the determining factor in describing how long that power or rate of energy conversion can be maintained. Redundancy is the spare or reserve features in a system which afford resilience in the face of internal failures or damage from without.

A GR (BEHAVIOUR) MODEL

There is much left unstated by the GR (Function and Form) Models. Systems have other universal characteristics concerned with their behaviour, including responsiveness, predictability, and many more. The purpose of the GRM is to take an internalized view of any system, and behaviour is in many ways an external, or emergent property view—see Vickers (1983). There seem to be some universals in human behaviour which could form candidates for such a model, for example: perception, memory, categorization, judgement. To these could be added: aggression, co-operation, stealth, temperament, friendliness, and many more. Clearly, these are not

---

[2] It can be shown that the maximum rate of such energy conversion occurs at 50% efficiency.

[3] The sea contains a vast amount of internal energy from solar heating, for example; this energy cannot be tapped unless it can be transferred from the sea to a colder sink. Without such a sink, it is inaccessible energy.

universal to all systems, however. Universals applicable to any system might include:

- Responsiveness—whether a system responds to stimulus, how quickly, how vigorously, indeed whether a system initiates—or appears to initiate—activity without external stimulus, whether response adapts to stimulus type
- Stability—whether a system is predictable, dependable, operates within prescribable limits

The development of a third model within the GRM set is a subject for on-going research.

USING THE GRM

The GRM is intended as a reference model for those conceiving, designing, comparing or evaluating systems, hopefully of any kind. The basic tenets of systems theory espouse the notion of emergence— properties of a system as a whole not ascribable to any one part of the system on its own. The essence of emergence is that it views a system *externally*. We can bring the GRM and emergence together as shown in Figure 4.3.

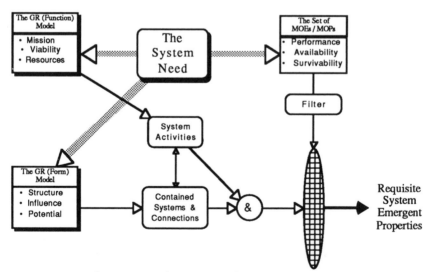

Figure 4.3 The GRM and emergent properties

Figure 4.3 shows a need, top centre. This need statement is used to generate both the *internalized* view (via the GRM) of the system to resolve the need, and the Measures of Effectiveness (MOEs)/

Measures of Performance (MOPs) by which the emergent properties,
or *externalized* view, of the system will be judged. The GRM is used
in the generation of the system concepts and design, while the
MOEs/MOPs are used—symbolically as a filter at the right of the
figure—to pass a suitable design solution. The MOEs/MOPs look at
the designed system from a different standpoint, often as shown in
figure 4.3 :

- Performance
- Availability (of performance)
- Survivability (of performance)

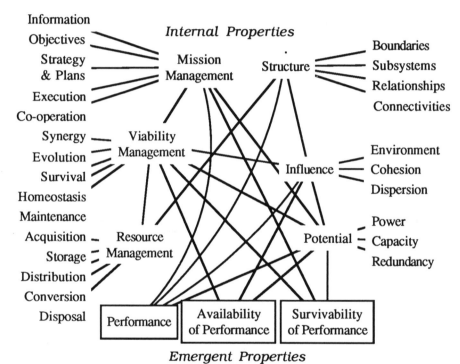

Emergent Properties

Figure 4.4 Notional mapping between GRM and emergent properties. The
GRM takes an internalized view of any system, the designer's view. The
emergent properties of a system, those apparent to an external observer,
arise through an often-complex mapping from and between elements of
this internalized view. Other, mundane, emergent properties tend to accrue
from internal elements, e.g. system cost, system mass, system consumption,
system dissipation, etc

These three MOEs present another N&S set, but categorized quite
differently from sets within the GRM. The MOE set is N&S because it
affords performance, as required to satisfy the need, is available

despite internal failure, and survives external threats, thereby assuring performance. Performance is derived from the GRM, for example, by a mixture of function and form; it does not appear uniquely in any one set.

Figure 4.4 presents a notional mapping between the elements of the GRM and typical emergent properties. The GRM is also used, as the figure indicates, to develop and elaborate the activities which the system must perform internally to achieve mission, maintain viability and utilize resources. For example, each of the individual activities in the management set can be developed as a process in its own right, so developing a deeper understanding and awareness of relationships, data, information, interfaces, etc. Elaborating processes is an essential step on the path to full architectural development.

Such concepts lead to the development of architecture—see Chapter 7.

CONCLUSION

A Generic Reference Model has been presented which describes the internal functions and form of a system with a view to understanding, conceiving, designing, comparing and evaluating systems. It is hoped that the model can find application to all systems, man-made, natural, ecological, social and socio-technological and in so-doing bring the different arms of the systems movement into closer harmony.

The internalized view of a system is that which, of necessity designers work from, but their success must be judged by their ability to achieve the requisite emergent properties of the system in question. The play-off between this emergent, or externalized view of the system and the GRM, or internalized, view of the same system is the key to its appreciation and understanding.

ASSIGNMENT

You have been made responsible for setting up the operations centre for a major disaster relief exercise. Your immediate assignment is to choose the organization within the centre to cover operations, administration, etc. The country has been ravaged by earthquake; roads are down, there is extensive flooding, communities are isolated. You have a number of heavy lorries, several Hercules aircraft, a dozen helicopters and plenty of bagged food at your disposal. A contingent of sappers is standing by with heavy equipment to restore infrastructure under your direction. All you have to manage is deciding which infrastructure to restore, getting the food distribution organized and evacuating the casualties to the nearby hospital. Your are on a green-field site—there is nothing there at present but bare earth. You are not responsible for maintenance of the various forms of transport.

Using the GR (Function) Model, identify all the organizational cells you will need in the operations centre to maintain a viable operation for the foreseeable future. (You will need at least one cell per item of the model, and possibly several cells for some items.)

Chapter 5.1
Efficiency, Effectiveness and Net Contribution

—Assessing the Worth of Projects and Systems

There can be no economy where there is no efficiency
Benjamin Disraeli, 3 Oct. 1868

INTRODUCTION

Situation

Analysts and designers compare potential solutions and potential strategies to exploit opportunities. We are continually seeking to improve our systems, to make them better. In industry, project investment options are compared to select the best—but what does "best" mean? We need yardsticks, measures by which to judge whether our actions will produce, or have produced, the expected results.

Need

Business, industry, finance and commerce need objective, substantial and traceable methods for assessing opportunities. Methods must stand up to scrutiny. This chapter briefly reviews the most-used measures, finds them wanting and introduces a new approach to assessment.

EFFICIENCY

Efficiency—Fashion and Fascination

There is at present such a fascination with organizational efficiency that one hardly dares to question the concept. Surely, an efficient organization must be better than one which is not?

Figure 5.1 shows the basis of efficiency. It is essentially dimensionless, since output and input should be measured in the same units, leaving simply a ratio. The value of efficiency seems to be that it indicates how much of the input is wasted because it never appears at the output.

Efficiency =Output/Input x 100%   (5.1)

What should typical figures for efficiency be? For a mechanical device, such as a pulley, they can be quite high—over 90%. Here, the concept of efficiency seems to be simple enough; that which is lost in the device is due to friction, converting kinetic energy to heat energy which is dissipated into the atmosphere and is not available for work. With even the simplest of electrical circuits, the problem becomes more complex.

Input → System ⊢ Output →

Figure 5.1 Simple Efficiency

Maximum power transfer occurs when the internal and external resistances are identical, which means that half the power is dissipated internally in the source, that is, it operates at only 50% efficiency. If we respond by cutting down the value of r, the internal resistance, the system overall delivers less power to the output R, even though its efficiency rises. Increasing r reduces efficiency *and* power transfer. Similarly, for the pulley, the maximum rate of energy transfer occurs when the effort is twice the load and the efficiency is 50%. In general, the 50% situation provides for the processing the greatest amount of power at the fastest rate, (Odum, 1971).

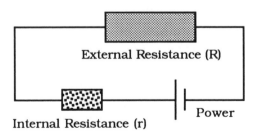

External Resistance (R)

Internal Resistance (r)   Power

Figure 5.2 Maximum power transfer. Maximum power is transferred from the power source to R when R = r

When the efficiencies of organizations are assessed, efficiency might be measured in terms of the overall cost of running the complete organization as "input", with the number of man-days of hands-on work as the "output". Or, from an accounting viewpoint, efficiency may be measured as follows:

$$\text{Efficiency} = \text{Direct Costs}/(\text{Direct Costs} + \text{Indirect Costs} + \text{Overheads}) \quad\quad (5.2)$$

which has the advantage that it is dimensionless. (The many items represented by costs are quite different in substance; the procedure merely provides an illusion of being dimensionless.)

Nature and Efficiency

Nature, on the other hand, does not seem to be quite so set on efficiency. That is not to say that Nature is profligate. Lotka (1922) showed early in this century that maximization of power for useful purposes was the criterion for natural selection, so developing Darwin's evolutionary law into a general energy law. However, as Table 5.1 shows, the efficiency of energy conversion in natural systems, even when artificially boosted by the use of fossil fuels for machinery and fertilizers, is modest.

Table 5.1 Magnitudes of primary production —(Odum, 1971)

SYSTEM	EFFICIENCY (%)
Subtropical Blue Water	0.09
Deserts	0.05
Arctic Tundra	0.08
Algal-Culture in pilot-plant scale	3.0
Sugar Cane	1.8
Water Hyacinth	1.5
Tropical Forest Plantation	0.7
Sewage Ponds on 7-day turnover	2.8
Coral Reefs	2.4
Tropical Marine Meadows	2.0
Tropical Rain Forest	3.5
Farms, US, un-subsidized by fossil fuels	0.03
Grain, Africa, as above	0.02
Rice, US, industrialized agriculture	0.25
Grain Average, N. America	0.12

Note: Efficiency is measured as a percentage of sunlight received, that being virtually the only source of energy entering each system

Judging by Table 5.1, some management experts might declare Nature to be so inefficient that it should be replaced. But Nature has a different goal—survival. In most natural systems, there is a host of sub-systems performing a variety of jobs; power is dissipated at each transition between sub-systems or processes. While this explains the seemingly low efficiencies, it also explains the robustness of natural systems. They contain *variety* and *capacity* sufficient to accommodate change and to resist threats. High-efficiency systems forego this robustness and do not survive for long.

The figures in Table 5.1 referred to plants. Animals, by virtue of their mobility, can have a broader approach to efficiency and survival. Birdsong takes a considerable amount of energy from a bird; during early spring, the amount of energy devoted to birdsong when food is not yet plentiful might seem to be profligate. Territorial birds use their songs to delineate no-go areas and thereby reduce or avoid the need to enter into physical dispute—an even greater use of energy. Thus birds use song to deter, rather than fight, as an *energy-efficient strategy option.* Similarly larks, noted for their soaring birdsongs, are actually fending off rivals for their territory. In so doing, they place themselves at risk from their principal predator, the merlin. Interestingly, fit larks continue to sing whilst being pursued by merlins; the merlins have come to recognize that a singing lark, being fit, is not worth pursuing. Here we have a truly efficient strategy for survival, combining as it does peer and predator deterrence.

Survival is a good business goal, too. If a business survives when competitors do not, clearly that business will "win" in some sense. Setting survival as the primary goal for a business does not mean that it should be inefficient, but it does put efficiency in perspective. Inefficiency, in the sense of needless waste, is clearly to be eliminated. But the elimination of useful *variety* can also occur in the name of efficiency, and that may militate against survival. Indeed, recent extensive efficiency drives in the UK may have rendered parts of UK Industry not so much "lean and hungry" as "emaciated and starved".

Natural systems also survive by a strategy of self-maintenance— they store some of their power/energy/wealth and feed it back into repair. Odum (1971) suggests six activities undertaken by natural systems in self-maintenance:

1 Fuel processing
2 Material processing
3 Synthesis of parts by combining materials
4 Rearrangement and connection of disarranged parts
5 Energy storing for necessary fuel reserves and necessary structure
6 Removal of worn parts

There is a powerful analogy between that list and the equivalent for a business, organization, or man-made system. Pursuit of economic efficiency can sometimes relegate such essential maintenance to low priority, as with maintaining essentials such as roads, schools and sewers—all self-maintenance features for a nation.

Efficiency and Queuing Theory

Simple queuing theory addresses simple channels in which a server provides a service to each of a succession of entities (objects, people, etc) which form an orderly queue. For the simplest mathematics to hold, interarrival times and service times should be exponentially distributed and mutually independent. The following relationship then emerges:

$$\text{Number of entities in the system} = \rho/(1-\rho) \qquad (5.3)$$

As ρ, the channel utilization, approaches unity, the number of entities in the system (queuing and being served) goes to infinity.

A company may be analysed using queuing theory; it would, of course, be made up from many queues, not all of them simple. But the same general principle applies—as the utilization increases, the number of entities in the many queues rises exponentially towards infinity. It seems that we have to have a channel utilization of significantly less than one if we are to operate without massive queues (inventory in manufacturing, checkout customers in supermarkets).

To contain queue lengths to reasonable lengths, utilization rate must be less than unity, the server must therefore have unused capacity, and the server must, at times, be sitting idle. Efforts are often made to fully utilize staff and machines, with the consequence that queues do build up, but—more importantly from a survival viewpoint—the organization becomes unable to accommodate any change other than collapse. In many instances the number of entities in the system need to be kept reasonably low—an average of one entity is not uncommon per queue; this also corresponds to 50% channel utilization.

Efficiency from a Systems Viewpoint

No system sits in isolation; they are all mutually connected and contained within wider systems. Consider then the elementary diagram of Figure 5.3. The output from the first system must form the input to one or more systems downstream. Altering the efficiency of the first system will affect its output, which will impact on downstream systems. This is, of course, obvious. Or is it? The 43 police forces of the UK have been attempting to increase their efficiency (Operational Policing Review, 1990). In the process, some have introduced a scheme called the Administrative Support Unit (ASU) which, on the face of it, is a sensible scheme. The ASU is staffed by experienced, uniformed policemen. They take over paperwork associated with prosecution from the patrol officer who initiated the proceedings. ASU staff become adept at the paperwork. Patrol officers—beat policemen—are relieved of the paperwork burden and can spend more time on patrol, executing "self-

Figure 5.3 System changes—downstream impact

generated work". A benefit all round?

Reducing the paperwork burden on the beat officer encourages him to produce more output, which results in more cases being prepared for the Crown Prosecution Service (CPS)—the downstream system. The CPS, unprepared for this increase in input, is unable to accommodate the increase and queues develop until prosecutions "drop off the end" because of excessive delay in coming to trial. Unless all the systems in the pipeline downstream are geared up to the increase in output, there will be either a build-up of queues or a compensating change of downstream system response—which might not always be predictable or desirable.

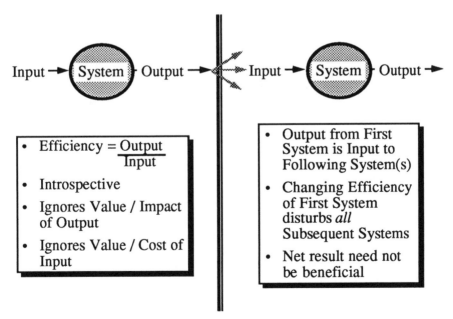

Figure 5.4 Efficiency as a measure

The Value of Efficiency as a Measure

Efficiency is evidently not the unassailable ethic that might be supposed. That does not mean that efficiency is of no value. On the contrary, it is a valuable tool in the armoury to improve system performance when it is used in conjunction with other measures. Like all tools, in the hands of the uninitiated or unthinking it can be a dangerous thing. The simple rule seems to be: use efficiency to seek out and eliminate waste in individual processes within a system/organization; avoid using efficiency to reduce variety within the system/organization. Again, use efficiency as a guide to choose between tactical or strategic options, as for the birds who choose to deter rather than fight. An overall view of efficiency is presented in Figure 5.4.

EFFECTIVENESS

Present Usage—Theory and Practice

Effectiveness presents a different viewpoint from efficiency. To begin with, it may not offer a simple, non-dimensional parameter by which to compare systems. Effectiveness, even at face value, is a more "thoughtful" measure; if efficiency is doing things right, then effectiveness is doing the right things. The implication of effectiveness is that it must somehow be judge by impact (effect) on something else. It offers an external view of a system. It assesses the system's emergent properties and is hence quite different from efficiency, even though the two words, efficiency and effectiveness, are often spoken in the one breath as though they were, somehow, two sides of the same coin.

Following the previous example from policing, consider the police process of crime screening. A scenes-of-crime officer awards points to crimes to develop a "solvability index". Crimes with a high index present more clues and are more likely to be solved. Investigating officers are allocated preferentially to such crimes, in order to increase the efficiency of the police in terms of clear-up rates, where that rate is measured as a proportion of the reported crime rate. The approach seems, on the face of it, to be nothing less than common sense: to allocate limited resources where they have the best chance of being successful.

Efficiency probably does increase. But effectiveness is an emergent property perceived, in this case, by the public. The public can feel neglected and disenchanted if the crimes to which they are subjected go unchecked. Often the general public, feeling it to be a waste of time, fail to report crimes which they feel that the police will not address adequately. The reported crime rate may be less than 10% of the actual crime rate according to some analysts, making a nonsense of the clear-up rates as a measure of either efficiency or effectiveness.

In general, it seems that efficiency and effectiveness, far from being similar in content, are uncomfortable bedfellows.

The Problem of Evaluating Effectiveness

Continuing with the police example, the question arises of how to measure effectiveness. Consider a beat officer on patrol near a parade of shops. A robber, intent on holding up the local building society, sees the police officer and is deterred. The visible presence of the police officer has been effective in deterring a crime—but who knows about it? Similarly, the local beat officer becomes known on his "patch" and locals become more relaxed about giving information, know where to go for immediate help, feel more confident that they are unlikely to be "mugged", and so on. The beat officer is effective in bringing "tranquillity" (a police expression) to the community. How can one evaluate such valuable social responses in order to measure effectiveness?

The answers are not simple, but they are important. In the case of the police, various sections of the public have a mental image, or model, of what they expect from the police in terms of service and of personal standards. It is also possible to model the deterrent value of "visible" policing; the police themselves produce handbooks for beat-policing which tell the officer what duties he should perform, how to allocate his time, about making and maintaining local contacts, and so on. The process of evaluating effectiveness can thus be seen as comprising two parts:

- Establish an ideal model of the system in its environment, interacting with other systems in that environment
- Compare the proposed or existing system(s) against the model to identify and highlight differences

Given such a process, the difference between ideal and proposed or actual can be used to measure effectiveness and/or promote change. Effectiveness can thus be evaluated by combining measures of the degree to which a system's emergent properties meet—or fail to meet—an ideal. (In this way the deterrent value of visible policing may be considered, a distinct problem when looking at efficiency.) Measures may be combined in several ways which will be discussed below. The assessment of effectiveness seems to be best made under three headings: *contribution* to containing systems' objectives; *co-*

operation with sibling systems; *harmony* of contained systems. These three broad categories from the three-tiered nesting system model of Chapter 3 are expanded to meet the needs of particular systems.

Practical Effectiveness

Effectiveness can be evaluated in practice (Hitchins, 1986) by using templates such as that shown in Table 5.2, for man-made information systems, which allow practitioners to compare options against each other. Options may be evaluated by using either a conventional weighting and scoring approach, or using ranking methods; these have advantages of being less subjective.

Table 5.2 Effectiveness tradeoff table

DESIGN DRIVERS / EMERGENT PROPERTIES		SOLUTION OPTIONS	
		OPTION A	OPTION N
Performance	Capability		
	Behaviour		
Availability	Reliability		
	Maintainability		
Adaptability	Flexibility		
	Expandability		
Interoperability	Communication		
	Protocol		
Usability	Human factors		
	MMI/HCI		
Survivability	Avoidance of detection		
	Self-defence		
	Damage-tolerance		
Security	Data		
	Physical		
Safety	Development		
	Operation		
	Maintenance		
	Disposal		

MMI—Man-machine interface.   HCI—Human-computer interface

No matter how the numerical analysis may be performed, there are still certain limitations with this approach. The comparison of options is aimed at finding the best of the available solutions—the ideal model of the system in its environment, interacting with other systems, can be almost completely lost. There is, in consequence, an almost universal tendency for the most effective solution nominated by this approach to also be the most expensive.

The Value of Effectiveness as a Measure

Effectiveness is potentially a valuable measure because it should assess the degree to which a system or process serves its purpose and harmonizes with other systems and its environment. The measurement of effectiveness is not a simple process, requiring the establishment of standards which emergent properties should satisfy.

COST-EFFECTIVENESS

Why Cost-effectiveness ?

Cost-effectiveness reflects a natural interest in cost as being of prime importance and of money as being the universal exchange for goods, systems, etc., which we use *inter alia* to choose between options. Cost-effectiveness seeks to maximize "value for money", by maximizing the ratio of effectiveness to cost.   This is an important idea, since it allows more expensive options to be embraced if they offer proportionately more effectiveness.

While simple effectiveness is of considerable value in addressing emergent properties, cost-effectiveness adds the input parameter introduced under efficiency above. Cost-effectiveness can be seen as "valued emergent properties per cost", where valued emergent properties are those which serve higher purpose and harmonize with those of other systems.

How is Cost-effectiveness Assessed?

There is a broad consensus about the approach to assessing or evaluating cost-effectiveness. The usual approach is illustrated in Figure 5.4—from an idea by Philip M'Pherson of City University.

A variety of potential solutions is generated. Each is processed against a set of models to predict performance, availability and survivability to determine overall effectiveness and cost, these two being ratioed for each option, the highest value giving the preferred solution.

There are some difficulties. Models are not always available or substantial, making prediction difficult or crude. Aggregating the individual predictions for performance, availability and survivability tends to use algebraic weighting and scoring methods, often subjective. Cost predictions may be accrued for capital cost or for life-cycle cost, the two often giving contradictory results; sometimes the most expensive to buy is not the most expensive to own.

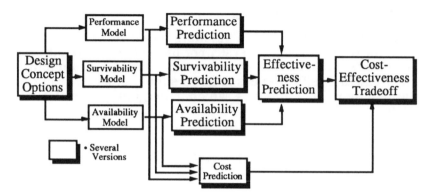

Figure 5.5 Cost-effectiveness Model

Further, the generation of potential solution options to compare is not always simple. Ideally, the options would be sufficient to address each of the principle design features; a requirement with, say, ten principal features (security, reliability, ease of use, etc.) would then generate at least twenty options as each parameter was individually set high, low and perhaps intermediate. Such a process can result in too many options.

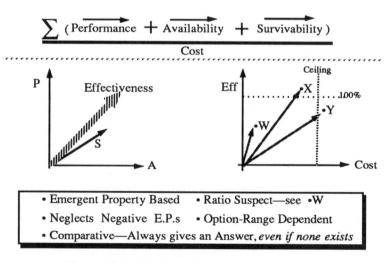

Figure 5.6 Cost-effectiveness perspectives

Some other features are shown in Figure 5.6. Cost-effectiveness is emergent property based, but there is a tendency in practice to accentuate the positive, and de-emphasize the negative.   This tendency is not implicit in the methodology; there is no reason why an examination of, say, performance for a sensor should concentrate more on range and resolution than on spurious emission, mass and shape but, unless care is taken, these tendencies are observable. It may be that the very idea of effectiveness is a positive idea and leads to playing down the negative aspects

The graph at the left of Figure 5.6 shows that performance, availability and survivability are not truly measurable on the same linear scale, and should be considered as vectors. The graph at the right shows that simply using a ratio can be misleading.   Of the three solutions, "W" has the highest cost-effectiveness ratio, but is relatively ineffective and may be so cheap as to be suspect, while "X" and "Y" are over-effective and over-cost respectively, presenting more difficulties. Last, the process of comparison tends to produce a solution, that which comes out best, even if none is truly worthwhile.   This arises from the lack of an absolute measure during the end process.   How low a level of effectiveness is not effective?

The Value of Cost-effectiveness as a Measure

Cost-effectiveness is, despite its limitations, a useful measure and one to which many systems practitioners subscribe.   That it addresses emergent properties as well as cost is admirable. It is, however, open to abuse and to misinterpretation and, as our systems become more complex, it is being seen to fail. Government strictures to be more cost-effective, for example, are not resulting in universally better systems. If a number of industrial organizations individually follow the path of cost-effectiveness, is their *aggregate* performance improved? Does such an approach benefit the society within which such businesses operate in terms, say, of improving the economic and transportation environments? The answer tends to be: NO. A number of organizations, independently choosing options which are cost-effective from their perspective, can aggregate to provide overall-unpleasant emergent properties.

Similarly, if the manufacturers of various parts for a man-made system independently produce cost-effective products, which perform well, are reliable, are not overly expensive and which interface correctly, will the resulting integrated system satisfy its customers and users? Not necessarily. It is not the performance or reliability of the parts which is ultimately important, but how those features contribute to the effectiveness of the overall system.   A super new radar may give an aircraft better "eyes", but can the aircraft materially improve *its* performance as a result? Can weapon performance (for a military aircraft) take advantage of the new radar performance? Does incorporating the new radar actually improve *mission* performance? Last, but far from least, it is possible to misapply cost-effectiveness by choosing an item as part of a larger system so that, while the item may be cost-effective by comparison with similar competitors, its effect on the larger system is counter-productive. To address such issues, consider the concept of Net Contribution.

NET CONTRIBUTION

Net Contribution—Apportionment and Budgeting

The Net Contribution assessment process starts from a higher level in the hierarchy of systems than does either efficiency or effectiveness. In the example concerned with police effectiveness, we saw that some idealized "model of policing" was required against which to judge observed policing-in-action. Moreover, this model of policing could be developed only by placing it in context, with the police interacting with other systems in the community and in government. Given such a model, it would be possible to compare optional policing strategies by evaluating how far they fell short of (or exceeded) the ideal.

Broadly, the same approach must be appropriate for evaluating all systems. A model of the system-in-focus is required, operating with other (sibling) systems within its environment. In other words, we need to identify the parent or containing system and the sibling systems contained within it, and to so apportion their attributes that the containing system's requisite features are realised. This can be seen as a budgeting process, illustrated in figure 5.7. The figure shows a matrix in which the columns at the right represent each of the sibling systems in the containing system. The left hand column contains a set of emergent properties for the system-in-focus. The example given of the budgeting process is an apparently simple one, in which the overall weight of the containing system is required to be 30 units, and the budget apportions these 30 units between each of the contained systems such that the system-in-focus, shown in the shaded panel, is identified as ideally weighing 5 units.

Although the example may seem simple, it need not be so in practice; to apportion weight sensibly requires knowledge of reasonable weights for each sibling system, otherwise ridiculous or unattainable weights might be targeted. For some emergent properties there exists a store of knowledge to ease the problem of estimating and forecasting. Figure 5.7 shows availability also; failure rates of man-made systems and products are often well known, and a sensible apportionment of failure rates between contained systems may be made in such cases, so that the overall system has *its* required availability.

Performance, a key emergent property, is likely to be less tractable; a model may be required of the containing system with each of its contained systems represented in its operational environment. The model will be used to vary the performance features of the contained systems so that the required overall performance of the containing system is achieved. The modelling process will result in definition of the performance features of each contained system including the system-in-focus, but can be directed to concentrate on the latter.

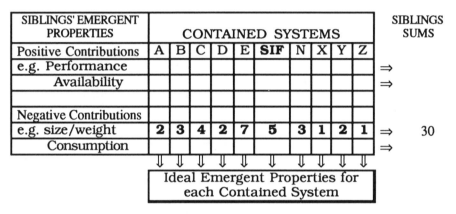

SIBLINGS' EMERGENT PROPERTIES	CONTAINED SYSTEMS										SIBLINGS SUMS
Positive Contributions	A	B	C	D	E	**SIF**	N	X	Y	Z	
e.g. Performance											⇒
Availability											⇒
Negative Contributions											
e.g. size/weight	2	3	4	2	7	**5**	3	1	2	1	⇒ 30
Consumption											⇒

Ideal Emergent Properties for each Contained System

Figure 5.7 Sibling contribution budget

Net Contribution—Evaluating the Options

The outcome of the budgeting process is an idealized set of emergent properties for the system-in-focus. The assessment process thereafter follows two steps:

1 Evaluate the optional solutions for the system-in-focus, judging shortfalls (or overruns) against the idealized emergent properties
2 Where shortfalls occur, seek to rebudget by trading with other contained systems

For example, excessive power consumption in one (otherwise suitable) option might be accepted if a compensating reduction in consumption could be made in one or more of the other contained systems. If no such compensation can be achieved then essentially the option must be rejected, and either the process of designing options must continue or a concession must be granted. (The granting of concessions may require significant understanding of their impact within the containing system, a theme which will recur below).

This approach overcomes some of the less desirable features of effectiveness and cost-effectiveness. A system-in-focus is selected/adapted/evolved which, by the process involved, must be both in harmony with its siblings and making the required Net Contribution to the containing system.

Accommodating Flows

There is one particular feature of interconnected systems which has already been mentioned and which must be accommodated within the Net Contribution process, that of downstream system flow. Since the output from any system may be the input to others within the container, it follows that the budgeting process above, and the subsequent re-budgeting advocated in Step 2, must take account of these flows. In particular where the system-in-focus provides an output to "downstream" systems which is different from the budget then either:

- The downstream system may be modified to accommodate the difference, or...
- A complementary system may be introduced to compensate.

Why Positive and Negative Contributions? Macro View

One of the deficiencies observed above in the practice of cost-effective analysis was the tendency to concentrate on positive aspects of effectiveness; in other words, the very term effectiveness leads to the positive, diminishes the negative. There is, then, simple advantage in separating positive from negative contribution in judging Net Contribution. But the concept runs much deeper than that.

Net Contribution operates within a three-tier system hierarchy: the containing system; the sibling, contained systems; and the sub-systems of the system-in-focus. If we can develop a practice of choosing systems-in-focus which show a net *positive* contribution, and if we choose the emergent properties of our systems appropriately, we can move towards a situation in which all system choices improve our economy, effectiveness, survival and environment.

A bold claim?. Not really. The notion of Net Contribution contains within it the simple idea of measuring value on a much broader basis than simply money—the myopic approach of cost-effectiveness practice. Cost-effectiveness need take no account of pollution, effluent, waste disposal, resource replacement, etc., since these tend to be negative factors. In a properly set-up Net Contribution evaluation process, such negatives would be put in the balance against the positives. Net positive contributors would be required to show that their benefits outweighed their disadvantages, including costs, since these are important. If the process were repeated at all hierarchy levels, the results must accrue to a positive net contribution at the highest national, international and world levels.

Why Positive and Negative Contributions? Micro View

At a more mundane level, positive and negative contributors tend to behave differently and to require different evaluation; the following section will enlarge upon this point. In particular, the way in which evaluations are viewed differs. Consider Figure 5.8. The figure shows, very notionally, how positive contributions tend to be viewed, using the broad term effectiveness as a measure. A ceiling is generally perceived, below which effectiveness is unacceptably inadequate. A notion of 100% effectiveness exists, which implies that a solution fulfils all expectations precisely. It then follows that effectiveness over 100% can exist too, where a specified requirement has been exceeded. 105% effectiveness may be more than required but—as the shape of the curve implies—if it can be achieved at little increase in cost, it may be worthwhile. By the same token, 90% effectiveness may be accepted if the cost reductions are appropriate—the so-called non-compliant solution. Acceptability for positive contributors tends, then, towards a logistic curve.

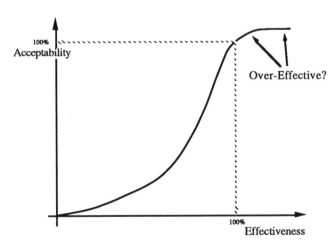

Figure 5.8 Positive contributor profiles

Figure 5.9 is more appropriate to a negative contributor, remembering that these tend to be incurred by accumulation, with weight, cost, volume, consumption, etc., all being accrued from the similar parameters of their contained parts by an accounting, or adding up, process. An ideal value is perceived, generally by customers, above which they are increasingly unwilling to pay, and below which they are increasingly suspicious that something is wrong. It is not in the nature of things business or physical for values to be too low, any more than it is acceptable for them to be too high.

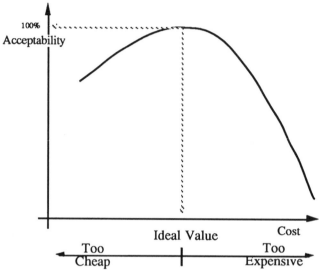

Figure 5.9 Negative contributor profiles

These differences between positive and negative contributors, combined with desire to avoid relatively diminishing the negative contributors, amply justifies their separation.

NET CONTRIBUTION—DELVING DEEPER

Assessing the Impact of Shortfalls and Overruns

The result of a simple approach to step 1 (above—evaluating the options against an ideal model) might be as shown in the following diagram, in which four optional solutions, A to D, have been evaluated by some process and the results have been tabulated against a set of emergent properties and their target values, as set by the containing system budgeting procedure (see Figure 5.10). (The example is grossly simplified to aid understanding.)

The usual approach adopted at this point by analysts using the cost-effectiveness approach is to select the "best" option by some form of weighting and scoring technique, in which each emergent property is given a weight according to perceived importance, each option is scored on some arbitrary scale, scores are multiplied by weights and the option receiving the highest weighted score is adjudged the winner. Weighting is, of course, highly subjective, and algebraic addition of weighted scores for such fundamentally different dimensions as, say, weight and survivability is questionable. But the most serious deficiency with the approach is that trading in this manner overlooks the impact on the containing system with its sibling systems to which the system-in-focus is connected.

Emergent Properties	Target	Optional Solutions			
Positive Contribution	Value	A	B	C	D
e.g. Performance	10	7	8	5	9
Availability	8	3	6	9	7
Survivability	5	5	5	6	4
Negative Contribution					
e.g.Cost	5	4	5	7	6
Size / Weight	10	6	11	10	12
Consumption	8	7	8	9	10

Figure 5.10 The sibling budget

Several features of the table are worthy of note:

- There is a tendency for positive contributors to undershoot and negative contributors to overshoot.
- In particular, the option which offers the best performance, option D, is over-cost, over-weight, over-consumption but under-available and under-survivable. (Although the figures are contrived, this situation is that which commonly arises, one of mutual incompatibility between the emergent properties.)
- There is no way of observing the *significance* of overshoot or undershoot. For example, how serious is option D's excess of 2 weight units?
- There is no way of seeing the *interaction* between parameters which have undershot/overshot, e.g. if the containing system were a satellite and option D a contained fuel system, how would option D's overshoot in weight affect the overall performance of the containing system, even supposing the performance of option D, considered in isolation, might be barely satisfactory?

In summary, the budgeting process is necessary but not sufficient, particularly as systems become more complex. Evidently, a better approach is needed for complex systems, where "better" implies that both the impact of undershoots/overshoots, and the interactions between parameter variations (such as weight and performance), can be sensibly evaluated and judged. Such an approach is introduced below.

The Contribution Balance

The value of separating positive and negative contribution factors can now be viewed from a different perspective. The accumulation of negative factors on the left of the scales in Figure 5.11 represent those features which are, generally, incurred in the process of realising a system. Incurring those features is worthwhile only if, as result, the system contributes positively to its parent (or containing) system, which can be best judged in relation to mission, viability and resource management.

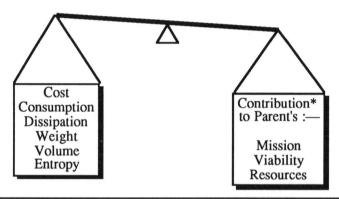

* Complementary to Sibling Systems

Figure 5.11 The Net Contribution balance

The GRM and Emergent Properties

The Generic Reference Model offers an internalized view of a system; it highlights features and activities within the system for it to exist and have purpose. The containing system described above is presented, as it looks inwards upon itself, with a view of the emergent properties of the system-in-focus. (For example, an aircraft or ship "sees" the thrust, weight, fuel consumption, heat dissipation, noise, etc., of its engine—these are engine system emergent properties. A company or organization "sees" divisional profitability, operational costs, work-in-progress, enthusiasm, resilience, etc—these are divisional emergent properties.

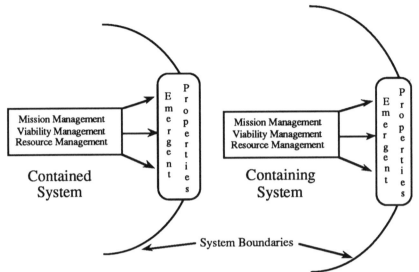

Figure 5.12 Contained systems contributing to their containing systems

What is the relationship between the GRM for the system-in-focus and its emergent properties? Figure 5.12 shows the relationship. At the left is a contained system, one of several—only the system-in-focus is shown for clarity. At the right is the containing system, which holds, owns, or contains its contained (or sub-) systems, including the system-in-focus. A need for a new, or changed, system can be represented in two ways: the mission, viability and resource management, or internalized, view; and the performance, availability and survivability, or externalized, emergent property view. Conventional cost-effectiveness analysis concentrates on the externalized viewpoint of emergent properties, while system designers and engineers seek to achieve those desired emergent properties by designing within the system-in-focus. In particular, the emergent properties of the contained systems—including the system-in-focus—contribute to the internalized management set of their containing system. This chain relationship can be continued up a hierarchy so that, for example, the management set of a module develops module emergent properties, which contribute to the management set of an assembly, which develop assembly emergent properties which contribute to the management set of a platform, which develop platform emergent properties ... and so on. Clearly, similar hierarchies exist for individuals, departments, divisions, companies, conglomerates, etc. This nested contribution hierarchy can be used as a basis for a powerful and rigorous evaluation procedure, illustrated in the following chapter.

Evaluating Net Contribution

As with efficiency, effectiveness and cost-effectiveness, Net Contribution can be reduced to a straightforward process of assessment and evaluation.

Table 5.3 Net Contribution table

	CONTAINING SYSTEM(S)	
SOI EMERGENT PROPERTIES	**GR(Function)M**	**GR(Form)M**
Contributors to:		
Containers' objectives		
Sibling co-operation		
Sub-system synergy		
Positive contribution		
Detractors from:		
Containers' objectives		
Sibling co-operation		
Sub-system synergy		
Resource efficiency		
Negative contribution		
NET CONTRIBUTION		

As Table 5.3 shows, SOI emergent properties in the first column are evaluated on the basis of their contribution to their containing systems' Generic Reference Models, that is, to their internal features. Positive and negative emergent properties are handled separately. Cost is seen in perspective; it generally contributes negatively to containing systems' objectives.

Consider, for example, a rowing eight, which we might loosely describe as "a human-powered system for racing on water"; this is to be our containing system. Suppose we wish to evaluate a member of the crew. First, we would identify the sibling systems and the environment, including the other crew members, the blades and rowlocks, the sliding seats, the boat hull and the wind/water state. Then we might budget for the emergent properties which we expected for the particular crew-member under examination, in terms of power, style, co-ordination, stamina, weight, height, flexibility, etc. Efficiency would mean little, cost-effectiveness even less. Net contribution, however, easily lets us separate the positive contributions to the containing system from the negatives. Given an ideal budget for each, we can simply assess the particular crew-member's characteristics against the budget and mark them accordingly.

The Value of Net Contribution as a Measure

Net Contribution seeks to overcome the deficiencies of efficiency, effectiveness and cost-effectiveness, and to evaluate systems in absolute, as well as comparative terms. Like cost-effectiveness, it can be complex if it carried out rigourously, owing to the need to predict outcomes using models. There is no panacea that will resolve that issue—complex problems generally invoke complex analysis and solution. On the other hand, Net Contribution can be

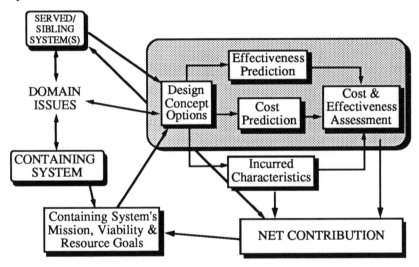

Figure 5.13 Net Contribution and cost-effectiveness

reduced to the sensible development and use of the processes illustrated above without the analyst(s) being concerned about the niceties and theory of systems. In summary, the Net Contribution process may be viewed as shown in Figure 5.13. The figure shows the containing system, the sibling systems and the domain issues which have resulted in the perceived need for the system-in-focus, at left. At bottom left are the containing system's management set to which the system-in-focus is required to make a contribution. That Net Contribution is shown being accrued, at the centre bottom, from effectiveness, cost and incurred characteristics of the system in focus. Cost is itself an incurred characteristic, of course, but it is shown separately in the figure to highlight the commonality between Net Contribution and cost-effectiveness, represented by the shaded panel. As the figure illustrates, Net Contribution works from a broader and higher perspective than cost-effectiveness and enables both the good to be weighed against the bad and—illustrated by the connecting, two-way arrow between Net Contribution and the sibling systems—balance to be achieved between the contained systems. Lastly, note the term "served sibling systems", drawing attention particularly to the "downstream" systems which will receive the output from the system-in-focus and which, are in consequence, particularly vulnerable to system-in-focus shortfalls, overruns or other imperfections.

CONCLUSION

The paper has examined efficiency as a measure of systems and found it wanting. The pursuit of efficiency, far from enhancing organizations, can reduce their resilience and robustness to the point that they cannot accommodate change. Efficiency is an introspective and potentially dangerous measure which, if confined to individual processes, can be used *with caution* to reduce unnecessary waste.

Effectiveness (which often runs counter to efficiency) has significant merit, examines emergent properties of systems and presents some difficulties in measurement. Effectiveness is essentially an external measure of a system's worth or impact as perceived by a viewer outside the system. To evaluate effectiveness, an idealized model of effectiveness is required, against which to judge actual and proposed systems. Such an idealized model may prove difficult to build, not because of technical difficulties but in reaching agreement as to what constitutes effectiveness in the first place. The effort is seen as worthwhile.

Cost-effectiveness highlights the cost aspect by developing a ratio of effectiveness to cost such that maximizing the ratio should maximize value for money. There are practical pitfalls in the simple ratio approach which can be overcome by complication, but the process contains more serious flaws. It is essentially comparative and addresses the question "which of the proposed solutions is the best". It does not address the question "is the best of the options good enough in absolute terms". It is also in the nature of effectiveness to accentuate the positive aspects and to play down the negative aspects, to the detriment of a sound result. Neither efficiency nor effectiveness takes much account of other systems with which they will interact in the environment.

Net Contribution provides an absolute measure, by asking the question "how do the emergent properties of the system-in-focus contribute to its containing system?" Solution options can be compared by how they contribute respectively to their containing system. Like effectiveness, Net Contribution requires some ideal model against which to judge putative solutions.

The rôle of cost is placed in perspective by Net Contribution. Cost is important, but spending wisely is a better concept. Net Contribution places the cost of the system-in-focus in the context of the overall cost of the containing system. If a putative solution to the system-in-focus costs less than the corresponding containing system budget, but contributes fully in concert with its siblings, then it achieves the goal. If it costs more but that cost can be offset by savings in associated siblings, and it contributes fully in concert with its siblings, then it also achieves the goal. If it contributes inadequately, and is over cost, it fails. If it contributes inadequately and is under cost, it fails, unless siblings can make up the contribution shortfall.

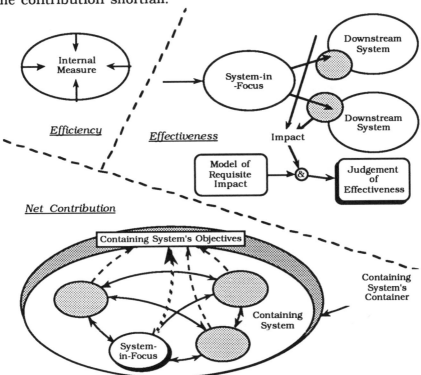

Figure 5.14 Efficiency, effectiveness and Net Contribution

If all systems were evaluated correctly using Net Contribution, and only net positive solutions accepted, then—owing to the recursive nature of the technique—a hierarchy of net positive systems contained within net positive systems must develop. Thus Net Contribution presents a high degree of implicit integrity in its effects on environment, its use of resources and its development of effective, enduring systems. This integrity of judgement is the Holy Grail for which Net Contribution is searching.

Chapter 5.2
Efficiency, Effectiveness and Net Contribution

—A Comparative Analysis of a Marketing Department

There are only two qualities in the world: efficiency and inefficiency; and only two sorts of people: the efficient and the inefficient.
George Bernard Shaw, 1856-1950

INTRODUCTION

This section illustrates the differing ways of evaluating systems, using a marketing department within an industrial organization as an example. The marketing department will be examined in terms of efficiency, effectiveness and net contribution.

EFFICIENCY

Efficiency as a measure uses the basic notion that:

$$\text{Efficiency} = (\text{Work out})/(\text{Effort available}) \times 100\% \qquad \textbf{(5.4)}$$

Calculations could be based on timesheet records. Suppose records show that, on average, each marketeer works 132 hours per calendar month in a 52-week year, 40-hour week. This gives:

$$\text{Efficiency} = (132 \times 12)/(52 \times 40) \times 100\% = 76\% \qquad \textbf{(5.5)}$$

This information is easily obtained, but is of little value in isolation, since we may have no idea what would constitute a "good" efficiency. A series of efficiency measurements over a period of time might reveal a trend which, on further examination, could reveal changing levels of absenteeism, training, etc. Again, this inform-ation is of little use in isolation, since there are no absolute standards by which to judge such levels. Efficiency, remember, is an internal view of a system and finding reference standards will always be difficult

EFFECTIVENESS

Evaluating effectiveness requires that we take an external view of a system, and that we have some idealized model which represents "100% effective", against which to judge our marketing department. If we can consider effectiveness to be comprised of performance,

Table 5.4 Marketing department effectiveness calculation

PERFORMANCE		EVALUATION (%)	ALERT(†)
CAPABILITY	Forecasting		
	•	70	
	World/National Trends		
	• Markets	80	✓
	• Technology	25	*
	• Resources	30	*
	Analysis		
	• Competition	65	
	• Niches	45	*
	Judgement		
	• Business	85	✓✓
	• Risk	25	* * *
	Specification		
	• Product & Service Characteristics	0	* * * * *
	Skill		
	• Bidding	80	✓
	• Negotiating	60	
BEHAVIOUR	Market Stance		
	• Aggressive	35	* * *
	• Covert	35	* * *
	Responsiveness		
	• Repeatability	60	
	• Speed	35	* * *
	Acquisitiveness	40	* *
	Energy	85	✓✓
	Co-operation	55	*
EFFECTIVENESS RATING		51%	

(†—The analysis not only results in a figure of merit, but much more importantly it also indicates areas of concern, marked with "*" and areas of excellence, marked with "✓".)

availability of performance and survivability of performance, then these factors have to be considered in respect of a marketing department. This we can do by breaking each of the headings down further, and conducting an audit of the department against the resulting model. Table 5.4 shows only performance, but would in practice address both availability and survivability.

Comparison between this marketing department and another operating in a similar business environment can be made against the same model. The judgement by the audit team may be subjective, and the breakdown of effectiveness into the parameters shown in the table is itself subjective, but the process of developing the model has resulted in an "ideal"—the 100% reference—and any subjectivity is now open to scrutiny and detection. Moreover, the profusion of parameters makes it difficult for an audit team to maintain a particular stance, favourable or unfavourable, without that stance being evident in their results.

The external view of the marketing department, as seen from the point of view of the company as a whole, is clearly valuable. On the other hand, it is evidently more difficult to derive than was effectiveness, and it lacks any measures of the relationship with other departments in the organization—an isolated marketing department would have no purpose.

COST-EFFECTIVENESS

Cost-effectiveness is generally used to choose between options. In this particular example, there are no options (unless we were to speculate about the ideal marketing department and cost that as a reference). To illustrate the point, suppose the marketing department costs its organization £500 000 p.a. then we could derive a cost-effectiveness quotient as:

$$\text{Cost-effectiveness} = 44\%/£500\,000 \qquad [£^{-1}]$$

Clearly, if we were comparing similar marketing departments, different quotients would be of interest, with higher values indicating better value for money from the viewpoint of the owning organization.

NET CONTRIBUTION

Introduction

The assessment of Net Contribution commences by identifying the System of Interest (SOI), its containing system(s)—in this case taken to be simply the organization—and its sibling systems; these are identified in Figure 5.15. Note the natural flow of activities from

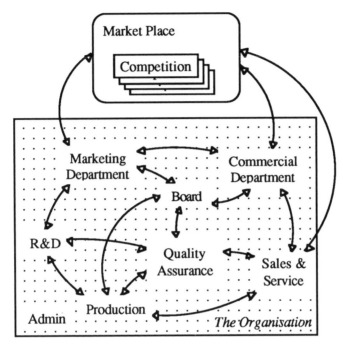

Figure 5.15 Company Organization

the market, through marketing, Reasearch and Development (R&D), production, sales and service and back to the market. Note too, the focal position of the board and quality assurance, with the commercial department in the loop to manage risk. Administration, shown unconnected, is connected to all departments. Finally, note that no hierarchy is visible in the representation.

Next it is helpful to establish the Prime Directives—see Chapter 10—of both the containing system and the SOI, which might be as follows:

- Organization's Prime Directive: "To survive and flourish in a changing market environment".
- Organization's strategy:—"To anticipate the need for change by always marketing a contemporary range of products."
- Marketing department's Prime Directive: "To position the company to best exploit business opportunities"

Evaluating Net Contribution

Figure 5.16 illustrates the evaluation process. At the top of the tree sits the containing system, the organization. Viewed internally, it has three main functions: mission, viability and resource management—see Chapter 4. The tree shows, as a partial example only, how the marketing department makes its contribution to that element of mission management concerned with mission objectives (or just objectives for brevity).

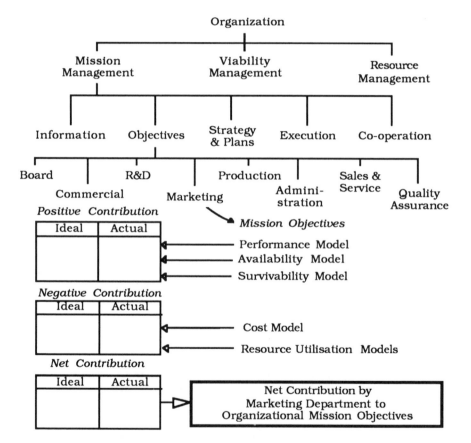

Figure 5.16 Evaluating Net Contribution. The marketing department is only one of the contributors to organizational mission objectives; any or all of the other departments may contribute too. The proportional contribution by the marketing department can be evaluated using models of performance, availability and survivability. The marketing department can then be assessed for actual contributions against the ideal.

Contributions to objectives might come from all or any of the Siblings. These are also shown in the tree as potential contributors. Figure 5.15 excludes any external siblings such as, for instance, an external marketing intelligence agency. In practice, agencies should be included. The example omits such external factors for simplicity.

Evaluating the marketing department's contribution to objectives requires understanding of the department's rôle in the organization as an ideal model, as a standard against which to judge. As the tree above shows, this can be reduced to performance, availability, survivability and cost.

Figure 5.17 is a simple model of performance in establishing mission objectives. It expresses what *should* be done. It represents a strategy too; obsolete products must cease production soonest to release manpower for new design, development and production. Marketing should identify the onset of obsolescence and specify the replacement item to be designed and manufactured, but clearly other departments contribute too. The commercial department, for example, might contribute to the judgement of obsolescence.

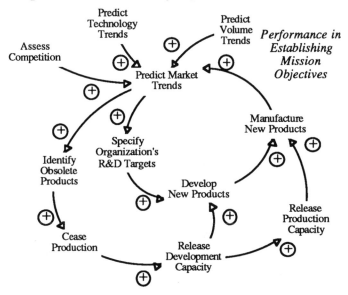

Figure 5.17 Modelling performance in establishing corporate mission objectives

It is similarly possible to model availability of performance and survivability of performance in the establishment of objectives. Using these modelling approaches it is possible to establish the ideal relative contributions of various departments to the organization under discrete headings as well as their mutual interchanges and exchanges—for a method, see Chapter 6. Unlike any other approach, Net Contribution concentrates on the usefulness and value of contributions *from the perspective of the containing system, the organization.*

Table 5.5 shows a typical aggregation of data, best done using a spread sheet to simplify the operation. This aggregation is for objectives only. The table shows the departments in the organization, with columns under for ideal contributions and actual contributions. The first column identifies the emergent properties of these departments (there could be many sub-headings). The "ideal" columns contain assessments, based on the models, of the ideal contribution from each department to the setting of mission objectives. The rows of ideal contributions sum to 100. The "actual" columns contain evaluations of the contributions observed by audit, using the models as a guide to evaluate contribution by the marketing department alongside contributions made by the other departments. The sum of any "actual" row may well be less or more than 100 since the organization, taken as a whole, may under- or over-contribute.

So, in Table 5.5, ideal performance in setting organizational objectives would have rated a 45% contribution from the marketing department, whereas the audit showed only 35%. Availability is calculated similarly. Positive and negative contributions average their scores separately—note that it is proper to add the percentages for capital and operating costs, since they are percentages of *contribution,* not of money. Finally, the Net Contribution is calculated by differencing the positive and negative scores.

Table 5.5 Part of a Net Contribution spreadsheet

Setting Organizational Objectives	Marketing Department		Commercial Department		
	Ideal %	Actual %	Ideal %	Actual %	Ideal %
Performance	45	35	20		25
Availability	65	45	10		15
Positive Contribution	55	40			
Capital	40	45	15		35
Operating	55	50	10		5
Negative Contribution	48	48			
Net Contribution	7	(8)			

Net Contribution rates the department in absolute terms as making a net positive, net negative or neutral contribution. The negative value of (8) in the "actual" column of the table indicates that the department is under-effective and over cost in this singular contribution. Its Net Contribution is poor. A "perfect" department would have scored 7 (see "ideal" column), i.e. would have made a net positive contribution.

This example evaluation looked at only one of the 15 headings under mission, viability and resource management. Full calculations would involve repeating the process, keeping positive contributions separate from negative contributions for clarity, and finally aggregating the scores and algebraically adding the resulting positive and negative values.

SUMMARY AND CONCLUSIONS

Four approaches to evaluating a marketing department in a product-manufacturing organization have been presented, with the following results:

- Efficiency was very easy to calculate, but of little value except, perhaps over a period of successive measurements to observe trends

- Effectiveness was seen as a valuable measure, given a reasonable model of an ideal system. Its potential limitation is lack of focus on true value—it would be easy, for example, to promote increased effectiveness without having a measure of the real value of that increase.

- Cost-effectiveness was inappropriate for assessing a single system, but might be useful to observe trends. The current preoccupation with cost-effectiveness as some sort of ultimate arbiter of good is clearly misplaced. There is no reason why several individually cost-effective departments or organizations should be cost-effective when viewed as a group, since there is nothing in the cost-effectiveness approach which considers harmony and interchange with siblings in an environment. Alternatively, combining separately optimized parts does not result in an optimized whole.

- Net Contribution assessed the value of the department to its owning organization, considering that its only real value lay in its contribution to the organizational goals. The results gave insight into deficiencies, adequacies, their reasons and respective values in terms of the *business*, rather than in terms of marketing as some end in itself. Moreover, Net Contribution showed how the other sibling systems contributed too, thereby presenting the opportunity to judge the need for organizational change on an organization-wide basis

Of the analysis methods presented in this example, only effectiveness and Net Contribution were of significant value and of these, only Net Contribution offered sufficient insight into the business objectives to be valuable, but at an inescapable complexity in the process of evaluation. Since so much depends on proper evaluation in so many walks of life, that penalty must be paid as the price for improved systems which give more than they take.

Chapter 6
Process and Structure Models

Life is one long process of getting tired.
Samuel Butler, 1835—1902

INTRODUCTION

Process models are used extensively to describe and manage the set of activities which together result in a desired goal. Flow charts, networks, work breakdown structures and many other forms of process model exist and are well known. Developing a robust process model is not always that obvious, however. First, where does a process model fit into the scheme of things. As Figure 6.1 shows, a process model is part of a system capability description, the other part being the structure model. A process model is concerned with the activities that are to be undertaken—it is functionally oriented. The structure model is concerned more with the organization of tangible assets, men, machines, materials and money, that will enable the activities delineated by the process model to occur.

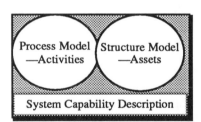

Figure 6.1 System capability models

THE STRUCTURE OF A PROCESS MODEL

A process model may be thought of as comprising a number of sequential phases, each marked by the achievement of an objective such that the objectives sum to be the goal of the process represented by the model. The process model thus describes a system, or perhaps a meta-system, for *producing* a system—the goal. Objectives are sometimes referred to as milestones. The end-system—the goal of the process—may be a product, a set of procedures, a new organization, or almost anything, and is hence best considered as a system.

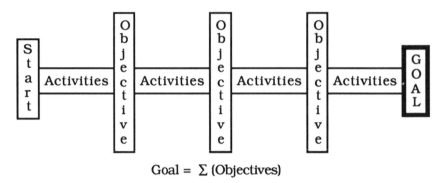

Goal = Σ (Objectives)

Figure 6.2 The structure of a process model

DEVELOPING A PROCESS MODEL

The following five steps may be used to develop a process model coherently. They are based on the USH Principles of of Chapter 3:

1 Start at the end—define the end-system that the process model is intended to produce, its siblings, containing system(s) and their objectives, contained systems and environment(s).
2 Synthesize strategies and consequent activities to create the end-system's intrinsic and emergent properties and overcome threats to their achievement.
3 Consider the process as a system—define its system features, siblings, containing system and objectives, contained systems and environment
4 Develop a process model strategy and framework acceptable within their containing system, harmonized with siblings
5 Sequence end-system activities into the process model framework to achieve objectives on the path to the goal.

Figure 6.3 shows two quite separate sources for the process model—the end-system which is the Goal to produce, and the process as a system in its own right.

The procedural steps may appear simple, but may prove less so in practical application. For example, multiple containing systems may complicate the determination of a full set of end-system emergent and intrinsic properties. Different end-system properties reflect differently into the process model, too. If the end-system is a complete run or batch in some continuous process producing several identical products, for instance, emergent properties such as production rate, per unit cost, consistency of product, etc., become relevant. Some end-system properties reflect into the design process, whilst others reflect into the development, or implementation processes.

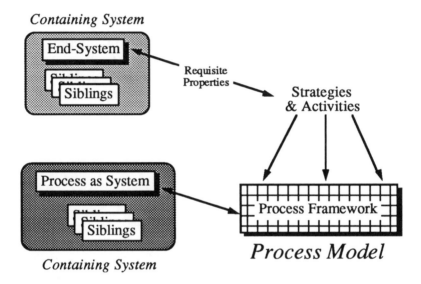

Figure 6.3 Process model procedure

End-system properties might be considered under two headings:

(a)   Features which make the customer/user satisfied with their acquisition. For example:

- Prestige gained by acquiring/owning the end-system
- Effectiveness as a system
    - Performance, judged against containing systems' objectives
    - Availability (reliability, maintainability, etc)
    - Perceived quality
- Contribution to containing systems' goals
- Compatibility with existing and planned siblings
- Capital and running costs in relation to affordability and alternatives

- The overall deal from the customer's[1] viewpoint, which may in some multi-lateral deals, contain elements seemingly unrelated to the end-system
- The degree of meeting the customer's stated objectives
- The degree of meeting the customer's real objectives—the so-called hidden agenda
- Etc.

(b) The partitions within the end-system which:

- Enable design, development and end-system production
- Enable phased introduction to meet manufacture capability, customer priorities, progressive design evolution, etc.
- Minimize risk, waste or difficulty in development, manufacture and procurement
- Ease integration
- Ease support, logistics, maintenance, etc
- Etc.

ILLUSTRATION

Consider setting up an international conference. Such conferences require considerable organization and skill, and it would be usual to employ experts to address much of the routine. Nonetheless, it is common for organizing committees to be set up to manage the overall exercise. The process model is to describe the activities to be undertaken by the organizing committee in conjunction with the professional conference organizers in achieving the end-system—a successful conference.

A number of objectives has been identified in step 1 as important attributes (emergent properties) for the conference. These have been arranged into a self-explanatory intent structure in Figure 6.4. Examination of the figure shows that outcomes are at the top of the figure, while pervasive objectives, those which we might describe as systemic in nature, are at the bottom. Each box is transitive, so that objectives at the bottom contribute to all those above them reachable through the arrows and boxes.

Since the upper objectives are outcomes, we may use them to establish a mission statement for the organizing committee: "to create a profitable conference which addresses the major issue

---

[1] In this context, "customer" is whoever receives the end-system; in a series of processes, each process is the customer of the prior process

effectively, highlighting present causes of dysfunction and identifying areas for advance".

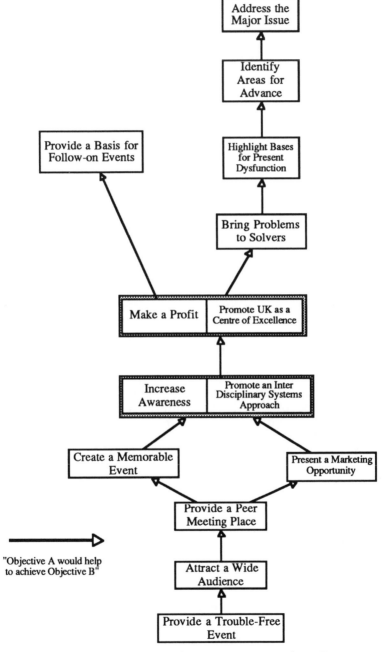

Figure 6.4 Intent structure for an international conference

That is not to say that the objectives in the middle are unimportant, but they are evidently less pervasive and the tend to follow as a result of the five listed above. We may proceed using the five steps for developing a process model. On the other hand, systemic objectives which will lead to the achievement of that mission are principally those at the bottom of the intent structure:

- Provide a trouble-free event
- Attract a wide audience
- Provide a peer meeting-place
- Create a memorable event
- Present a marketing opportunity

Step 1

Start at the end—define the end-system that the process model is intended to produce, its containing system(s) and their objectives, siblings, contained systems and environment.

The end-system is the successful conference. The containing aystem(s) are the institutions or organizations creating, "owning" and providing the conference. Their objectives as learned societies are to further understanding and share knowledge, while as organizations their objectives are to make sufficient profit to enable future similar conferences. Siblings are the transport and accommodation systems which bring people to the conference and house them, together with the conference venue itself. Contained systems are the exhibition to be included in the conference, the system for presenting papers and the system for replenishing the delegates. The environment can be considered in two ways: it is the locale of the conference centre; it is also the competition from other conferences for the pool of potential conference delegates.

Step 2

Synthesize strategies and consequent activities to create the end-system's intrinsic and emergent properties —taken from Figure 6.4— and overcome threats to their achievement.

Objective: Provide a trouble-free event
Threats/obstacles:
    Subject matter which attracts unwelcome attention
    Poor travel arrangements

Poor accommodation

Poor conference facilities

Poor security
Strategies to overcome:

1 Omit politically-controversial subjects

2 Secure the conference centre thoroughly

3 Vet accommodation

4 Provide comprehensive travel information

5 Provide transport from BR for luggage, participants, spouses

6 Provide comprehensive conference communications: telephone, fax, datapost, photocopying, etc

7 AA/RAC signposting.

8 Issue books of papers at commencement

Objective: Attract a wide audience
Threats/obstacles:

Cost of publicity

Ineffective publicity

Lack of subject-matter appeal

Cost of attending

Low perceived value in attending
Strategies to overcome:

9 Choose subject with multi-disciplinary appeal

10 Direct publicity to likely audience:

Institutions, academia, customers, users

Industry—internationally

11 Advertise keynote papers from respected authorities in their fields

12 Run parallel, theme-based sessions

13 Offer on-line translation

14 Use inexpensive accommodation as basic, with more expensive options

15 Focus the subject into several clear, related themes known to be areas for concern/research

16 Run associated "classified" day for sensitive subjects

Objective: Provide a peer meeting place
Threats/obstacles:

Failure to attract professionals of sufficient standing

Lack of opportunity for peers to interact professionally

Strategies to overcome:
   17 Provide workshops as part of overall programme.
   18 Identify peers; invite directly to attend, present papers

Objective: Create a memorable event
Threats/obstacles:
   Lack of social activity
   Lack of quality in the papers
   Lack of conference prestige
Strategies to overcome:
   19   Include sponsored social events in programme
         —Reception, historic dinner, spouse activities, theatre, etc
   20   Offer included weekend breaks in conjunction with
         operator.
   21   Keynote papers from respected authorities—see 11 above.
   22   Careful peer selection of submitted papers.
   23   Prize(s) for best contribution?
   24   Celebrity dinner speaker.
   25   Celebrity to open conference.

Objective: Present a marketing opportunity
Threats/obstacles:
   Dilution of perceived professional activity status of conference.
   Lack of space for exhibition
   Lack of interest
Strategies to overcome:
   26   Encourage sponsorship of social events
   27   Establish an exhibition or advertising area of services,
         methods, products directly related to the conference topics.
   28   Ask industry for demonstrations to conference
   29   Invite industry experts to speak
   30   Encourage industry to provide prize(s) for best
         contribution.
   31   Invite book publishers to display

N.B. Each of the strategies will clearly lead to a set of activities too
numerous to detail; it is these activities which will eventually be
interleaved into a detailed plan along with those emerging from step
4 below.

Step 3

Consider the process as a system—define its system features, siblings, containing system (s) and their objectives, contained systems and environment.

The process is that system which undertakes the activities resulting in a successful conference. It is to complete its organizing work in 12 months. It comprises (i.e. the contained systems are) the organizing committee and the professional conference organizers, each represented at the other's meetings and given details of all activities. The maximum sensible number of organizing committee participants is fifteen and they are further grouped into subsystems for publicity, vetting proposed papers, and organizing sessions.

The containing system(s) include the institution or organization which engenders the organizing committee, but in a more subtle way it is also possible to consider the organizations that support and employ the members who participate in the organizing committee as also containing, since these other organizations could certainly stop the event. The objectives of the Institution are to ensure an economically viable conference and to enhance their own reputations as seats of learning and dissemination. The organizations employing the committee members have as their objectives the professional development of their employees and the potential for marketing and publicity.

Siblings include similar groups in other Institutions with whom a relationship exists or might exist, publicity or marketing agents, potential sponsor groups, exhibiting organizers, the conference venue owners and organizers, relevant accommodation and transportation systems, etc. The environment is that experienced by the conference-organizing system, effectively that presented by the institution. In this example, we may say that the institution is a learned society and is therefore predisposed to support scientifically advanced and respectable activities only.

Step 4

Develop a process model strategy and framework acceptable within their containing system, harmonized with siblings .

Objective: Establish an effective organizing committee
Threat/obstacle:

   Mismatch between committee members and the tasks to be
   undertaken
Strategy:

Invite members known for organizing capability and for professional authority in the conference subject matter

Objective: Control the effort required by committee members who will be committed to other work
Threat/obstacle:

Too much work, too many meetings, disorganization, insufficient use of professional conference organizers
Strategy:
Establish minimum set of meetings:

Inaugural meeting to establish the policy, nature and structure of the conference and to initiate actions on: the call for papers; the selection and invitation of keynote speakers and prestigious guests; publicity and advertising; organization of the vetting of papers, once received; subdivision of the Organizing Committee into Publicity, Financial, Paper Vetting, Workshop Organizers, etc.

Second meeting at Conference venue to approve the site and accommodation, to confirm the vetting of received paper synopses, to group them into session themes, to identify workshop features and participants, to review and approve/redirect advertising, publicity, etc.

Third meeting to vet full papers, redirect worthy, but off-the-mark papers, rejig session contents, assess impact of advertising and redirect, etc.

Fourth meeting, possibly, to assess redirected papers, review progress, etc.

Step 5

Sequence end-system activities into process model framework
Each of the strategy statements implies a number of activities: it is these that are interleaved in Step 5. With so many strategies and consequent activities, the resulting sequence would be rather too complex for illustration purposes. As an example, the following strategies will be addressed only:

Strategy 11   Advertise keynote papers from respected authorities in their fields

Strategy 27   Establish an exhibition or advertising area of service methods, products directly related to conference topics.

Figure 6.5 shows the various activities for each stratagem identified by a different box—rounded for Strategy 11, square for Strategy 27— so that the interleaving may be clearly seen. Traditionally, such figures are presented with the initial activity at the top, in the manner of a flow-chart. Each set of activities may be read separately by starting at the top and working downward, choosing only the particular box-shape of interest.

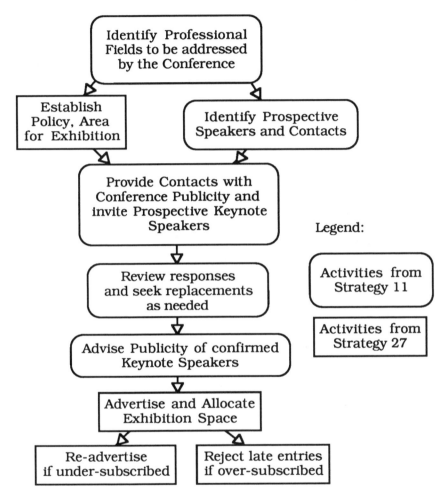

Figure 6.5 Process model: activities from strategies 11 and 27

The reason for restricting the number of strategies used in the example should now be evident; the activities resulting from the complete set of strategies would be so complex that the picture would become cluttered. In practice, this clutter is such that the various strategies may become invisible, and the activities flow chart is often presented as a PERT network or GANTT chart, which may totally conceal any strategy. While such representations may be necessary to control the organization and flow of work, the concealing of underlying strategy is to be deprecated; people using these representations should be aware of the strategies concealed within them if the people are to be effective.

Finally, note that the last two activities at the bottom of the process model are alternatives—a fact not well indicated by this type of representation—and that phasing of activities will be addressed below.

Such process models are derived by identifying the relationship between all activities on a pairwise basis, i.e. by asking "does activity A precede activity B, or does activity B precede activity A, must they occur at the same time, or are they unrelated?"

PRESENTATION OF PROCESS MODELS

There is a simple presentation, derived from software engineering (see Alford, 1985) and called an R-Net (or Requirement Net). As the inset panel of figure 6.6 proposes, the Software Requirements Engineering Methodology (SREM) is delightfully simple and clear, and allows branching either as an AND, i.e. taking both all branches or as an OR, i.e. taking any of the routes. The point at which a number of activities come together presents itself as a natural end-of-phase, which is a most convenient planning feature. There are two ways to establish process model phases: either of these may be chosen to suit the needs or practices of the process-containing system; or, and often more effectively, the phases may be allowed to emerge naturally from the coming together of a number of activities at a logical activity node.

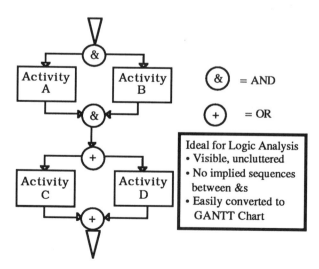

Figure 6.6 Requirement networks—R-Nets

STRUCTURE MODEL

Figure 6.7 shows a notional structure model. The partitioning in the process is visible, as are the milestones. This representation suggests that the phases are like pipes which channel the activities, while the structure essentially supports and holds the pipes end to end, so that the goal may be achieved. The whole is founded upon the available assets of people, tools, methods and resources. The notion is real enough; the best process model is worthless unless it can be put into effect in a resource-bearing structure.

Developing a structure model should be straightforward in principle, once the functional process model is established. Unravelling the requirements of the process model has established the base data for the structure model, too, in terms of durations, per unit costs, quality, etc. It remains to "enable" the process model by supplying men, machines, materials and money (Jenkins, 1972) for each activity and organizing these resources into a system. One approach to the task is developed in figure 6.8, which should be self-explanatory. Note that the TRIAD building system generates all the elements of both structure and function, but does not order them into sequence or architecture.

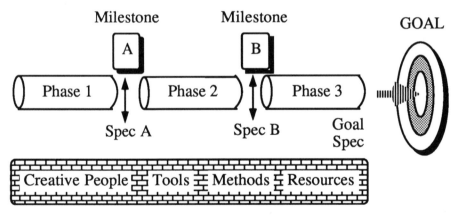

Figure 6.7 Structure model concept

Risk Management

The seemingly-simple TRIAD building system can be immensely powerful in practice. It operates at any level within an organization or hierarchy, and can be continued until as much detail is generated as situation demands. Risk management is implicit, since threats are identified and addressed at all levels in the process. The procedure provides implicit traceability, too; each activity, no matter how far down the chain, is traceable back to the original prime directive.

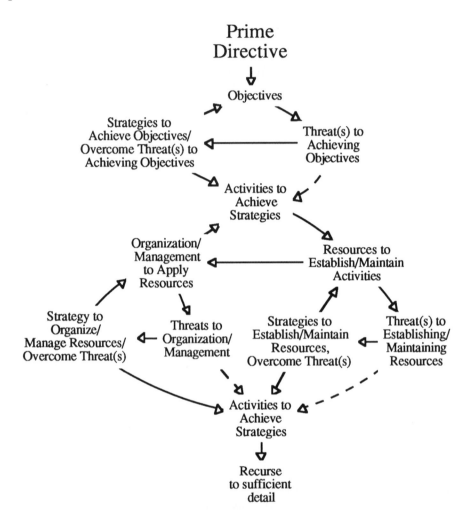

Figure 6.8 The TRIAD building system for structure models. The diagram is read from the top, with a Prime Directive (see Chapter 10.1) or ultimate statement of purpose being broken down into objectives. Threats are identified to each objective and strategies are formulated both to overcome each threat and to achieve the objective. The term TRIAD reflects the repeated three-part structure which persists throughout—objective, threat, strategy

ASSIGNMENT A
THE INTELLIGENT BUILDING

Scenario

A major intelligent office building is required as a prestige project by an international developer. The building is expected to evolve during its expected 30 year life-span, with a major internal refit anticipated every 5 to 7 years, during which only the building fabric would remain unchanged, to install new communications and environmental control facilities as they came on the market.

The specification is intentionally broad. The building is to house some 350 people in ultra modern office accommodation, with individual access to personal (micro) environmental controls and all conceivable communication facilities. Security is to be paramount, with control of access and egress to and from the building and similar control of individuals to within their authorized areas within the building. It is likely that this will entail some form of individual tracking. The building is to contain its own recreational facilities and vehicle parking within the security cordon, together with a nuclear fall-out shelter to house and sustain all occupants for up to 7 days. The building is to harmonize with its Central London surroundings, yet to be distinctive as befits its prestigious nature.

Situation

You are new to the building design consultancy, but have made friends with 3 or 4 others in your area. Together, you are given the following assignment :

- Develop a process model for the design of the building, to be presented, after approval by your Board, to the developer and to civic and social pressure group representatives
- Develop a structure model for the design, construction, operation, periodic refit and eventual replacement of the building as a basis for estimating the through-life cost of building ownership
- Develop sketch designs for the building layout, and special features
- Present your initial findings to the board in only 7 hours!

ASSIGNMENT B
THE CORPORATION DUST-CART

A process model is required for the design of a new corporation dust-cart. The corporation has a variety of waste collection and disposal systems, but local population has increased, new estates have grown, and current facilities are inadequate. Any new system must be compatible with other waste collection systems for private residences. Capital and running costs are to be minimized for the new dust-cart, consistent with effective waste collection from private dwellings and minimal disruption to local traffic. The corporation has its own waste dump, some miles from the area of collection; the dump is known to have soft ground and present dust-carts regularly bog-down.

The corporation has indicated likely prices and delivery schedules, but competition is likely to be fierce, so these indicated figures are not set in concrete. The corporation is also proud of its amenities and likes to be thought of as progressive.

Develop a process model for the design of a new corporation dust-cart. Remember that the dust-carts will form a fleet of vehicles; you are an employee of the manufacturing company, and must therefore consider production runs as part of the manufacturing process, *insofar as they might affect design.*

Chapter 7
Systems Architecture

Architecture in general is frozen music
Friedrich von Schelling 1775-1854

ARCHITECTURE

Structure, Balance and Flow

There are features about any good design which seem somehow "right". We are familiar with aircraft and ships being the "right shape", for example. So it is with systems. A well-designed system exhibits three characteristics: structure, balance and flow. This discussion is substantially about realizing the substance of those three words—first, structure.

Pervasive Architectures

Architecture is a widely used term, implying many things to many people. Consider Bronowski's viewpoint, (Bronowski, 1973):

> The notion of discovering an underlying order in matter is man's basic concept for exploring nature. The architecture of things reveals a structure below the surface, a hidden grain which, when it is laid bare, makes it possible to take natural formations apart and assemble them in new formations. For me this is the step in the ascent of man at which theoretical science begins. And it is as native to the way man conceives his own communities as it is to his conception of nature.
>
> We human beings are joined in families, the families are joined in kinship groups, the kinship groups in clans, the clans in tribes, and the tribes in nations. And that sense of hierarchy, of a pyramid in which layer is imposed on layer, runs through all the ways we look at nature.

A view of balance, at a different level, is expressed by Edward Rubenstein (1989), Associate Dean at Stanford University School of Medicine:

> How does nature encompass and mould a billion galaxies, a billion billion stars—and also the earth, teeming and exuberant with life? New insights into how nature operates come from parallel

advances in particle physics and in molecular biology, advances that make it possible to examine the fundamental physical and biological processes side by side. The resulting stereoscopic view reveals a previously hidden, unifying logic in nature; its paradigm for construction.

What nature does, in essence, is to make assemblies. It relies on the same template of programmed actions in each step of assembly along the way. Continuing sequences of assembly are the veins of evolution. Biological evolution is the result of natural selection operating on random variations. Physical evolution is a similar process of construction: a chain of chance associations from which new structures arise. Whether these objects survive or vanish depends on their environment.

... Physical evolution and biological evolution are both characterized by common descent, natural selection and the eventual—and apparently inevitable—expression of symmetry.

My view of structure and balance as essentials of good architecture embrace both Bronowski's and Rubenstein's views. But first, what is architecture in a visual sense?

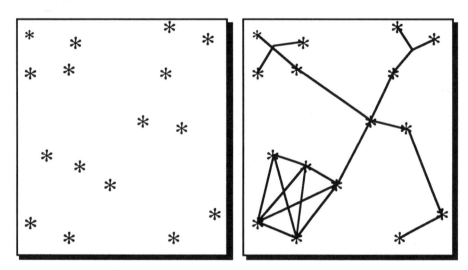

Fig ure 7.1 Basic architecture—clusters and links

In figure 7.1 at the left is a set of entities. There is no inter-connection. There is no architecture. On the right, the same entities have been connected in patterns which reveal two features: clusters of entities, and both cluster intra-connections and inter-connections. There is architecture. Architecture at its most elemental, then is clustering and linking. For artefacts, clustering and linking are purposeful, where purposeful includes aesthetics. Entities, at this level of definition, may be physical chunks, activities, people, ideas even. Architecture can be comprised of heterogeneous entities, so long as purposeful clustering can take place.

Binding and Coupling

Entities bind together when they share common processes, interfaces, communication links, physical features, etc. Functionally-bound entities are candidates for physical grouping in order to reduce the end-system interface complexity. Figures 7.2 and 7.3 show sets of modules to illustrate ideas of binding and coupling—ideas which are recognized by software engineers but which have much wider connotations in the development of architecture. At the left is a set of fully interconnected modules, suggesting closely interwoven mutual dependence. Binding is an intra-cluster concept.

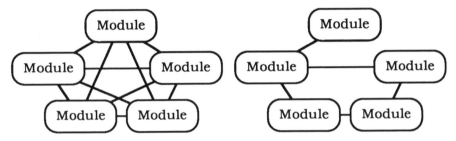

Figure 7.2 Functional binding. At left, the modules are fully-interconnected, or tightly-functionally bound. At right, the modules are loosely functionally bound

At the right, the same set of modules—sub-systems or parts—is only partially interdependent, or loosely functionally bound.

Coupling presents the inter-cluster viewpoint, showing how much sets might be related one to another. As Figure 7.3 shows, sets can be tightly coupled or loosely coupled. Design ideals are envisaged; a system should be partitioned so as to encourage functional binding, and reduce functional coupling. In practice, these aims are rarely realized. However, we can say:

- Partitioning is a crucial system design activity
- Objective is to partition so as to:
  + Maximize binding
  — Minimize coupling
- Functionally bound module sets are candidates for aggregation
- Aggregation implies boundaries
- Coupling implies across-boundary linkages :

+ Interfaces
+ Protocols for interconnection
+ A flow—of information, sometimes of substance
• Together, coupling and binding develop architecture

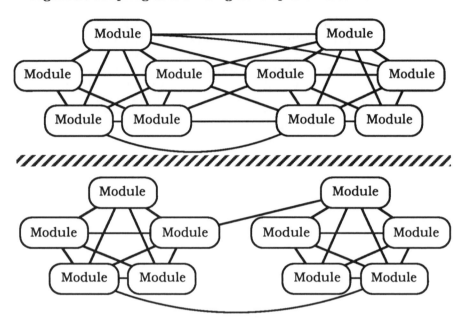

Figure 7.3 Functional coupling. Above, the two sets of modules are tightly coupled. Below, the sets are loosely coupled

Coupling is the degree of interaction between entities in different groups, and it is generally considered desirable to reduce coupling (of this variety) also to reduce complexity of interface and communications infrastructure. The concepts can be applied to software, hardware and to higher hierarchy-levels of architecture, including grouping of humans into organizations

Figures 7.4 and 7.5 illustrate the N^2 chart which is associated with Robert Lano (q.v.) of TRW, but which is now used world-wide. The N^2 chart is an incidence matrix comprising N rows and N columns—hence N-squared squares. Entities are recorded on the leading diagonal and interfaces between them occupy the other squares in the matrix. By convention, all outputs from an entity are on the row containing that entity, while all inputs to an entity are on the columns containing that entity. Each square (other than those occupied by entities) thus stands at the coincidence of an output from, and an input to, two entities; it thus represents the one-way relationship between those entities.

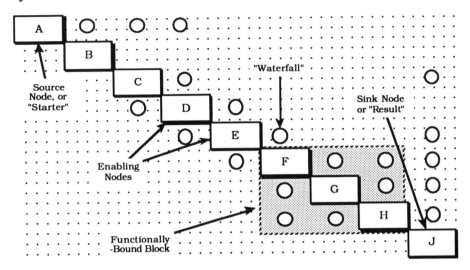

Figure 7.4 Typical N^2 chart interface patterns

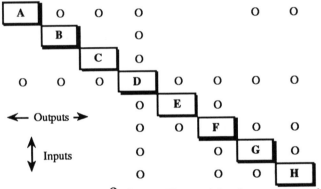

Figure 7.5 Clustered N^2 chart. The matrix shows F,G and H to be functionally bound since all their respective interfaces, represented by 'O', are filled in. D is a system nexus or node since it has interfaces to and from every other entity on the chart; D would be a candidate for special interest, since its loss would split the system into two. A is a source node, since it "supplies" the other entities

Lano observed that relationships, or interfaces in the software jargon, formed patterns when mapped on to the N^2 chart. These interface patterns may not be evident initially, but appear if the entities are suitably rearranged, and can reveal binding, coupling and other features, This is a powerful technique, which becomes very much more powerful when coupled with the speed of a computer, since there are some N!/2 (factorial N divided by two) permutations of entities which, for a large matrix can become extremely unwieldy. Techniques have been developed for characterizing the shapes of the various clustered patterns formed on the N^2 chart, for identifying missing interfaces and repairing such omissions, for developing clusters with different characteristics, and many more. This subject will be expanded below.

Examination of the clustered N^2 chart shows that it can be reduced to the simpler chart of Figure 7.6 by recognizing that the entities with filled-in mutual interfaces are tightly functionally bound and may usefully be considered as one macro-function. This aggregation process is synthesis, the opposite of analysis which breaks things down into parts.

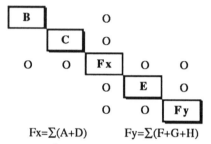

$$Fx = \Sigma(A+D) \qquad Fy = \Sigma(F+G+H)$$

Figure 7.6 N^2 chart. First stage of synthesis

In the first stage of synthesis, F, G and H are combined, and so are A and D which also bind functionally. This is not the only synthesis path at this point; note that D, E and F also exhibit tight functional binding. Synthesis involves choice, as does analysis.

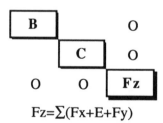

$$Fz = \Sigma(Fx+E+Fy)$$

Figure 7.7 N^2 chart. Second stage of synthesis

The second stage of synthesis, Figure 7.7, combines Fx, E and Fy, since these now form a functionally-bound block. It is important to maintain interface consistency throughout the process, and interface aggregation occurs as part of synthesis. Comparing the final chart with the original shows that a very considerable simplification has occurred. No information will have been lost in the process, since the previous charts act as reference. This process of synthesis is vital in the development of systems architecture, and further technique will be presented below.

Scoring N² Charts

It is possible to introduce the concept of scoring an N^2 chart. To score a chart, one simply determines the distance of each interface from its associated entities in terms of the number of squares, and multiplies the number in the interface by some function of distance. The sum of all such scores for all interfaces makes the N^2 chart score. The process is illustrated in Figure 7.8. The number, X or Y in the figure, represents some characteristic of the interface as viewed from system level, such as strength of association, priority, etc., determined in a systematic marking scheme. Typical functions, f, of distance would be direct proportionality, square or cube. If two interfacing entities are separated on the chart by a number of intervening entities, then the interface joining them will score high due to the distance functions, dx and dy above. If they were adjacent, their interface score would be low. It is therefore possible to arrange the entities on the chart so that the chart has an overall lowest score. In this configuration, all interfaces connecting entities will be grouped such that their scores are low; competition between entities, each trying to occupy the same position relative to a third entity will be resolved by the strength of their respective interface.

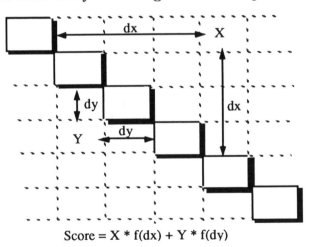

Score = X * f(dx) + Y * f(dy)

Figure 7.8 Scoring N^2 charts

The reason for the function of distance can now be explained. If the distance function is made a square instead of linear, then tighter clusters result. The cube function produces even tighter clusters. If the N^2 chart is considered like a lattice, then the leading diagonal containing the entities is a central septum. Taking a linear function of distance about this septum equates to taking moments, and is a torque, or first moment function. Squaring the distance equates to an inertia-type, or second moment function—and so on.

Automatic Clustering of N^2 charts

The ability to cluster automatically and according to a selection of simple rules presents great architectural richness. Entities present system-level emergent properties not visible in any other practical way, as clusters, often quite unexpected, appear. The clustering has, however, come about on the basis of relationships and strengths identified individually by the would-be architect, and any supporting tool simply reveals the structural implications of his or her supplied information.   It is a remarkable feature of this approach that all the information is supplied directly by the user but that he or she may be quite unaware of the implications of their piecemeal knowledge.

Repairing Flawed Architecture

Clustering enables the detection of missing interfaces. The Figure 7.9 shows architectural imbalance, since interfaces almost

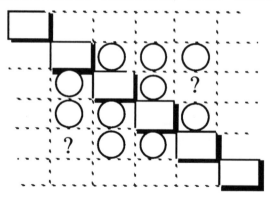

Figure 7.9 Identifying missing interfaces The human eye-brain combination is excellent at recognizing patterns, even where only partly formed. The figure shows two interfaces which stand out by their absence from an otherwise symmetric figure

invariably occur in pairs[1], a "send" interface from entity A to entity B and a "reply" interface from entity B to entity A. These interface pairs appear also as corresponding links in control loops. A concept-developer seeing the Figure 7.9 would have to question

---

[1] See dyadic reciprocity—Chapter 2

deeply the validity of the missing interfaces. While such missing interfaces can occur occasionally, for example, in the case of remote sensors which are totally open loop, i.e. not controlled at all, they are rare and generally non-robust. Where the missing interface refers to human interchange, the absence of an interface in one direction suggests that A is passing information to B, quite unaware of whether it is being received or, if received, whether it is satisfactory. Such lack of feedback causes human links to fade.

The usual practice, then, on seeing missing interfaces either in a node or in a functional block, is to fill them in. For complex systems, automated support for clustering becomes almost essential; without tools there would not be such visibility of clusters, and the human skill at pattern recognition would not be brought into play.

WORKED EXAMPLES

The Presentation

Three examples will be presented below, one simple, the others less so. The simple example is concerned with structuring a presentation from amongst its topics, to understand relationships and promote flow. The chart at the left shows the topics unclustered, while at the right they are clustered into tight patterns. The result gives a chapter sequence, from bottom to top in this instance, since the N^2 clustering approach does not recognize top from bottom of the chart. The result is useful, promoting ease of presentation for the author and ease of understanding in the reader.

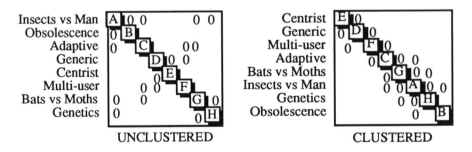

Figure 7.10 Clustering presentation topics. Topics are entered in any order at the left, and their mutual relationships identified in the N^2 chart. Re-arranging the topics develops a natural flow, by clustering the topics toward the entity-diagonal, leading to a waterfall sequence which is ideal for presentation purposes

Repairing Inadequate Architecture

The second example presents the results of an unofficial study, undertaken as an exercise, into a crisis management system for the Channel Tunnel (Chunnel) to anticipate terrorists, failures catastrophes, etc.

```
Damge Cntl     1    N                    6            6
Interpol       2       D      3        9      3 3
Activ Sens     3          H          8 8           8 9
Envir. Sens    4             G       8               9
Customs        5       3        B 3      7    1 3
Bag.Insp       6              6 C
Safety Cntl    7                     I               2
RailOps        8                   9 O               9
Intel          9                       J           9 8
Logistics      10   2                      L       2 6
Immgrtn        11      6      1        7     A 6
Local Pol      12      6      2        9     2 E   1 4
Emgy Svcs      13                              F     4
Security       14         1          7 7      3    M 8
Operations     15   9    1 2       9 7 5      4 4 9 K
```

Figure 7.11 Unclustered N² chart. The (hypothetical) chart represents the views of the operations officer in terms of which interfaces were important, and what was their relative importance to emergency operations, represented on a 0-9 scale. (Direct copy from computer printout.)

```
Bag.Insp       1    C 6
Customs        2    3 B 1 3 3 7
Immgrtn        3      1 A 6 6 7
Interpol       4      3 3 D 3 9
Local Pol      5      2 2 6 E 9     1 4
Intel          6            J       9 8
Emgy Svcs      7                F     4
Activ Sens     8            8   H 8 9 8
Security       9          3 7   1 M 8           7
Operations     10         4 5 4 1 9 K 7 9 2 9
RailOps        11                 9 O 9
Safety Cntl    12                 2   I
Envir. Sens    13                 9 8   G
Damge Cntl     14                 6       N 6
Logistics      15                 2 6     2 L
```

Figure 7.12 Clustered N² chart. The rearranged chart shows a major cluster in the top, left-hand corner and a major node around the operations officer. The two structures are coupled via the local police and intelligence, while security presents a partial system node. (Direct copy from computer printout.)

The conception of architecture started with the development of an N^2 chart in which the information flowing through the interfaces was described in words: logistics passes information about resource availability and constraints to operations, for example. This word-based N^2 chart was then converted to a numbered chart, figure 7.11, by the simple ruse of establishing a numbering scheme and allocating numbers to each active interface: in this case, the numbers represented the degree of importance ascribed by operations to the particular information flow.

Clustering the numbered N^2 chart results in the re-arranged chart at figure 7.12, which shows the pattern necessary to establish physical structure.

Advanced Architecture Design Concepts

Since the concept of clustering and linking is fundamental to architecture, it should be applicable to the most advanced of projects. In such cases, the challenge and demand might be much greater, but the concept should be similar. The following example is taken from an advanced avionics architecture project concerned with physical relationships and positioning of avionics devices—boxes—inside the fuselage. There are many influences on positioning:

- Antennae must be at the fuselage skin
- Receivers must be near the antennae to avoid unnecessary signal loss in the connecting cable
- Displays and controls must be near the crew
- Critical devices must be replicated and isolated to avoid a single hit from damaging performance
- Centre of gravity must be maintained within limits, etc.

As can be seen, while some factors tend to cluster, others tend to repel. Clustering can be made to accommodate this feature by a simple change of numbering scheme, as follows:

9. Proximity essential
8. Proximity v. important
7. Proximity important
6. Proximity useful
5. Proximity convenient
4. Don't care
3. Distance convenient

2. Distance useful

1. Distance vmportant

Effectively all that has happened is a shift of origin to the middle of
the range; this does, of course, exclude zero as an option and in
consequence every interface is filled, making clustering by eye and
simple matrix manipulation virtually impossible. To a suitable
clustering tool, however, nothing has changed.

With the more complex situation presented by avionics
architectures, it also becomes swiftly evident that we are not in the
realm of "right answers". There is no correct answer to architectural
problems; some are simply better than others in some respects.

Consider the following situation. An avionics system is
comprised of a number of discrete modules which can be put
together to build operating functions. There are 15 such modules in
this case; they are as follows:

A power amplifier (PA)	A CNI* receiver
Two antennae	A radar receiver (Rx)
A special transmitter	Two TX/RX controllers
A special receiver	A frequency synthesizer
A radar transmitter (Tx)	Crew displays and controls
A CNI* transmitter	Weapons

* Communications, Navigation and Identification

Adding the aircraft fuselage and the crew themselves completes the
picture. The first moment cluster, relatively loosely-bound, shows
several interesting architectural features:

• The transmitters have been grouped with one antenna and one
  controller
• The receivers have also been grouped with the other antenna and
  the other controller
• The fuselage is a pivot, around which the design clusters.
• The displays and controls, the crew and the weapons are grouped
  remotely from the transmitters with their unwelcome and
  potentially hazardous radiation
• The controllers have been mutually separated for survivability

The groupings are unconventional. It is more usual for each
transmitter to be grouped with its respective receiver, since both are
often made by the same manufacturer. The clustering process has
suggested the different arrangement because it worked at a higher
system level, that of the aircraft as a whole. At the least, the
technique is assisting lateral thinking. It could even be proposing a
much more robust design approach. And it used only information

provided by the avionics experts who used the technique—they alone selected the entities and chose the numbers in the N^2 chart

CONCLUSION

Architecture is fundamental to systems. An understanding of architecture is an essential precursor to analysing, conceiving, designing and synthesizing systems. The science of architecture is not well developed but there are methods of analysing and synthesizing which reveal latent structure and deficiencies. Architectural features may combine in a combinatorial explosion to generate seemingly unmanageable complexity, but this richness is valuable and there are methods of addressing the complexity, sometimes tool supported, which come into their own only when the richness appears, as subsequent chapters will show.

ASSIGNMENT

Using the organizational cells generated in Chapter 4's assignment, set up an N^2 chart and identify, in words, the information which must flow between the various parties within the Operations Centre and those interacting with the Centre. When complete, re-arrange the N^2 chart columns and rows to develop a suitable organizational architecture.

Part C
System Synthesis

Outputs

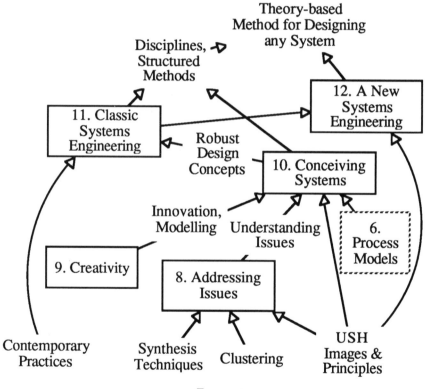

Inputs

Chapter 8.1
Addressing Issues

" ... giving them patience under their sufferings and a happy issue out of their afflictions.
Prayer Book, General Thanksgiving

INTRODUCTION

The world is full of issues. Issues abound in the affairs of man, in technology, the workplace, families, communications, politics, crime, government, religion and in all walks of everyday life. Issues represent actual or potential disharmony, different point of view, the causes of dispute and conflict, mismatch, imbalance, and so on. Issues are the stuff of life, the hurdles to be overcome or circumnavigated—resolved, solved or dissolved, according to Ackoff (1981). Ackoff defined his terms, in respect of problems rather than issues, as follows:

> To resolve *a problem is to select a means that yields an outcome that is good enough, that satisfices. Ackoff called this approach clinical because it relies heavily on past experience and current trial and error for its inputs. It is qualitatively, not quantitatively, oriented; it is rooted deeply in common sense; and it makes extensive use of subjective judgement .*
> To solve *a problem is to select a means that is believed to yield the best possible outcome, that optimizes. Ackoff called this the research approach because it is based largely on scientific methods, techniques and tools. It makes extensive use of mathematical models and real or simulated experiments; therefore it relies heavily on observation and measurement.*
> To dissolve *a problem is to change the nature of either the entity that has it or to alter its environment in order to remove the problem. Problem dissolvers idealize rather than satisfice or optimize because their objective is to change the system involved, or its environment, to bring it closer to an ultimately desired state, one in which the problem cannot or does not arise. Ackoff called this the design approach. Designers make use of the methods, techniques and tools of both clinicians and researchers, and much more, but they use them synthetically, to build, rather than analytically, to decompose. They try to dissolve problems by changing the characteristics of the system that contains the part with the problem. They look for dissolutions in the containing whole rather than solutions in the contained parts.*

Given the almost limitless scope for issues, it seems unlikely that a sensible approach to issues, if possible at all, could hope to be founded exclusively in either the clinical approach or the research approach. The clinical approach must founder because of its dependence on experience and trial and error in unknown and sensitive situations and in the knowledge that complex systems behave counter-intuitively (see Forrester, 1972).

The research method must similarly fail where observation and experiment are inappropriate, and because its goal, optimization, is at best a localized phenomenon. Experiment will fail where the conditions for conducting experiments cannot sensibly be established. Social systems satisfy this criterion; to conduct experiments on, say, an angry group of prison inmates in order to solve an issue would be inappropriate. Physical systems may also satisfy this criterion; much of astrophysics research has to be accomplished without satisfactory experiment because of the impossibility of the scale involved.

Practical as both the clinical and the research approaches might be in appropriate circumstances, neither offers a sound base for a general theoretical approach to issues. Kerlinger defines a theory as:

> *a set of interrelated constructs (concepts), definitions, and propositions that present a systematic view of phenomena by specifying relations among variables, with the purpose of explaining the phenomena.*

Present methods for addressing issues do not seem to live up entirely to this definition.

Anticipating Counter-intuitive Results

Present methods may tackle only parts of an overall issue. This tendency arises where several problem themes contribute to one issue and the complexity implied by addressing all of the problem themes together may seem too high. Selecting one, or even several, of the overall set of problem themes risks counter-intuitive results, however. A sound method would *not* select, but would address the complete issue, with all its problem themes and their mutual interactions, as one.

Lack of Theory—Implications

Nonetheless, the lack of any theory, resulting in the employment of essentially *ad hoc* methods, is a fertile ground in which to produce less than ideal results. Not only might recommendations be less than ideal, they might conceivably offer quite incorrect advice. Without a theory, there is little prospect of judging:

- If an issue has been, or can be, sensibly addressed at all
- Whether an issue is potentially solvable, resolvable or dissolvable
- What activities, actions or occurrences might affect the issue
- Whether "reasonable" recommendations are likely to offer genuine help or be counter-productive in the short or long term
- Whether recommendations, judiciously followed, were responsible for subsequent results, good or bad, owing to parallel, on-going changes in the relevant systems

With such a wide market, a theory-based approach to issues could be invaluable.

WHAT IS AN "ISSUE"?

First, the dictionary:

- "Cause, affair, business, concern, matter, argument, controversy, proposition, question"
- "Outcome, end, consequence, result"

Clearly, there are two basic meanings represented here: problem-related, and outcome-related. This chapter is concerned with understanding in relation to the first meaning, with a view to beneficially affecting outcome, the second meaning.

Interacting Systems

In systems terms, using the systems images presented in Chapter 3, an issue may be thought of as an irritant, perturbation, imbalance or disturbance in the fabric of interacting systems. In the first sense of issue, perturbation may be more readily identified than outcome, the second sense of issue.

Viewpoints

The concept of generating different viewpoints to encompass a wider spectrum of information and to broaden understanding is worthy and is to be found in a host of software engineering tools. But is it new in the context of systems? The hierarchy principle of systems, Checkland (1981) and Boulding (1956), is a well established model, as is the consequential concept of simultaneous multiple containment of one system by many containing systems. There seems to be little substantial difference between the notion of

Weltanschauungen and the notion of multiple containment. Perhaps *Weltanschauung* is a descriptor of a particular containing system.

"Issue" Source Possibilities

If issues are evidence of imbalance or disharmony, then we should be able to locate the possible sources, using the USH systems images as a model. Issues are, at the abstract level, a strain in the fabric of interacting systems. As such, the strain could arise because of stresses within the systems or between them in their interchanges. An issue could arise from changed "pressure" on or from a system, or asymmetric "pull or push" acting on a system, to use physical analogies. An isolated, or closed, system could not be said to exhibit imbalance or disharmony, since both terms imply a relative measure, between two or more systems.

For an issue to have its source *within* a system, the system must exhibit disturbed emergent properties arising from an imbalance between its contained systems. For interacting systems, then, an issue within a system can be reduced to an imbalance between systems by hierarchy shift. Hence:

> *Issues arise from an imbalance in the relationships and interchanges between interacting systems, these relationships and interchanges being mediated by environment*

This statement is axiomatic, given the definitions and USH system images upon which it is based. Moreover, there is more than a hint in the argument above that issues may be highlighted by continued reduction in hierarchy level until systems are revealed between which imbalance can be recognized.

Imbalance and Hierarchy Level

If imbalance between systems is the source of issues, then the question arises about location. Can imbalance occur only at a single hierarchy level, i.e. between siblings, or can it occur also "up and down" hierarchy levels, between a contained and a containing system? The second question reveals its own inconsistency. While relationships and interchanges exist between systems at the same hierarchy level, they cannot be said to exist *in the same way* between hierarchy levels, since the containing system is the aggregate of the contained systems and their intra-relationships, exchanges and environment.

Imbalances, then, occur at a given hierarchy level and impact upon emergent properties of the containing system(s), i.e. one hierarchy level higher.

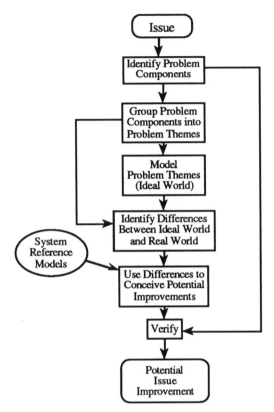

Figure 8.1 Addressing messy, complex issues

ADDRESSING ISSUES

Figure 8.1 shows a broad approach to addressing what Checkland refers to as messy problem situations—indeed the diagram could apply to SSM at some level of abstraction. However, the approach adopted below is unlike SSM in several important respects. First, it does not select problem themes and address them separately, but seeks to advance understanding on all fronts at once. Second, it invokes methods and tools to manage the resulting information expansion. Third it uses the images from USH (Chapter 3) and the concept of interacting open systems. Fourth, it uses causal loop modelling in place of conceptual modelling, to seek cause and effect.

Within this broad structure, how might we unravel problems and seek to understand complex interactions between systems. How can we detect, identify and locate issues? In much the same way as a doctor goes about diagnosing a patient, perhaps:

1 Find individual *symptoms*
2 Form a *set* of all *symptoms*
3 From this symptom-set, infer the *likely cause*
4 Use knowledge of the *relationships* [1] between symptom-sets and the *whole body*
5 Employ known characteristics of the *particular* body/patient
6 Employ knowledge of the *environment* to which the body/patient has been subjected

Symptoms

A symptom is an indication of dysfunction. If two interconnected systems are in tandem, then an increase in the output from the upstream system might well appear as an inability on the part of the downstream system to accommodate sufficient input. If, instead of two systems in tandem, several systems are mutually inter-connected in a network, locating the source of imbalance may prove more complex.

On the other hand, if all the symptoms associated with an issue could be identified then the set of symptoms *taken as a whole* may indicate dysfunction of appropriate contained systems. This follows *because* of the complexity of the system. If a complex set of interacting systems develops an imbalance between two or more of its systems and if, as a result, many of the interacting systems are disturbed, it is likely that the result will be *characteristic* of the originating cause. There are, after all, many configurations which an interacting set could adopt in general, but only a few which could result from a particular imbalance. If the interacting set of systems were exclusively connected by negative feedback, then possibly only one characteristic configuration would result from one imbalance, but this would be a special case. In general:

One imbalance arising between a pair of systems in an interacting set will result in a finite set of characteristic configurations, given sufficient time for the interacting systems to settle after the disturbance.

In principle, then, it is possible to track down issues to a particular imbalance or disharmony between a particular subset of contained

---

[1] Item 4 in the list is an example of relationship between hierarchy levels, where the imbalance within the body, between the contained systems, contributes to whole body dysfunction, but imbalance cannot be said sensibly to exist between the contained systems and the containing whole. The containing whole *is* the contained parts plus their relationships and environment.

systems by assembling all the symptoms and inferring the cause by understanding or experience—this is essentially what general practitioners do. Of course, while one imbalance may map on to a finite set of symptoms, it does not follow that a particular set of symptoms maps uniquely to one imbalance. There may be, for example, preferred patterns towards which several quite different imbalances lead, making diagnosis by this method notoriously difficult.

Symptoms are often easy to find, on the other hand. We become aware of issues because of symptoms of unease, violence, disquiet, oppression, excess, shortage, defects, dominance, etc. So, while there may be difficulty in mapping symptoms to their cause, they are the starting point in a process-based theory for addressing issues. Following paragraphs categorize symptoms and present illustrative examples.

Self Reward

In the biosphere, flora and fauna exchange CO_2 and O_2 to their mutual benefit. A tree sheds leaves, bacteria (saprobionts) decompose the leaves into nutrients for the tree's continued growth—saprobionts and tree mutually thrive. An investor saves according to the level of his income, and receives interest accordingly, increasing his income. A schoolteacher praises the class according to their performance and receives improved effort, bringing forth more praise. A child is praised and responds with improved behaviour. A foreign visitor to a company is greeted in his native tongue, and responds with warmth, encouraging the company to repeat the exercise. A maintenance system keeps an aircraft system in good working order, thereby increasing the airline's profits and their ability to improve the maintenance system. All are examples of mutually self-rewarding relationships. They are the stuff of cohesive, binding, enduring system interactions—see the USH Principle of Cohesion, Chapter 3.

Inadequacy/Excess

Such cannot be said of all relationships between two systems. Interactions may be inadequate, that is the output from one system does not fulfil the needs of the other. Alternatively, the output from one system may be excessive, overloading or flooding the receiving system. Inadequacy and excess are best viewed as symptoms of change from a previously satisfactory state.

For example, oil production from the Middle East may be considered excessive by some OPEC members because it drives down the price per barrel of crude oil on the open market. This compares with a previously satisfactory state before production was increased. Or, consider the police who present criminal cases to the recently formed Crown Prosecution Service (CPS), to be processed through the courts. If the CPS elect not to proceed but fail to consult with, or advise, the police, the latter will perceive an inadequate interaction between the two systems. A bridge is to carry heavy loads and is constructed of excessively heavy cast-iron spans, so increasing the bridge's unladen weight and reducing its peak carrying capacity.

Inadequacy and excess tend to occur in matched interaction pairs. In the examples given, oil production was excessive, price inadequate. In the police/CPS example, excessive transfer of cases from police to CPS might reasonably result in CPS overload and inadequate consultation. The weight of the bridge was excessive, making its carrying capacity inadequate

Restriction

Some interactions between systems are restrictive, that is they reduce the activity, freedom, performance, etc., of the receiving system. A strut may be added to a set of interacting members to reduce vibration. A law may be enacted against retirement before a certain age. A curfew may be imposed. A closed-shop may be introduced. A green belt may be defined. And so on. Restrictive interactions tend, as the examples demonstrate, to be uni-directional rather than occur in pairs—although the imposition will inevitably engender a reaction of some kind. Restriction may refer to amount or variety in interaction or both.

Missing

Some interactions may simply be missing. Amongst a set of interacting systems, not all mutually interact. For a potential interchange to be classified as missing would imply that its absence is out of place. Identification of "missing" interfaces may provide valuable clues about the indirect relationships in a complex system, including the routes by which influence is exerted via other interacting systems.

Others

Not all system interchanges are problematic. In practice it is unusual for interchanges to be asymmetric; symmetrical relationships are as natural as action and reaction, and similarly occur in pairs. Control usually implies at a minimum two interchanges, from controller to controlled and vice versa. Goods exchanged for money or bartered form a symmetric relationship, and so on. In addressing issues, these "comfortable", symmetric relationships present a backcloth against which the asymmetric relationships point to imbalance. A previously acceptable control relationship could, for example, become disharmonious owing to the emergence of an excessive, inadequate, restrictive or non-self-rewarding relationship within the loop.

ISSUE HIERARCHIES AND SYMPTOM AGGREGATION

Implicit System Generation

We now have sufficient information to consider a systematic approach to Addressing issues, based on the models and constructs considered above. At sufficiently low level of hierarchy, issues display symptoms of imbalance between interacting systems. Hence any methodological approach starts with the identification of symptoms. Imbalance, at its most basic, is observable on a pairwise comparison between systems—fewer than two systems cannot exhibit imbalance or disharmony—see Figure 8.2.

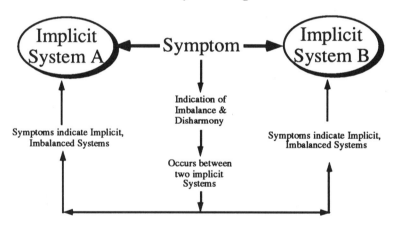

Figure 8.2 Symptoms 'generate' implicit systems

To identify the systems affected by an issue, then, it will necessary to identify and associate individual symptoms with a particular pair of systems. Each symptom may represent an imbalance between more than two systems in which event it will be repeated until all systems have been recorded. This progressive process reveals the implicit systems concerned with, and affected by, the issue. Thus, we can *identify the affected systems* by pursuing the symptoms emanating from the issue. Note that the systems so revealed are referred to as *implicit* because they may not coincide with the organized boundaries observable within man-made, or organizational systems.

Interaction Complexity

An entity of interest may exist in the webs of several systems at once. For instance, an individual person may be simultaneously in a work system, a travelling system, an economic system and a family system, and an issue could be associated with tensions between any or all of these systems. A ship's navigation computer could be simultaneously in a navigation system, a power consumption system, a cooling system, a steering control system, a maintenance system, and so on.

We thus face a problem in which the systems associated with an issue, having been identified by progressive decomposition, are likely to generate a high degree of complexity in their interaction.

Reducing Complexity by Aggregation

The symptoms which arise between interacting systems are special, disturbed relationships. They form the basis for clustering the systems into sets, so that a group of systems forms a higher level, significantly smaller set of systems and issues. A clustering process may produce several such higher level groups; the clustering process offers a way of synthesizing a much smaller set of interacting, issue-related systems. The process could be repeated for very large and

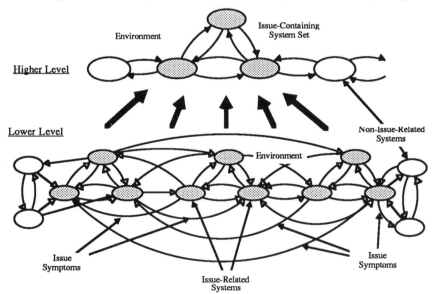

Figure 8.3 Aggregating interacting systems to a higher hierarchy level

complex systems, until a containable number of higher-level systems is obtained such that the analyst's mental capacity can encompass the interactions.

As Figure 8.3 illustrates, the high degree of potential interaction complexity at the lower hierarchical level is reduced if the nine lower systems can be sensibly aggregated to three higher level ones. Mathematically, the number of simplex intra-connections in the example would be reduced from a maximum of 72 to a maximum of 6—ignoring interconnections with other, non-issue-related systems. This is not a sufficient indicator of complexity—each of the systems is both open and transitive, and a change in any system may be felt in any other and in itself as effects reverberate through the interacting set—nonetheless, it is a significant step forward. Each of the aggregated systems contains a subset of the lower-level symptoms and systems.

The Rôle of Environment

Although aggregation may have reduced the apparent complexity of the interacting systems, there is still some way to go in order to address the issue. In real world terms, we have effectively reformulated the symptoms into a higher-level issue between fewer systems. How these systems will respond is a function not only of their mutual interactions, but also of their environment. They are still open systems; in Figure 8.3, interchanges with other systems at the higher level may be present. Moreover, the environment at this higher level of hierarchy may differ from that at lower level. For example, we may move from a micro-economic to a macro-

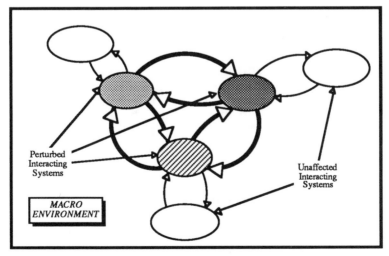

Figure 8.4 Interacting containing systems in a macro-environment

economic environment—see Figure 8.4—or from a pressurized compartment containing man-made systems to a hard vacuum environment containing a variety of systems, some perhaps internally pressurised, but with space between them. The type of social environment may change from a person-to-person environment, to many-on-many group interactions—and so on.

PROSPECTS FOR ISSUE RESOLUTION

The process of aggregating symptom-related systems to produce a simpler, higher level set of issue-containing systems can be achieved manually or with the aid of a computer to overcome the often-large interaction matrices. If the higher-level set and its environment are much simpler, more readily-understood, or similar to previous situations, it might be possible to postulate or perceive solutions to the disharmony at that higher level, and to propose remedies. Supposing this to be so, what would that imply for the lower-level set of issue-related, interacting systems? In principle, it must mean that they too would be resolved, solved or dissolved, provided that all of the issue symptoms had been assiduously uncovered and had been properly aggregated.

Feasibility and Validation

In practice, uncovering all symptoms, placing an objective interpretation upon them, identifying the systems between which they exist and aggregating these systems into a workable set may prove less than straightforward. Postulating a solution, even at the simpler, aggregated level, may be difficult or impossible.

It is, however, straightforward to test a potential, higher-level solution by the simple expedient of observing its effect at lower level, symptom by symptom, factor by factor. If every symptom/factor representing imbalance is solved, resolved or dissolved then the potential solution has merit. But the higher-level solution may also impact on other, interacting systems at that level; one potential solution may become the generator of another problem—that is inevitable, but in principle the theoretical perspective and methodological approach presented above can be brought to bear on this new situation, too.

The Hierarchical Issue Method (HIM)

The approach to addressing issues can be considered in seven steps, the Hierarchical Issue Method detailed in Table 8.1

Table 8.1 Steps in the Hierarchical Issue Method

Step	Hierarchical Issue Method
1	Nominate the issue and its domain
2	Identify the issue symptoms and factors
3	Generate the implicit systems
4	Synthesize implicit containing systems
5	Understand containing systems interactions
6	Address containing systems imbalances
7	Validate against issue symptoms

The process of addressing issues may also be presented in diagrammatic form as at Figure 8.5, giving more detail:

Step 1. *Nominate the issue and its domain.* The first step identifies the arena in which an issue exists. Identification is expressed in broad terms, generally by starting with an expression such as "A feeling of unease about ... ", to avoid preconception about the problems behind the issue

Step 2. *Identify the issue symptoms and factors.* Generally, a practical process of talking with involved, knowledgeable and concerned parties. In practice, symptoms and factors are easy to acquire, although they are generally accompanied by the donor's pet theory for resolving the issue, so that symptom has to be carefully separated from supposed conclusion. Factors are those elements that, although not seemingly disturbing, nonetheless characterize the situation. Factors often indicate excessive or inadequate relationships. Thereafter, treat symptoms as factors and vice versa.

Step 3. Generate the implicit systems. A creative step, requiring each symptom to be perceived as having been generated by at least two implicit systems in mutual imbalance. Where one symptom seems likely to have emanated from more than two such systems, the symptom may be repeated until all the candidate implicit systems have been generated. It is prudent to precede each implicit system title with the words "A system for .. ". This device has the advantage that it avoids confusing extant organizational boundaries with implicit systems.

Step 4. *Synthesize implicit containing systems.* The aggregation process, in which implicit systems with mutual relationships are clustered or grouped together so that the clusters may be identified/nominated as joint members of a higher-level system. Clustering may be undertaken by hand, or using a suitable tool/clustering method. This step essentially groups the original symptoms into sets within a systems framework. It is tempting to imagine that clustering the symptoms directly would be useful, but the systems framework is essential to an understanding of the mutual interactions between the *causes* of the symptoms and factors; symptoms generally appear "downstream" of their cause.

Step 5. *Understand Implicit containing systems Interactions.* A process involving the identification/creation of an environment in which these higher-level implicit systems interact, and the modelling of these Implicit containing systems to understand why they are in mutual imbalance. In essence, this step creates an ideal world of cause and effect, compares it with the real world as represented by the Implicit containing systems, and identifies their differences.

Step 6 *Address containing system imbalances.* A creative step in which the differences between the ideal and the real world are used to generate potential solutions at containing system level. This is potentially feasible because the aggregation process has reduced the number of interacting systems from at least two per symptom—resulting in, perhaps, dozens or scores of systems—to only a few containing systems, with which human intellect may cope.

Step 7. Validate against issue symptoms. Each potential solution from step 6 is checked to see that it addresses each and every symptom and factor from the original set at step 2.

Some points are noteworthy:

- The approach satisfies Ackoff's design paradigm, seeks to idealize, and accepts dissolving as a means of resolving issues. The term "resolve" is used here and in Figure 8.5 to encompass Ackoff's "resolve, solve and dissolve"
- Steps 3 and 5 seek to identify causation at contained and containing system level respectively
- Step 6 proposes that the issue may be addressed by introducing one or more complementary systems, by rebalancing interchanges between implicit systems or by simply removing the source of the issue, where that is feasible
- There is no certainty of success in resolving, solving, or dissolving an issue. Complexity may remain too great, resources may be inadequate, positions may be too entrenched, solutions may disturb the surrounding fabric too much, and so on
- Where success is potentially possible, the means of achieving it has to be addressed—see below
- The identification of a potential solution may arise by recognition of symptom-sets as being like a previous situation, may arise by analysis through modelling, may be intuitive, may seek to optimize or satisfice, and so on—no limitation is imposed by the process.

- Potential success is assessed—Step 7—by analysing the overall solution on each and every individual symptom/factor. This feature of the Hierarchical Issue Method amounts to self verification—a valuable feature of the method, in which any potential issue resolution is tested against the symptoms/factors which generated it.

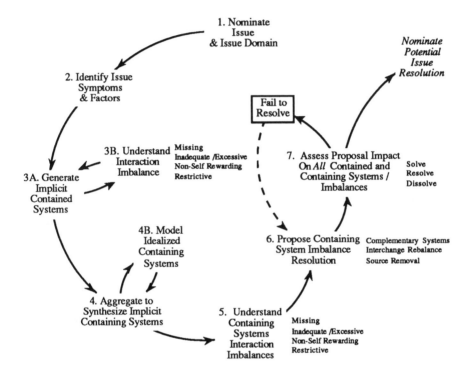

Figure 8.5 Hierarchical Issue Method (HIM)

EVOKING CHANGE IN A COMPLEX INTERACTING SYSTEM SET

Given a potential solution, how might it be realized? The USH images of interacting systems and the USH Principles offer some guidance in terms of likely outcomes and traps to avoid. The general approach which seems to hold promise is that employed by the biological world—antagonism. Within the human body, for example, virtually all change is controlled by processes working in mutual antagonism. We are familiar with this phenomenon in terms of muscles, which work in antagonistic pairs such that when both pull at the same time but in opposite senses the limb remains stationary, but when one pull exceeds the other, the limb may be moved under careful control. Our enzymes, hormones, etc., operate in antagonistic pairs, for example in the maintenance of body temperature, body fluid levels, blood-sugar levels, ionic concentrations, and many other physiologigal system balances. It occurs also in the eye, where light from a small, distinct object falling on the retina triggers a response, while the general level of light surrounding the object reduces retinal response, so enabling a limited retinal dynamic range to accommodate a wide range of illuminances.

It is rare for current system practitioners to employ this concept of antagonistic pairs when conceiving solutions to problems, but it has very great merit in complex situations, since small changes can be introduced and their progress controlled to observe the response of the interacting systems, which we know to be counter-intuitive. We have evolved such antagonistic systems within our societies, however, to deal with situations where outcomes are simply not knowable—in truth, the vast majority of real world situations.

We pay for an Opposition to the Government. The law is designed to support the small and weak against the large and strong. We appoint Ombudsmen. Managements evoke unions. And so on. Antagonistic pairs are also evident in engineering and mathematics—Newton's third law, Lenz's law, etc. But if we propose to introduce a new system such as a new power station, a new tax, a new motorway, a new health & welfare scheme, a new pricing system, a new law—then we seem not to think in terms of antagonistic pairs. Yet these are potentially very complex new systems in terms of their interactions with existing systems, and hence the outcome of such interactions may not be knowable. The method is clear in principle—we have some reluctance to use it in practice.

In USH, the term "complementary systems" is used instead of antagonistic pairs, being more in keeping with the underlying sense of harmony and balance. In the real world, a new or modified system is introduced to achieve a specific purpose—the change inevitably perturbs other, interacting systems in a way that is not necessarily the intention of the new system. Complementary systems are introduced or adjusted to anticipate and compensate for the unwanted side-effects of the new system and to connect sub-systems internal to the new design to the wider world. So, introducing a new power station will provide power—the desired objective. It will also disturb the local ecology, river/coastal/estuarine systems (for cooling), transportation, power distribution, economy, work patterns, centres of living, wealth distribution, etc., and mostly in an undesirable way. When introducing the power station, complementary systems would be introduced specifically to minimize the effects of these unwanted disturbances—see Chapter 12, where this example, and the notion of complementary systems will be expanded.

CONCLUSION

At the beginning, one definition, by Kerlinger, of a theory was offered. It is repeated here:

> *a set of interrelated constructs (concepts), definitions, and propositions that present a systematic view of phenomena by specifying relations among variables, with the purpose of explaining the phenomena.*

Accepting the definition, has a theory been presented? Certainly, a set of interrelated constructs, definitions and propositions has been presented, and these specify relations amongst systems with variables in both the systems and their interactions. The purpose has been more than to explain the phenomena—the purpose has been to reduce the perceived complexity of the phenomena so that they might be understood and resolved, solved or dissolved.

A methodological approach to issues has been revealed, which has foundations in general systems theory and in the Unified Systems Hypothesis. Moreover, a means of achieving controlled change between complex interacting systems has been highlighted, with excellent credentials in the social, engineering, physical and biological sciences.

To fully appreciate the merits of the approach outlined here, a case study or two will be necessary—this will be presented in the following chapter.

Chapter 8.2
Hierarchical Issue Method—Case Studies

It ain't what you don't know that's the problem.
It's what you know that ain't so. Will Rogers

INTRODUCTION

This chapter illustrates the approach to issues, presented in Chapter 8.1, by example. There are two case studies: the first concerns a real company and is a rare example of a real-world organizational investigation where the answer emerged as clean as theory. The second example concerns a nuclear processing plant, a different problem, based on fact, but developed to make it more complex.

CASE STUDY 1

Step 1. Nominate the issue and the issue domain

The issue domain is a leading systems company which has not been doing as well as its competitors in recent years. The engineers in particular seem to lack confidence in both themselves and the company. Staff turnover is high, with the younger staff being seduced by higher pay offers from competitors. The issue emerges as follows:

A feeling of unease and a lack of confidence about the direction and future of the company

Step 2. Identify issue Symptoms and Factors

The symptoms were volunteered eagerly by managers and engineers at all levels in the company—everyone not only knew what was wrong, but also knew how to fix it. Unfortunately, their views differed. The symptoms were collected and are listed in Table 8.2:

Table 8.2 Table of symptoms

Need clear, long-term objectives	Need clear short-term objectives
Poor wage levels	Overheads too high
Overlap between divisional business areas	Loss of (previous) software supremacy
High average age	Implicit unemployment
Lack of internal labour mobility	Too much argument about objectives
Business becoming tighter	Low morale
Stagnant growth	Facing changing markets

It is evident from the symptoms that there are several, mixed-up "problem themes" and it can be deduced which implicit contained systems are in imbalance by postulating "cause" systems and "effect" systems. Each of these implicit systems is purposeful or purposive so their titles may usefully be preceded by "A system for...". Hence a simple plan emerges for identifying implicit contained systems:

1 Identify symptom
2 Identify a possible cause of the symptom
3 Model the situation, either mentally or using causal loop modelling to develop understanding
4 Identify implicit contained systems from the model which may be prefixed by 'A system for...' This simple device helps to avoid a common trap—correlating an implicit system with an existing physical or organizational boundary. It is very unlikely that an implicit system, which is functional, will coincide with an actual boundary.

For example, "Need clear, long-term objectives" suggests that the corporate leadership is not insisting upon proper forward planning, from which such long-term objectives would emerge.

A simple cause and effect model might appear as in Figure 8.6. Evidently there is an imbalance between the leadership system (cause) and the planning system (effect) in that the former is giving inadequate direction to the latter. The model suggest other cause and effect system pairs, too; how about "A system for participative management" and "A system for promulgating common staff/management objectives"? This part of the Hierarchical Issue Method is creative, invokes knowledge and experience, and there are no simple right and wrong answers. By taking each symptom in turn, the relevant implicit contained systems in imbalance can be generated progressively. Remember that some ideal world is being created as a basis for comparison; it is intentionally *not* a real world and should not be confused with one.

(N.B. It is tempting to simply cluster symptoms as a way to identify problem themes. A little thought shows that this is unlikely to be effective because symptoms emerge "downstream" of causes. The Hierarchical Issue Method employs an underlying system model which depends upon the notion of containment—symptoms are not contained *per se*.)

Figure 8.6 Simple cause-and-effect model

Step 3. Generate implicit contained systems

Step 3 is best presented as a table (see Table 8.3), in which the symptoms are used to generate the systems, A and B, between which a symptom represents disharmony or imbalance. Note from the table that the implicit contained systems, A and B, have been given non-jargon names to avoid their being confused with departments or grades in the company:

- The leadership system is the system for leading the company at all levels, and is indicative of a style—authoritative, autocratic, consultative, participative, etc.
- The throughput system is the system for selling to the market and receiving the money in return for goods and services
- The operational system is the system for developing and making the goods and services to be sold
- The reassignment system is that which moves people about from position to position in the company
- The opportunity pursuit system is that system which goes after a business opportunity

• The internal changes system is that which adapts the company to meet the demands of the market and the competition

Table 8.3 —Symptoms and their respective interacting systems

Implicit System A	Symptom	Implicit System B	Relationship Deficiency
Planning system	1 Need clear, long-term objectives	Leadership system	Inadequate (IA), B to A
Participation system	2 Need clear, short-term objectives	Leadership system	IA, B to A
Reward system	3 Poor wage levels	Value system	IA, A to B
Leadership system	4 Overlap in divisional business areas	Participation system	Non-self rewarding (NSR)
Throughput system	5 Loss of software supremacy	Market system	IA, A to B
Re-assignment system	6 Lack of (internal) labour mobility	Operational system	NSR
Work allocation system	7 Implicit unemployment	Work evaluation system	NSR
Recruiting system	8 High average age	Reassignment system	NSR
Market system	9 Business becoming tighter	Throughput system	IA, B to A
Work allocation system	10 Overheads too high	Work evaluation system	IA, B to A
Opportunity pursuit system	11 Lack of marketing aggression	Reward system	NSR
Throughput system	12 Stagnant Growth	Operational system	NSR
Internal change system	13 Facing changing markets	Market system	IA, A to B
Leadership system	14 Too much argument about objectives	Participation system	IA, A to B
Value system	15 Morale is low	Reward system	IA, B to A

- The participation system is that which enables the subordinates to join in the decision-making processes in the company
- The reward system is that which provides each person with a return for his efforts invested in the company. Reward can cover much more than simply money—praise, satisfaction at a job well done, promotion, esteem, recognition, etc.
- Lastly, the value system is that which the individuals use to judge their status and circumstances compared with others in the company and outside and with their personal expectations and aspirations

Note also that the contained systems are not distinct from each other and may overlap so that an individual can find himself or herself in several systems at once. Moreover, it may be that some of the systems are contained within some others, indicating a multiple hierarchy. All of these features are to be expected, and represent information rather than problems.

Step 4.   Synthesize implicit containing systems

So far, we have been examining symptoms and their inter-relationships at lower level, relating individual symptoms one to another. (In complex situations, models may help to identify implicit contained systems from symptoms.) The next process is to cluster or group the symptoms and their associated systems from the table in such a way as to identify the systems which contain them—to synthesize by moving up one level of hierarchy (see Figure 2.7).

The contained systems generated in Step 2 were entered in an

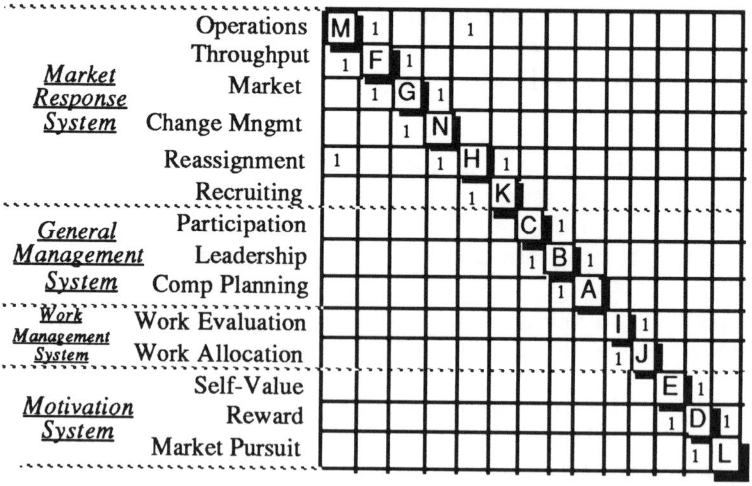

Market Response System	Operations	**M**	1			1												
	Throughput	1	**F**	1														
	Market		1	**G**	1													
	Change Mngmt			1	**N**													
	Reassignment	1			1	**H**	1											
	Recruiting					1	**K**											
General Management System	Participation							**C**	1									
	Leadership							1	**B**	1								
	Comp Planning								1	**A**								
Work Management System	Work Evaluation										**I**	1						
	Work Allocation										1	**J**						
Motivation System	Self-Value												**E**	1				
	Reward												1	**D**	1			
	Market Pursuit														1	**L**		

Figure 8.7 The clustered N2 chart revealing implicit containing systems

incidence matrix (N^2 Chart) in the order indicated by the letters in the highlighted squares above, with "A—Company planning" originally at the top-left and going alphabetically to "N—Change management" at the bottom.   The presence of a symptom of disharmony or imbalance was recorded in the appropriate square between the respective systems; for example, the "1" in the top row and the fifth column represents Symptom 6, "Lack of internal labour mobility". The initial pattern was disordered. The various systems were rearranged, preserving their inter-relationships, until that shown above was derived which represents the most ordered, or tightly-clustered, set.

As the matrix shows at the left, containing systems can be identified by observing the common nature of those systems which cluster together. We appear to have four containing systems—systems which, between them, contain all the reported disharmony and imbalance:

- The market response system. This comprises the systems shown in the matrix.   Within it, the most significant system is evidently the reassignment system in the sense that it is pivotal to success since it joins together more systems (M, N and K directly and F and G indirectly) than any other

- The general management system. Leadership is pivotal in this system to the achievement of company plans through workforce participation

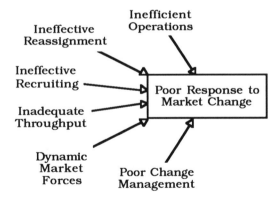

Figure 8.8 Initial "laundry list" for poor market response

- The work management system. This system appears to be isolated; in fact, it is part of the operations system, and is a lower hierarchy phenomenon rather than a separate system

- The motivation system. Reward is pivotal within the motivation system, both to increase self-value among the staff, and also to evoke more aggressive response to the pursuit of market Opportunities. This system is not so much isolated as pervasive of the others—it represents a different viewpoint or *Weltanschauung* e.g. "The company is a system for motivating and rewarding people who compete in the market place"

Understanding interactions between the various systems is best achieved through causal-loop modelling (see Chapter 9) of an idealized implicit containing system.   First, a "laundry list" of factors contributing to the market response system—see Figure 8.8. To develop the full causal loop, as shown in Chapter 9, it is useful to model the mutual relationships between the contributing factors first.

The developing models are shown in Figure 8.9, from which it is possible to see the progressive build-up to the (later) full model. The simplest of the loops below proposes that an increase in operations will cause a rise in throughput, which will cause an increase in sales revenue which will/can cause an increase in operations. This is a simplistic view, perhaps, but the reverse *is* true. A reduction in operations *will* cause a drop in throughput *will* reduce revenue *will* reduce funds for operations. Note that, in forming the loops, words from the laundry list such as "poor" and "ineffective" have been expunged, so that the bias implicit in such words is removed in forming the loops.   The other two loops in Figure 8.9 show the process of developing cause and effect relationships between the other factors from the matrix.

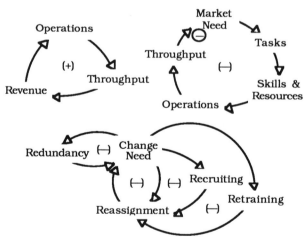

Figure 8.9 Initial causal loop part-models

Finally, the part-models are integrated around the concept of interest, represented at the right of the initial laundry list—in this case, poor response to market change, but again removing the bias implicit in the words.

The result of the integration is shown below. A closed-loop model emerges which represents an ideal world towards which we might aspire. By comparing this ideal world with the real world we can see how our real world falls short and hence where we might seek to improve our situation. It would be ill-advised to react directly to the simple diagram below, however, for two reasons: first, it is only part of a set of interacting systems, so we must repeat the operation for all of the systems clustered in the N^2 chart above and then examine the whole problem as one; second, it may be necessary to delve deeper into aspects of each causal loop model to explore in more depth. This might be accomplished using a variety of methods, including simulation and mathematical modelling,.

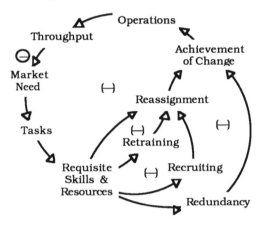

Figure 8.10 Market response system—idealized

Figure 8.10 proposes that the fundamental cause of poor company performance is lack of responsiveness to market place needs, and that once tasks have been identified which will result in saleable goods and services, then a change process should follow in which staff will need to be recruited, retrained and reassigned to follow (or lead) the market. Increased operational effectiveness will increase throughput and reduce the degree of poor market performance.

Figure 8.11 proposes the causal relationships between management style, morale and unity of effort, which some of the symptoms questioned. The proposition is that commitment to company goals and objectives is based on participation in planning those objectives and that the complete process is self sustaining—positive feedback—once this loop is set up. Morale rises as a result of concerted achievement, with *concerted* implying that the team spirit and the feeling of belonging are appropriate as well as success. Clearly, morale is also coupled with self-value, but the causal relationship is not understood—in any event, as the figure shows, they are closely coupled in the regenerative loop. Note that this causal loop model accommodates two of the implicit containing systems, the motivation system and the general management system.

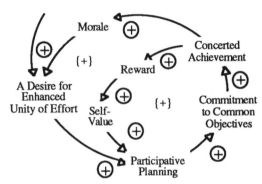

Figure 8.11 Management and motivation—idealized

Figure 8.12 is concerned with work allocation and evaluation, and is related to the symptom 'implicit unemployment' which suggests that people are not gainfully employed for an adequate portion of their time—they are, in effect, stretching the job to cover the hours, a typical "cost-plus" attitude. This is inefficient in the true sense of that word, but worse, it prevents the redirection of effort to new areas to achieve the much-needed change to which many of the symptoms obliquely refer. Once again, the figure suggests that the loop could be self-sustaining, positive feedback, once set up. A way to achieve regeneration would be to reward those in the loop, *including those who are the time-wasters,* for the identification of waste. This would necessitate the time-wasters being assured of reward or support in the event that their rôles were seen to be redundant.

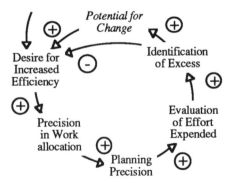

Figure 8.12 Work management—idealized

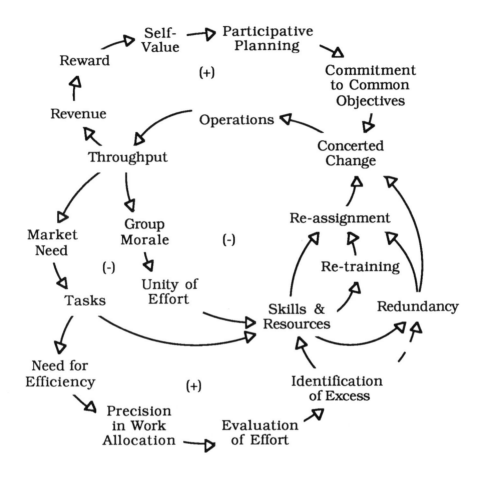

Figure 8.13 Idealized company change model

Step 5. Understand containing system interaction imbalances

Having developed individual CLMs, the first step on the road to understanding containing system interaction imbalances is the integration of the idealized causal loops from Step 4.

The overall CLM of Figure 8.13 shows how, using the original symptoms as a basis, the company might respond in some ideal world. A summary diagram is presented in Figure 8.14. It illustrates the containing systems existing against the backcloth of an environment with high competition, dwindling defence market, falling pools of skilled engineers and a dearth of skilled engineer

managers. The figure spells out the higher-level issue facing the
company, evidenced by the lower-level symptoms.

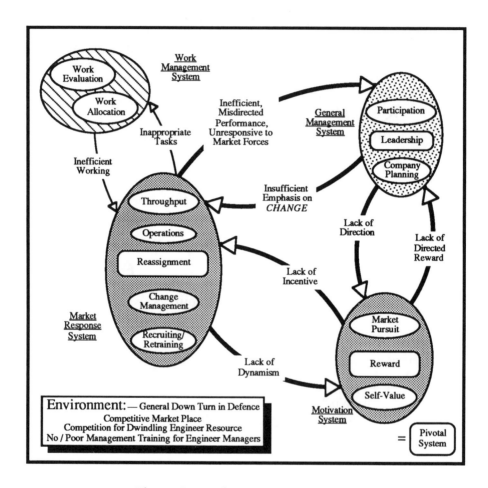

Figure 8.14 The interacting systems

Step 6. Propose containing system imbalance resolution

There are several threads to addressing the issue, remembering that
we may resolve, solve or dissolve the issue which, you will recall,
was *a feeling of unease and a lack of confidence about the direction
and future of the company.* We can pick up all the threads by
addressing Figure 8.14. (Note that the market place, although it does
not explicitly appear, is implied in the system interaction model.)
The systems shown in the figure do not map on to the company

organization—it does not, for example, have a market response system as a unit of organization. Nonetheless, the analysis and synthesis processes reveal that such systems exist in principle, in the sense that the rôles are performed, although the participants are spread about within the company and do not think of themselves as in the same system. The method of addressing issues has identified this *de facto* system and highlighted it as one which contains many of the ills proposed by the symptoms, taken as a set. Consider each of the systems in turn:

A *General management system.* The keynote is a change of emphasis in management *style* more to one which encourages workforce commitment through participation in the planning, as well as the execution processes. Participation is not the same as consultation, which is asking what is wanted but not allowing staff to join in the consequent planning. Participation means the workforce become *involved* in planning and setting their own objectives—and not just the higher or middle management. This must pervade the company to be successful, led, guided and encouraged by management at all levels. The long-term plans, short-term objectives, and arguments about them will not then present problems because everyone in the company will "own" the company's problems. Clearly, this contributes to the next system, too

B *Motivation system.* The keynote is reward. To be effective, reward should be used to reinforce required behaviour. So, those pursuing markets vigorously—not just marketing staff—should be rewarded, so that others see the effects. Those increasing efficiency and reducing "implicit unemployment" should be rewarded, also visibly. And in view of the alleged problems with excessive age and poor wage levels—which are coupled, since older staff expect more money—older staff should be motivated by retraining and reassigning them. In any event this will become necessary because of the environment, with its dwindling pool of engineers, so make a virtue of necessity; pensioning-off older engineers, a possible approach in the past, is no longer a sensible option

C *Work management system.* Evidently in need of a shake-up. Eliminate all cost-plus and similar contracts which encourage sloth. Introduce incentive bonuses for saving time against the plan forecast, subject to quality being maintained. Reward those identifying waste in processes, and particularly those able to turn that waste into throughput

D *Market response system.* The major area for improvement has been left to the end. The company seems to have an inability to change quickly and effectively in response to the market and the competition. Such an ability is vital. A recommendation might be that a *change management system* should be designed, set up and properly resourced, and that it should act as the first of the causal-loop diagrams above—company changes. The start-point must be a review of work done in the company against goods and services which are selling well in the market place—in other words, which efforts are effective and which are directed to

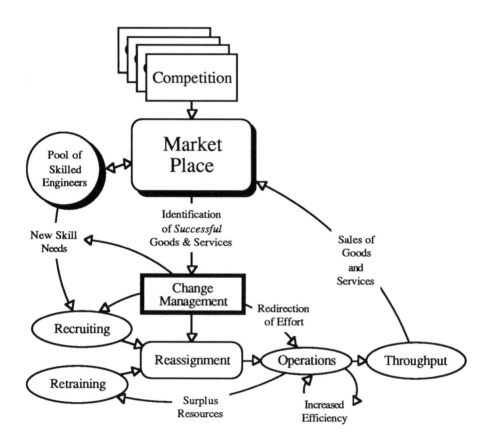

Figure 8.15 Change management system

produce unwanted, or at least unprofitable, goods. Once misdirected effort has been identified, it can be put to more productive work. The keynote is the reassignment system, and that can get under way immediately, reassigning people to refresh their experience. The reassignment system will need to be fed with new and retrained resources as change progresses—it is an *enabler* system, whereas the suggested change management system is a director/co-ordinator system. See the Figure 8.15.

Complementary systems

The proposed changes will evoke the need for some complementary systems, either new or changed from the current status quo:

- Recruiting and retraining need considerable boost, since they must accommodate the need to change, and must feed the Reassignment system; this system will need teeth so that staff can be prised from the clutches of individual project managers in the interests of the company and the individual, who must be kept interested and motivated if he or she is to stay with the company
- Management need trained in organization for, and methods of, participative management. It is unlike the autocratic or authoritative styles of management with which many engineers have grown up, nor is it like the service discipline which many ex-servicemen bring with them into industry. Creativity and innovation die under such regimes, and without innovation the company will not recover
- Personnel assessment systems need to change so that reward can be given more readily to performers rather than by grades—these have no real relevance to making the company more responsive and dynamic, quite the contrary
- A system is needed to review the company's output from a market viewpoint, to see if it is what the market wants. It is unlikely that such a system could exist within the company. It would be required initially, to trigger the change, and then every 6-12 months to keep the change process charged up
- Sales will need to accommodate change in the goods and services it will receive from the operations system. In *hi-tech* defence companies, the sales force is very largely comprised of engineers, untrained for the job. The shortfall on training will require amending

A composite design for all these systems, either separately or (better) together, would be undertaken using the GRM of Chapter 4 to generate functions and form, the architecture of Chapter 7 to aggregate the parts and the process model from Chapter 6 to develop a coherent plan for risk-controlled implementation. See Chapter 10.3, where this further process is illustrated.

Step 7. Assess impact on all contained and containing systems

The assessment of impact of potential solutions on all contained and containing systems is presented in Table 8.4

Table 8.4 Symptom/cure match

Symptom	Addressed By
1 Need clear, long-term objectives	Participation in planning/leadership style
2 Need clear, short-term objectives	Participation in planning/ leadership style
3 Poor wage levels	Reward system geared to Performance
4 Overlap in divisional business areas	Participation in planning
5 Loss of software supremacy	Market pursuit and recruiting
6 Lack of (internal) labour mobility	Reassignment system
7 Implicit unemployment	Efficiency incentives, retraining system
8 High average age	Retraining, reassignment systems
9 Business becoming tighter	Change-management system
10 Overheads too high	Consequence of misdirected effort— see market response system, above.
11 Lack of marketing aggression	Reward system
12 Stagnant growth	All
13 Facing changing markets	Change-management system
14 Too much argument about objectives	Participative management
15 Morale is low	See motivation system

So, the original symptoms have indeed been addressed.

Summary, Case 1

In this event there appears to be a cogent approach to the issue. It may be, however, that the proposed approach is culturally, organizationally or procedurally unacceptable in some way—that would remain to be explored. Note the use of the USH Principles throughout the development of a potential solution

CASE STUDY 2

In the second example, the procedure will be presented in a more compressed form so that the reader may see the whole procedure in a compact, more digestible form.

Step 1 Nominate Issue and Issue Domain

A hypothetical county, somewhere in the heartland of England, which happens to house a government nuclear R&D complex. People living in the shadow of the complex have been nervous for many years, despite there having been no significant incidents on which to found their disquiet. Local politicians are similarly frustrated, and find themselves facing competing demands for the slender resources of this busy, but essentially rural, community

The Issue

A feeling of unease about the preparedness and the effectiveness of measures to be taken in the event of a nuclear disaster or major incident at the local complex.

Step 2 Identify Issue Symptoms and Factors

1　"We all know that place is a time bomb"
2　"The traffic congestion is bad enough around here without any disaster adding to it"
3　"How would I know?　Round here, I don't even know if the weather's on the turn—I'm over seventy, you know, and deaf"
4　"We have other priorities for our slender resources—we have the poll tax to contend with now"
5　"Such events are so improbable as to be discountable"
6　"We certainly couldn't afford a standing army sitting around waiting for that once-in-a-blue-moon event, now could we?"
7　"Let's hope the emergency services know what they're doing"
8　"This one's been a hot potato for years—political dynamite"
9　"Evacuation is seen as a major issue—look at Chernobyl"
10　"It's doing anything fast enough that's the problem"
11　"What we need are highly trained crews available at a moment's notice to go straight into the problem area, neutralize the problem and safeguard the public—nothing less will do!"
12　"Group control of rescue and emergency services is all very well, but that's vulnerable too"
13　"Depending on CB and ham radio operators for emergency communications assumes that the CB isn't blocked like it usually is and that the hams can get to their radios to operate them—not too clever, if you ask me"

14 "Evacuation is all very well, but where to? With fall-out and wind, we could jump out of the frying pan into the fire"

Step 2B, Step 3 Generate Implicit Systems and Imbalances

Implicit systems may be generated using the 4-step procedure given in the first case study (see Table 8.5).

Step 4 Synthesize and Model the Implicit Containing Systems

Analysis of the clustered pattern of interfaces above is not quite so straightforward as in the first example (see Figure 8.16). Note that the following are at the centre of interface crosses, indicating pivotal systems: Local living, transport, threat and local politics. Also, emergency services and local publicity, together with traffic management and road systems are isolated and peripheral—i.e. relegated to the edges of the cluster. Emergency transport and transport management cluster as functionally-bound. Threat system, emergency command and control, and C^2 radio are in a waterfall relationship, indicating that the threat could disrupt the flow of information. These factors lead to the initial systems interaction model, Figure 8.17, which shows the result of aggregation. Note that:

- The threat has been set aside as essentially different in character from the other systems, being the fundamental source of the issue

- The emergency services are not shown as part of the crisis action system, suggesting that the initial symptom-set was in some way inadequate

- The local road system sits uncomfortably between the others, owned by the socio-political system, used by the crisis management system, loved by neither.

- Pivotal systems are shown in rounded-corner boxes

Table 8.5 Nuclear plant symptoms and implicit systems

Implicit system A	Symptom	Implicit systemB	Imbalance
Threat system	1. We all know that place is a time bomb	Value judgement system	Excessive, A to B
Traffic management	2. The traffic congestion is bad enough, without...	Road system	IA A to B
Public alerting system	3. How would I know?, I am old and deaf...	Local living systems	IA A to B

Local political system	4. We have other priorities for our money	Value judgement system	NSR
Local political system	5. Such events are so improbable.....	Value judgement system	NSR
Local political system	6. We couldn't afford a standing army....	Local economic system	NSR
Emergency services	7. Let's hope the emergency services know what.......	Local publicity system	IA A to B
Local political system	8. Political dynamite	Local economic system	NSR
Local living systems	9. Evacuation is seen as the major issue	Transportation systems	IA B to A
Transportation systems	10. It's doing anything fast enough.....	Local living systems	Excessive B to A
Transportation systems	10. It's doing anything fast enough.....	Transport media, road, air, river...	IA B to A
Transportation systems	10. It's doing anything fast enough.....	Emergency transport management system	IA A to B
Immediate action system	11. What we need are highly trained crews available at a moment's notice......	Local living systems	Missing
Immediate action system	11. What we need are highly trained crews available at a moment's notice......	Threat system	IA A to B
Emergency C^2 system	12. Group control is vulnerable	Threat system	Excessive, B to A
Emergency radio communication system	13. Depending on CB and hams is not good	Threat system	Excessive, B to A
Emergency C^2 system	14. Evacuation requires fall-out knowledge	Local living systems	IA A to B
Emergency C^2 system	14. Evacuation requires fall-out knowledge	Transportation systems	IA A to B

Step 4B Crisis Management—Idealized

See Figure 8.18—model notes:

- Road evacuation impracticable for some events
    - —Radio alerts will exacerbate traffic congestion
    - —Traffic management inadequate
    - —Roads inadequate, too slow
- Air evacuation more viable—need air transport

```
Traffic Mangnt     1    B 1
Road Systems       2    1 L
PA System          3        C   1
IA Systems         4          H 1
Loc Living         5        1 1 F   1 1
Em TrnspMan        6              P 1
Transpot           7          1 1 G 1 1
Em C2 System       8          1   1 I   1
Transpot Media     9              1   O
Threat System     10                1   A 1 1
Em Radio com      11                    1 J
Value Judgemnt    12                    1   K 1
Loc Politics      13                        1 D 1
Loc Economics     14                          1 M
Em Services       15                              E 1
Local Publicity   16                              1 N
```

Figure 8.16 Clustered N^2 chart (taken directly from program)

- Need air transport to bring in incident specialists, too
- There is a standing army at the scene—the plant employees
    - —Use escaping employees to evacuate locals?
    - —Train some employees to fly air transports out?

Step 4B Local Socio-political System

See Figure 8.19—model notes:

- Perceived risk related to incidents—few, minor incidents, little risk ...

- Competing demands for local government resources very strong indeed
- Local social concern failing to influence local politics sufficiently:

  —Political suicide to advocate heavy spend on crisis management system to detriment of other social demands
- Much easier to spend on publicizing the minimal risk

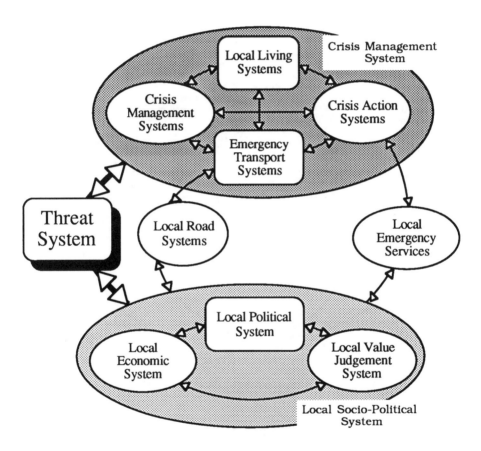

Figure 8.17 Interacting systems/problem themes

Step 5 Understand Containing Systems Interactions

We can now examine the interaction imbalances at containing system level, Figure 8.20, by comparing the idealized models with the observed situation derived from the original symptoms and factors. At the same time, it is essential to carefully identify the relevant environment against which these interactions can be seen. The result might appear as shown above

Step 6 Propose containing system imbalance resolution

Bearing in mind the USH Principles, two approaches present themselves, the first being simply a change to the interchange between systems (A below) and the second being the introduction of a complementary system to neutralize the issue (B below):

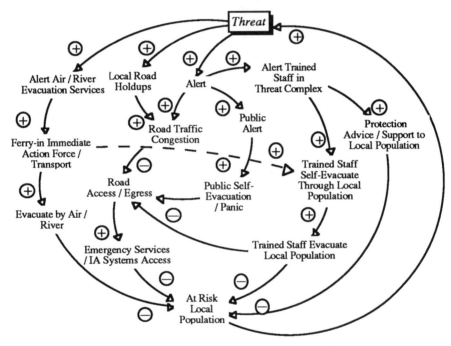

Figure 8.18 Crisis management causal loop/influence model

A Open doors at complex to public, schools visits, Greenpeace, etc. Outcome either:

   1 Reduction in local concern, need evaporates, or......

   2 Social concern rises, political will to spend emerges

B1 Augment inadequate present crisis management system with military resources becoming available as "peace dividend".

   —Army and RAF helicopter transport

   —Sapper, SAS/SBS skills & resources

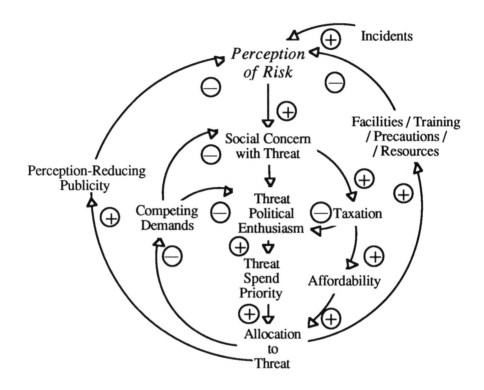

Figure 8.19 Socio-political model

B2 Use Army to train complex employees in self and local   public
evacuation, with periodic exercises, publicity

—Little cost to local taxation if central government agrees

—Worthy peacetime rôle for military

Step 7 Assess proposal impact on all contained and containing systems

Analysis at containing system level is evident; implicit system
analysis is given in Table 8.6.

Summary, Case 2

Within the constraints of the simplified set of symptoms available,
a reasoned, traceable approach to the issue has been identified.
There may be many other potential resolutions; in this case for

example, the removal of the issue source—nuclear complex itself—is one logical, if politically difficult, choice. As is inevitably the case, potential approaches raise many more questions, all of which will be addressable using the Hierarchical Issue Method.

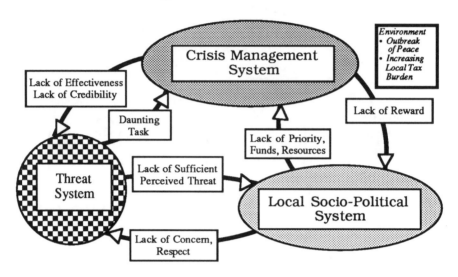

Figure 8.20 System interaction diagram

Table 8.6 Verification Table

	Symptom	Potential Solution
1	We all know that place is a time bomb	A
2	The traffic congestion is bad enough, without...	B
3	How would I know?, I am old and deaf...	B
4	We have other priorities for our money	A
5	Such events are so improbable.....	A
6	We couldn't afford a standing army....	A/B
7	Let's hope the emergency services know what.......	A
8	Political dynamite	A/B
9	Evacuation is seen as the major issue	B
10	It's doing anything fast enough.....	B
11	What we need are highly trained crews available at a moment's notice ...	
12	Group control is vulnerable	B
13	Depending on CB and hams is not good	B
14	Evacuation requires fall-out knowledge	B

CONCLUSION

- The Hierarchical Issue Method HIM *delivers*:
  - —It is theory-based
  - —It enables issues to be addressed methodically
  - —It generates richness and complexity
  - —It manages that complexity
  - —It is self-validating
- HIM provides a framework for creative thinking and synthesis
- HIM encourages team-work and openness of method and results
- HIM is tool-supportable
- In these examples, and generally, HIM verifies potential solutions—if such exist—which nonetheless require to be tested for practical, political, economic and cultural acceptability. There is a long way to go from issue to final solution.

ASSIGNMENT

ISSUE DOMAIN

The company has been reorganized recently, along project lines. efficiency experts have been through the company, reducing wastage in manpower and resources. systems engineers are "owned" by a central group and deployed into projects as these arise.

ISSUE

A dislike of the new organization by systems engineers, who feel that the project managers' drive to meet time and budget constraints is at the expense of quality.

SYMPTOMS

- "We don't spend nearly enough time establishing the requirement and developing the design"
- "We have to use company products now, even if they're not really suitable"
- "Marketing have screwed up the design before we've even met the customer"

- "Oh! At least you got to meet the customer!"
- "Project managers don't understand systems engineering—they're so busy bashing ahead that they don't anticipate problems
- "Systems engineering ends up as progress chasing"
- "Systems engineering has no rôle between the end of system design and the start of integration and test"
- "The quality just isn't there—the customer might be satisfied with the product, but the user sure as hell isn't"
- "We're totally overloaded towards the end of every project phase"

TASK

Using the case study as a model, complete Steps 2-7 of the Hierarchical Issue Method,

Chapter 9
Creativity

I must Create a System, or be enslaved by another Man's;
I will not Reason and Compare; my business is to Create.
William Blake, 1757-1827; Jerusalem

CREATIVITY AND INNOVATION

Creativity is about generating new ideas and ways of approaching activities and problems. Most people are creative, even if many of us had our creativity suppressed from an early age in the mould of conformity imposed by short-sighted elders. We can all enhance our creativity by learning to recognize our self-imposed constraints which we bring to any situation. Figure 9.1 suggests some of the ingredients of creativity.

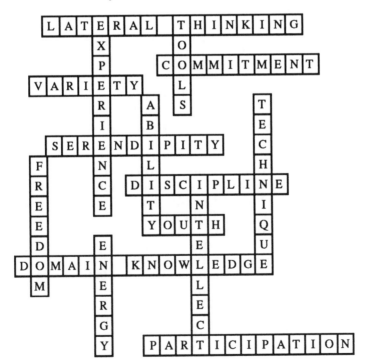

Figure 9.1 Ingredients of creativity

As Figure 9.1 shows, there is a wide variety of factors. Some are intentionally orthogonal: youth and experience; freedom and discipline. Some support each other in the same direction: tools and techniques; commitment and participation; serendipity and lateral thinking; variety and domain knowledge. No such figure can be comprehensive, but the themes run throughout this paper.

Creativity can be a two-edged sword; there are times to be creative and times to pursue a plan relentlessly. Creativity is not confined to the initial stages of any situation or project, however; creative ways of operating, maintaining and even of recycling and disposing of systems abound. But creativity is of little use on its own in the real world.

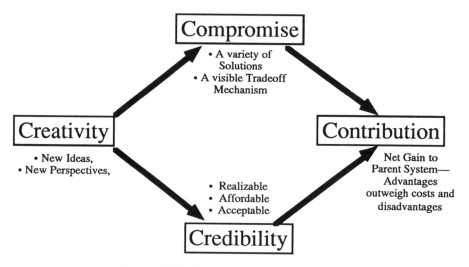

Figure 9.2 The four Cs of innovation

Figure 9.2 illustrates the point: creativity may generate the ideas, but these ideas have to be credible if others are to support them and their originator may have to make some compromises in adapting the ideas to the real world. Contribution is the crucial test; creative ideas are of real value only if they make a positive contribution, a difference to "the bottom line".

Innovation is vital to any modern company. Taking customer's solutions "off-the-shelf" is tempting—after all, a lot of time and effort went in to putting them there. But that is the point; if they are on the shelf, available now, they are old designs in a very fast-moving world. How can they be of sufficient quality? The components may work, but be going out of stock, making maintainability poor. The performance could not have taken advantage of recent improvements in design methods for ease of manufacture, reliability, etc. "Off-the-shelf-syndrome" is understandable, but doomed to failure in the long term.

CREATIVE METHODS

Causal-loop Modelling and Influence Diagrams

One valuable approach to unravelling problems is Causal Loop Modelling (CLM). The idea is simply to connect factors by a signed arrow where a causal relationship can be established between them. Often causation is hard to establish; we may be assured that one factor influences another, but be less certain about causation. Such diagrams, where influence is involved are called Influence Diagrams, or sometimes 'signed digraphs'. Influence is much easier to identify, of course, but two factors which seem to influence each other may in fact both be related to a third, unseen, causal agent. Causation, difficult to establish, is worth the effort. Causal loop diagrams may be similarly difficult to form, but are also well worth the effort.

We tend to develop a "laundry-list" mentality as we go through life (see Richmond, Peterson and Boyle, 1990 for the most excellent explanation and guide to dynamic systems). Figure 9.3 illustrates the point.

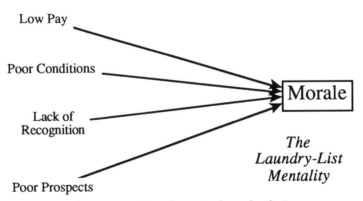

Figure 9.3 Developing a laundry list

One limitation of the laundry-list is that it overlooks the relationships between the components. In the figure , there seems to be a relationship between lack of recognition and poor prospects, for example. If, instead of the laundry list, we develop the notion of causal, or even quasi-causal, loops then a much more useful representation emerges. The four simple loops emerge by considering relationships between each of the contributing items in the original list. Note, however, that the loops contain nouns or noun-phrases and that "bias" words such as 'low' and 'poor' have been dropped. Each loop is, by chance, a positive feedback loop as indicated by the bracketed symbol. By removing the bias words, the loops work for increasing as well as decreasing change.   So, good prospects lead to good performance, but equally poor prospects lead to poor performance.   Each loop, of course, comprises items which contribute to the original target of the model—morale. It follows, therefore, that the separate loops can be combined and that morale can be added.

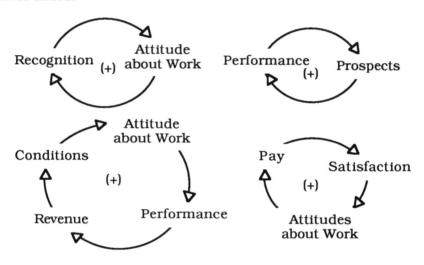

Figure 9.4 One laundry list, separate causal sub-loops. A systems view must address the relationships between the causal features from the laundry list

Combining the separate loops and adding morale results in the composite causal loop diagram, Figure 9.5 The diagram is very much more explicit and meaningful than the laundry list it replaced; it presents the understanding of its author quite clearly, and it shows how morale is in a self-perpetuating closed loop— which works towards good morale as well as poor.

Feedback loops occur widely in living and non-living systems. They come in two forms—negative feedback, which regulate towards some norm, and positive feedback, which may tend to run towards extremes if not associated with other controlling effects. We have seen the establishment of cybernetic negative feedback loops in Chapter 1, and now positive feedback has been presented. By modelling in loops, another advantage accrues: the need to weight and rank is reduced or eliminated. Weighting and, to a lesser extent, ranking are subjective and hence suspect. Modelling in closed loops obviates the need to weight and rank, by the nature of the loop.

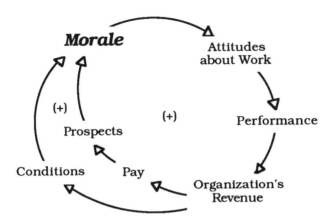

Figure 9.5 Synthesized causal loop set

Some find causal loop modelling difficult at first. The following approach makes the process relatively straightforward:

1 Identify the entity to be modelled (morale above)
2 Establish a laundry list of contributing factors
3 Develop a series of simple CLMs combining contributing factor, using nouns or noun phrases only and dropping any features from the laundry list which suggest bias, such as 'low', 'heavy', 'poor', 'hot', etc
4 Integrate the set of simple CLMs into a fuller single version, including the entity to be modelled

With practice, step 2 above can usefully be dropped. CLM is a useful technique for addressing complex issues at the initial stages of understanding and, in common with most methods, it has to be used carefully since it can lead both the originator and the reader to believe that they understand a problem or situation when they have not really explored in sufficient depth.

Where more depth of analysis is required, CLM provides a sound input to a more comprehensive tools such as STELLA®II, a computer tool running on the Apple Macintosh for modelling dynamic systems. STELLA® diagrams have been introduced in Chapter 3. The basic approach adopted by such methods is to establish levels and rates, so that quantities are stored in reservoirs to which are connected inflows to add more "stuff" and outflows to remove it. Using this simple notion it is possible to produce models of surprising robustness, enabling the modeller to understand and explore systems where the response might well be counter-intuitive.

Another example of CLM, in a quite different arena, is given below; it tackles the thorny problem of why we humans are, as Desmond Morris so aptly described us, "naked apes". This unique characteristic amongst the primates is a puzzle, but its not the only puzzle. We also, uniquely amongst the primates, have developed subcutaneous fat. This evolutionary development has been used in the CLM below to explain why it is (might be?) that man is naked. But man is not entirely naked; we still have hair in some areas of the body. The CLM proposes that these areas are important to the secretion of pheromones, those subliminal sexual odours which attract our mates, and that the remaining hair is concerned with retaining those pheromone odours in order to support the increased sexuality required of the naked ape by the new, carnivorous lifestyle.

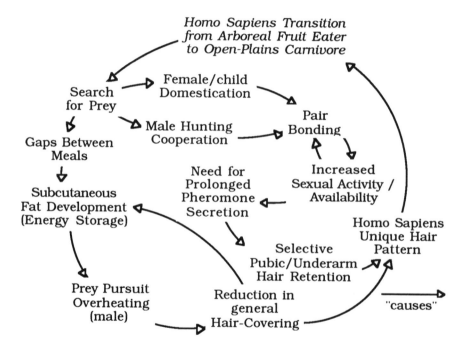

Figure 9.6 Cause of nakedness in *homo sapiens sapiens*(?)

Clearly, the diagram is not strictly causal—there is no consensus about the cause of our relative nakedness. But one of the assets of CLM is that it generates loops, which drive or are driven, hence revealing the underlying dynamics in relationships. In this instance, the unwritten driving force is natural selection—the "causal agent".

Finite State/Transition Diagrams

Many creative methods exist, but few examine discontinuities. CLM above, for example, tends to lead thoughts in the direction of continuous feedback, positive, negative, or both. Many real systems behave non-linearly, explosively or catastrophically, and new theories are emerging to explain these non-linear, chaotic phenomena (see Bak and Chen, 1991).

A compact and expressive way of presenting non-linear interacting systems that I have adapted from classical physics is the finite-state transition diagram. A simple example is given in Figure 9.7. The diagram shows the relationships between various states of theatre and global conflict, shown large in the centre of each square. Arrows between squares show at their source the cause of transition between states. Arrows re-entering the same square show causes for remaining in the present state.

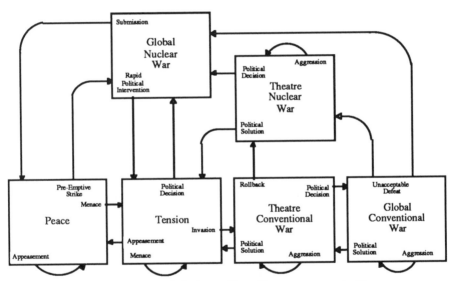

Figure 9.7 Finite state transition diagram—war in Europe

This technique is interesting not only because it represents non-linear behaviour, but also because the diagram presents so little room that only the highest level causes of transition can be entered, so encouraging the highest level of abstraction in analysis.

Ishikawa's Fishbone Diagram

Professor Kaoru Ishikawa, University of Tokyo, is credited with the fishbone diagram, a creative method for developing ideas. At the

top of Figure 9.8 we see the fish-head and the spine, presenting poor
systems engineering as an example problem. Figure 9.8 shows the
main causal branches of this phenomenon, according to the
analysis, while Figure 9.9 presents the next stage in analysis

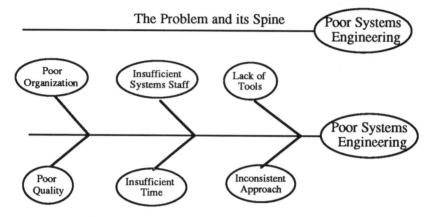

Figure 9.8 First two Ishikawa fishbones—poor systems engineering

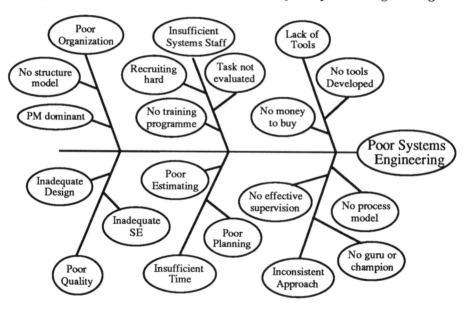

Figure 9.9 Developed systems engineering fishbone

The approach is deceptively simple; many people can work at once
on the diagram, bringing group creativity to the problem. Often a
gap is left between the stages of developing the diagram, to allow for

thought; this has the added benefit of allowing participants to forget who proposed what, so developing group ownership of the problem.

Stakeholder Analysis

To overcome too narrow a view, employ stakeholder analysis. Ideally, all principal stakeholders in an issue or problem should be gathered together and their respective objectives identified, so that all viewpoints and hence all objectives can be considered. (How these objectives might be aggregated will be addressed later in this chapter.) Finding appropriate stakeholders is best done by considering the subject at issue as a system and then identifying the system's containing system(s) and *their* objectives. For an intelligent building project, for instance, stakeholders would include social/environmental systems, employment systems, commercial systems and the building development system in the locale where the new building was to be erected. Sometimes, genuine stakeholders—i.e. those with something to lose—may be unavailable and surrogates must be employed. Even in this event, stakeholder analysis is valuable—see Chapter 10, Creative Entropy.

Brain-Storming

A well-tried and trusted method of generating ideas is brain-storming. Brain-storming is, in practice, rather difficult to undertake well, and a session needs to be carefully prepared and managed.

The notion is simple enough; a group of "experts" comes together in a creative environment and generate as many ideas as they can about a particular topic. But what constitutes an expert, what is a creative environment, how are ideas to be generated, rather than suppressed by the team members, perhaps for fear of peer ridicule?

Effective brain-storming seems to work best when the group has variety in terms of disciplines, ages and experience, and when there is a discipline of "no negative thoughts allowed"—a task for the person running the session to ensure. But first, the group needs to be worked up. There are many ways of doing this. One approach is to ask the group to generate as many ways of using an everyday object as possible in a very short time; for example, to generate as many ways as possible of: using three tennis balls which have been cut in half; using table tennis balls; moving water uphill; and so on. Having got the group going, the plan is to move swiftly on to the problem in hand while the creative juices are flowing.

Some participants may have a penchant for "putting down" those whom they consider inferior, or for attacking particular ideas they do not like. *In extremis*, it may prove necessary to banish such a disruptive influence which, since the miscreant is probably senior, requires firm management. The "no negative thoughts" rule is essential. All in all, it has to be said that brain-storming is not all that it is frequently said to be.

Idea Generation

A better approach than brain storming, in terms of achieving effective generation of ideas, is—not surprisingly—"idea generation" (Moore, 1987). This is a simple concept in which some form of trigger question is agreed between the assembled group, each of whom has a sheet of paper in front of him or her. Participants are then required to write down ideas relating to the question. After, say, two minutes, the pieces of paper are rotated around the group, and the idea-generation continues.

This process may be repeated three or four times. In each case the person receiving a sheet of paper sees others' ideas which may initiate new thoughts, and should certainly prevent excessive repetition between participants. At the end of the generation process, ideas are read out and assembled as a group exercise without difficulty, there being no idea-"ownership" difficulties since the source of an idea is not evident.

Nominal Group Technique (NGT)

NGT, invented by Delbecq et al. (1975), comprises five basic steps (Janes, 1988):

1 Clarification of a trigger question
2 Silent generation of ideas by each participant
3 Round-robin discussion of the ideas on a flip-chart
4 Serial discussion of each idea for clarification and editing
5 Voting to obtain a preliminary ranking of the ideas in terms of importance

In Janes view, NGT is particularly valuable when used in conjunction with interpretive structural modelling—see below.

Force-Field Analysis

Force-field analysis, Lewin (1949), is from the behavioural science camp and seeks to represent an organization in equilibrium under a set of balance and opposing forces. If we can identify the opposing forces, those urging us on and those restraining us, the we can select one or more of the forces to adjust in order to move in the desired direction. Again, the idea is seductively simple but, in the hands of the right expert, can be a powerful stimulus to understanding and action.

Red Teaming

The concept of red teaming is summarized in Figure 9.11. Essentially, the idea is to create a surrogate customer who is both knowledgeable and sceptical, and who therefore is going to view a proposal, or design, or solution through critical eyes.

Red teaming can be powerful, but it is not without its drawbacks; for a red team to be effective, there must be sufficient substance in the subject under review for sensible comment, but there must also

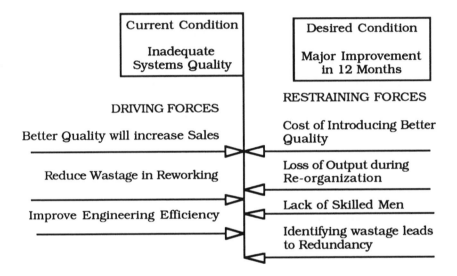

Figure 9.10 Lewin's force-field analysis. In practice, work to reduce a restraining force rather than increase a driving force

be sufficient time to correct any blunders. Thus the timing of red team activity is crucial. It is also difficult to man the team effectively; members must be both expert and uninvolved. One approach, used by some systems houses to good effect, is to turn parallel design teams on to each others' projects periodically, such that each design team looks at another design team's work. This ensures design competence, but of course there must also be representation from commercial, marketing and other interested parties. In summary, red teaming can be a powerful stimulus to enhanced creativity and performance in bidding, design and related enterprises, but it needs to be understood and managed carefully.

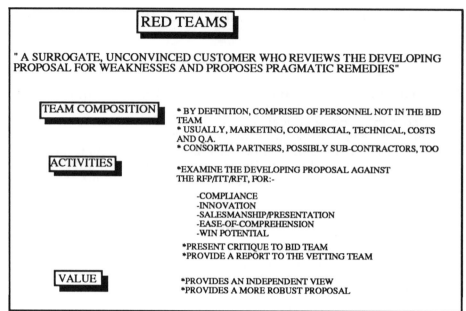

Figure 9.11 Red-teaming

STRUCTURE DEVELOPMENT

Interpretive Structural Modelling (ISM)

There is a variety of ways of aggregating entities, each having its
merits and demerits. One way is Interpretive Structural Modelling
(ISM) (Warfield, 1973 and 1989); (Janes, 1988). Using the ISM
technique, factors are related by their respective contribution, one
to another.

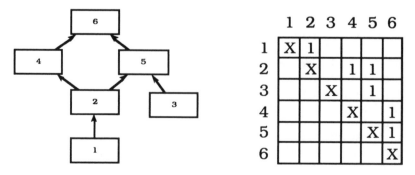

Figure 9.13 Network and its contribution matrix

The result may be represented in many ways.   Janes uses an approach similar to those in Figures 9.12 and 9.16. At the bottom of the diagram are those factors which are most pervasive, i.e. will make the widest contribution. At the top are those factors to which most others will contribute. Items which contribute mutually, one to another are entered in the shadowed boxes and are said to be "in a cycle". The result is a clear and persuasive structure showing what we might call the most strategic, far-reaching factors at the bottom and the potential results towards the top—a valuable insight has been gained by this   structuring and clustering technique.To understand this powerful technique, consider first a simple network as shown in figure 9.13. The network may be represented in matrix form, as shown on the right of Figure 9.13, where contributions are shown on the horizontal. So, "1" contributes to "2" in square x = 2, y = 1.

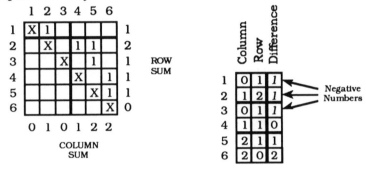

Figure 9.14 Developing contribution rank order

In Figure 9.14, the sums of the "1"s in each row and column have been derived, and—at right—differenced to produce a rank order. (In this instance, the rank order is as given in the figure, since we started from an ordered network. In normal usage, we would have started with an unstructured set of entities, found their relative contributions in a matrix, and then worked back to the network.)

Now consider a real-life example. The contribution matrix of Figure 9.15 is derived from some work on the introduction of a coordinated transport scheme to a city where presently the various forms of public and private transport operate quite independently. Using NGT (see above), it is possible to identify a range of factors relevant to the issue. These can then be related to each other by identifying their pairwise contribution. So, if factor "a" contributes to factor "b" then a "1" appears in the appropriate contribution matrix. If the reverse contribution does not exist, then a "0" would be entered in the relevant matrix position.

The so-called reachability matrix is copied directly from a simple computer tool which is used to assist in the acquisition, processing and handling of the information. The reachability matrix shows which entities—the factors in the left hand column—can be reached via which other entities. For example, there is a route from "Carried?" (short for "What is to be carried?", which is too long for the computer tool) to "City Needs", via the second "1" on the top row, left hand. Clearly, there are many routes from "Carried?" to "Sale-ability to Investors", the 22nd entity. If these alternative routes are suppressed by considering intervening boxes to be transitive, then we may draw direct from the chart by inspection—Figure 9.16

Factor	#																						
Carried?	1	1	1	1	0	1	1	1	1	1	0	0	0	1	1	1	1	1	1	1	1	1	1
City Needs	2	0	1	1	0	1	1	1	1	1	0	0	0	1	1	1	1	1	1	1	1	1	1
Comm Replenish	3	0	1	1	0	1	1	1	1	1	0	0	0	1	1	1	1	1	1	1	1	1	1
Aesthetics of LR	4	0	0	0	1	0	0	0	1	1	0	0	0	1	1	1	1	1	1	1	1	1	1
Scheduling	5	0	0	0	0	1	1	1	1	1	0	0	0	1	1	1	1	1	1	1	1	1	1
Mode Transfer.	6	0	0	0	0	0	1	1	1	1	0	0	0	1	1	1	1	1	1	1	1	1	1
Journey Times	7	0	0	0	0	0	0	1	1	1	0	0	0	1	1	1	1	1	1	1	1	1	1
Conv. Loss	8	0	0	0	0	0	0	0	1	1	0	0	0	1	1	1	1	1	1	1	1	1	1
Energy Costs	9	0	0	0	0	0	0	0	0	1	0	0	0	1	0	1	1	1	1	1	1	1	1
Nat/EECStnds	10	0	0	0	0	0	0	0	0	0	1	0	0	0	0	0	0	0	0	0	1	0	0
Ownership	11	0	0	0	0	0	0	0	0	0	0	1	0	0	0	0	0	0	0	0	0	0	1
Min Disruption	12	0	0	0	0	0	0	0	0	0	0	0	1	0	0	0	0	0	0	0	0	0	0
Veh.Tech.	13	0	0	0	0	0	0	0	0	0	0	0	0	1	0	0	0	1	1	1	1	1	1
Bus Percept	14	0	0	0	0	0	0	0	0	0	0	0	0	0	1	0	0	0	1	1	0	1	1
Economics	15	0	0	0	0	0	0	0	0	0	0	0	0	0	0	1	1	0	1	1	0	1	1
Light R ROCE	16	0	0	0	0	0	0	0	0	0	0	0	0	0	0	1	1	0	1	1	0	1	1
Vandalproof	17	0	0	0	0	0	0	0	0	0	0	0	0	0	0	0	0	1	0	0	1	0	0
Green City	18	0	0	0	0	0	0	0	0	0	0	0	0	0	0	0	0	0	1	1	0	1	1
Road Levies	19	0	0	0	0	0	0	0	0	0	0	0	0	0	0	0	0	0	1	1	0	1	1
Safety	20	0	0	0	0	0	0	0	0	0	0	0	0	0	0	0	0	0	0	0	1	0	0
CC Residence	21	0	0	0	0	0	0	0	0	0	0	0	0	0	0	0	0	0	0	0	0	1	0
Invest.Saleabilit	22	0	0	0	0	0	0	0	0	0	0	0	0	0	0	0	0	0	0	0	0	0	1

Figure 9.15 Rank-ordered contribution to city-centre light rail scheme

Priorities

An alternative use of ISM is to examine relative priorities between, say, projects competing for limited funds. An example which is topical at the time of writing might concern a secondary school which has to face the new situation of managing its funds, and allocating priorities. Suppose the list of competing school projects or demands on funds were as follows:

- School play
- Text books
- Library books
- Music lessons
- New trampoline
- New sports gear
- Redecoration

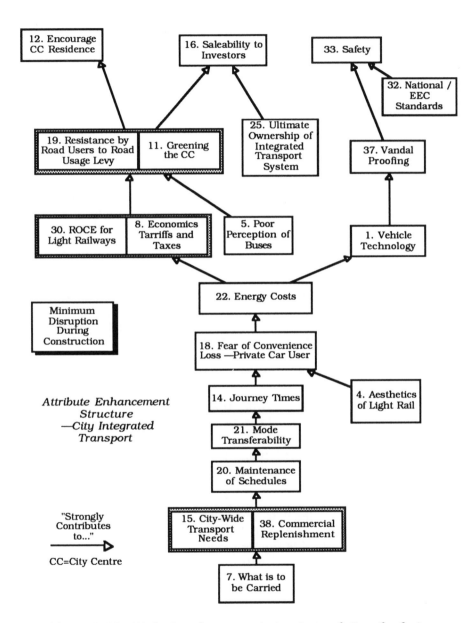

Figure 9.16 Attribute enhancement structure relating the factors contributing to the viability of a city-centre light rail scheme

- New toilets
- Lollipop lady
- Theatre trips (English studies)
- Annual sports day
- Fire equipment
- New 'A' level
- Supply teachers
- A second groundsman
- French trip (French studies)
- Skiing trip
- Special careers room
- Support to school secretary
- Laboratory equipment

The available money will not cover even half the estimated cost of all the projects. Which to choose? How to choose them? Evidently, there are several "pet projects" on the list, and some staff, parents and pupils are going to be disappointed.

One approach would be to hold an interactive management session with the staff, parents and pupil-representatives, to compare the relative importance of the various projects by discussion. Projects would be discussed on a pairwise basis—"Is Project A more, or less, important than Project B". The idea of "more important" is itself difficult, and should not be imposed on the group, but should be allowed to emerge. Suppose the following criteria emerged:

1 One-off projects are less important than those with an enduring effect

2 Projects where parents could reasonably be expected to pay should draw less on school funds and were less important for the allocation of school funds

3 Projects which benefited more pupils were preferred to those benefiting less

Using these criteria, Figure 9.17 might be the outcome of an interactive session, at least in terms of a diagram ranking projects as most important at the top, least at the bottom. The priority structure of Figure 9.17 is not self-evidently logical. It is the result of reconciliation of local partisan pressures. This reconciliation is the *real* result—all of the group have participated in the resulting priorities, all have had their point of view considered, and all have reason to be committed to the result. Were such an approach to be used in schools, it would draw together the three parties (pupils, staff and parents) in a way seemingly difficult to realize at present. Note in the figure that the two lower arms are skewed—the skiing trip is at a higher level than music lessons, for example—so that a complete ladder of priorities is presented, except for the second and third rows from the top where equal weightings have been given within the respective rows. Since individual costs have not been included up to this point, costs can be used as a secondary discriminator—a distinct improvement over spending only on the affordable in order of cheapness!

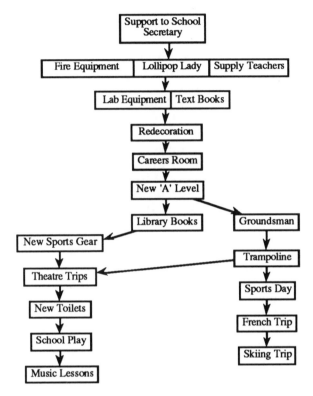

Figure 9.17 School budget priority structure

CREATIVE ENVIRONMENTS

Hitchins' Systems Laws

Hitchins' First System Law: Creativity is inverse to experience

Hitchins' Second System Law: Comprehension is inverse to promotion level

Hitchins' Third System Law: Size of cock-up is inverse to elapsed project time

Hitchins' Fourth System Law: Efficiency is inverse to effectiveness

Hitchins' Fifth System Law: Decision time is inverse to decision importance

Hitchins' Fifth System Law: A locally optimal system contains sub-optimal parts

Everyone has their pet "laws"; mine are presented above and are distilled from observing humanity at work trying to design systems. A certain amount of cynicism might be forgiven, but the laws are not just cynical—they might be useful, too.

- *Hitchins' First System Law* proposes that we had better blend youth and experience in such a way that the younger element in an organization can be creative without being crushed or ignored by older, experienced people who "fly by autopilot", assuming answers to problems that they only *think* are like ones they have previously conquered.
- *Hitchins' Second System Law* is not meant to be unkind, but it is true that as we progress up the promotion ladder we have less time to keep in touch, less time to freshen our skills, less time to invest in understanding a problem. Living on memory lasts only for so long in a fast-moving technological world. Seniors should remember that they are out of date, and not make judgements based on out-dated knowledge and understanding
- *Hitchins' Third System Law* is the *raison d'être* of systems engineering. In general, we are far too keen to rush into jobs without properly understanding. How often do we pick up half-baked ideas, use them as though they were essence of wisdom and then discover later, after much time and effort, that they have totally mislead us? Marketing staff are classic offenders in a systems company, returning from a visit to a new customer with a grubby piece of paper containing a block diagram of the proposed system clutched proudly in their hands, unaware that they have undertaken in the course of seconds the design of architecture—perhaps the most difficult, far-reaching and demanding task in system design.
- *Hitchins' Fourth System Law* observes that attempts to increase efficiency generally reduce effectiveness. The reasons for this were given in Chapter 5.1, but the usual cause is that efficiency drives, in their laudable aim to reduce internal waste, also reduce variety in the system, and hence robustness and the ability to respond to change. When that change comes, the organization lacks the reserves, and cannot cope.
- *Hitchins' Fifth System Law* observes people's penchant for excessive concentration on things they can understand easily and quickly. Committees can spend much more time on such issues as hard or soft toilet paper, while major investment decisions go through "on the nod" by comparison. The underlying reasons for this widely observed and repeated

phenomenon is unknown to me, but it is possibly related to Klein's work, see Chapter 2, with the committee-room presenting an expert with a stressful situation requiring decisions about complex issues while under time pressure—result, Recognition-Primed Decisions.

- *Hitchins' Sixth System Law* is well known, but bears constant repeating—complex systems cannot be optimized. Local optimization is a fleeting phenomenon achieved at the expense of de-optimizing something else. The law is intended to make designers realize the nested nature of the problem; if they seek and find the contained, sub-optimal system and "put it right", guess what they have done to the containing system?

Creating the Creative Environment

The keynote of creativity must be youth—not necessarily youth in years, but in attitudes of mind. Some will always be more creative by their very nature; but the organization can be set up to be creative too. It is a simple statement of fact that there are more people at the *bottom* of the organizational pyramid than at the top, and that these people are *younger*. It is also a simple statement of fact that achievement of actual work progresses *across* the pyramid, not up and down—these activities are reporting and control, not actual progressive work. It therefore follows that the creative, innovative power-house of any organization is in the lower strata, as illustrated in Figure 9.18.

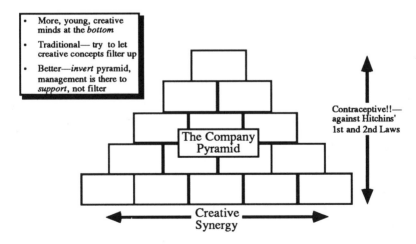

Figure 9.18 A pyramid view of companies

If the organization does not recognize this self-evident fact, then the comment made against the vertical arrow in the figure will be all too true. A model of the organization in which the pyramid is

inverted so that management *supports* the innovative process by
enabling, resourcing and encouraging, would be an improvement—
see Figure 9.19. For such a figure to be representative of the real
world, it would be necessary for managers to think of themselves as
serving their employees. At one time, the ethic of public service was
one of service, and a stroll around any reasonable town in the UK on
a Saturday morning will reveal a myriad of volunteers testifying to
the fact that many people in the UK are still dedicated to helping
each other. Politicians, on the other hand, are fond of saying what
they intend to do "when we get into power"—this sort of comment
sits at odds with any notion of service! I am not at all sure, in a
democratic society, that the notion of power and service are
compatible.

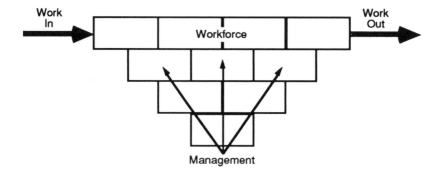

Figure 9.19 The management-in-support concept

SUMMARY AND CONCLUSIONS

This chapter has presented something of a kaleidoscope of ideas and
techniques for creative thinking and working. The profusion of
topics is to be expected; the very notion of creativity is right-brain,
unstructured and frenetic—were it otherwise, we could parcel up
creativity and supply it in a bottle or in a computer program. The
underlying essence of creativity, as exemplified by all the
techniques presented, is that it need not be a solo affair; it is
unlikely that any one person has the monopoly on good ideas.
Instead, every technique presented encourages group cooperation
and participation so that, not only are new and innovative ideas
generated, but the generating group becomes committed to their
realization.

ASSIGNMENTS

A. An Intelligent Building (IB) is proposed for the sea-front at Blackpool:
   1 Treating the IB as a system, identify its containing system(s)
   2. Conceive the containing system(s) objectives
   3. Develop an intent matrix, inter-relating the various objectives by asking the question: "Does Objective A help to achieve Objective B, or is it the other way round, or are they unrelated?'"
   4. From the intent matrix, draw an intent structure
   5. On the intent structure, identify the pervasive objective(s), any pivotal objective(s) and the mission
   6. Comment on the merits of this approach c.f. weighting and scoring or ranking methods.

B. Develop a causal loop model addressing the success of a degree course:
   1 Establish a laundry list of factors strongly contributing to/causing/enabling a successful degree
   2 Develop sub-CLMs relating the various causal factors to each other
   3 Integrate the sub-CLMs
   4 Comment on the value of the full CLM, (cf the laundry list) and its limitations.

Chapter 10.1
Conceiving Technique

Whether it be in the heart to conceive,
the understanding to direct,
or the hand to execute
Julian of Norwich, 1343—1413

THE PURPOSE AND ROLE OF A CONCEIVING SYSTEM

Between enquiring systems which seek to understand, and creating systems which seek to implement, is a gap; the purpose of a conceiving system is to fill that gap.

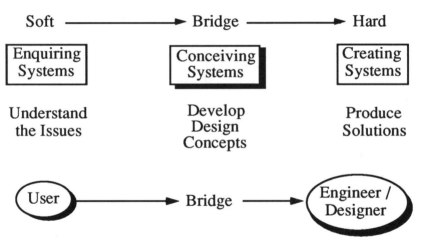

Figure 10.1 Conceiving systems

A conceiving system is intended to bridge the gap from soft issues where there is no established requirement, simply a problem situation suggesting a need, to the development of a substantial design concept for a solution to (part of) the problem. A conceiving system should also, by virtue of its concern with operational domain issues, provide a bridge between user/operators, those who understand the domain, and designer/engineers, those who understand the technology. A conceiving system is a metasystem, too.

Coherency requires that a design concept be realized comprehensively and traceably and that each step of the path be justifiable. In the real world, as experiences with creating systems testified, work is more often carried out by the inexperienced, rather than the experienced designer, particularly where innovation is the order. Coherency therefore must be judged relative to the inexperienced.

PLANKS IN THE BRIDGE

There is a series of steps in the process of conceiving systems:

- Understand the issues - a soft task
- Generate a broad, but solution-relevant, information base
- Develop a clear description of purpose
- Generate and develop a variety of system concepts
- Develop the human system(s) first
- Support the human system(s) with technology as/if needed
- Develop the human and technology systems as one
    - Develop system performance (hard-ish)
    - Develop system effectiveness (hard-ish)
- Select the preferred system by relative comparison (hard)
- Determine the absolute value of the preferred solution (soft)

BRIDGING CONCEPTS

Middle-Out Design

Top down design is a fundamental feature of the contemporary systems engineer's philosophy; it implies a high level of abstraction at the start so as to free the mind of prejudice and to encompass all aspects of the subject. Top down, improperly applied, can be a disaster of overkill and misdirection. It is essential to have some knowledge of "the bottom" if top down is to be given sensible direction; understanding the bottom equates to having good domain and subject knowledge.

Most people, if they are honest, do not work top down. While it is often sensible to present the results of work top down, analysts faced with a new problem generally seem in practice to start somewhere in the middle of a problem, choosing a topic with which they are reasonably comfortable, so easing their way into the overall problem, as indeed proposed by Descartes. It is the mark of good analysts that they can retract from this early effort and move up to the top level once a greater degree of understanding has been achieved without retaining undue allegiance to their initial work.

The real world in which design solutions have to be conceived operates under budget and time pressures. A method that does not make the best use of time will prove impracticable. It is a characteristic of some soft methods that they produce at the beginning a vast array of problem situation data much of which is subsequently discarded. It can also be argued that, unless the full spread of situation factors is uncovered, it will be difficult to discern the issues. A compromise is needed which directs attention of analysts towards factors which could be relevant and away from factors that cannot be relevant.

S-O-I Prime Directive
Semantic Analysis
of
Prime Directive

Strategy for Achieving Prime Directive

Behaviour	Strategy	Management Set
Aggression	Strategy options	Mission management
Discretion	Unifying concepts	Viability management
Co-operation	Innovative approaches	Resource management
Measures of S-O-I effectiveness	Negative contribution factors	Threat to achieving PD
Performance	Cost	External
Availability	Mass/weight/volume	Internal
Survivability	Complexity	Environmental
	Failure modes/criticality	Political/economic/ social/technical

Figure 10.2 A system requirement template

For similar reasons of time and budget, and with the added incentives of traceability and completeness, it is important to employ formality in the concept evolution process. The software industry is introducing formal methods for mathematically provable software design and test. The move is inevitable where a soft engineering practice meets stark reality in business. The process of conceiving designs is not at a stage of development where such formal methods could be applied, but a simpler form of such formal methods is a minimum requirement.

A suitable approach to the kind of relaxed formality appropriate to conceiving systems is that of the template. The template is simply an empty set of pigeon holes, suitably annotated with headings indicating the contents with which each hole is to be filled. A requirement template, available from the start of a concept formulation exercise, will enable analysts to concentrate their early work towards the intermediate goal of filling the template pigeonholes. Further templates, available from the start of the exercise, will guide the effort after filling the Requirement Template towards filling the solution templates.

Completing templates also provides milestones of achievement and progress, which are necessary even in this essentially creative process. A requirement template, at high level, might appear as shown in Figure 10.2; typical solution or tradeoff templates have already been introduced in Chapter 5.

The Continuum Concept

Some methodologies have very few, individually large steps. The would-be analyst has to progress from step to step, iterating where need be, but essentially he is using his own intellect to find his way in a very loose framework. Advocates of such frameworks would say that it is the very "looseness" that provides the ability to address a wide variety of "soft" problems. But it is also true that these frameworks are suitable structures only for practitioners of substantial, and unusual, intellect; what of the rest?

In real-world problems, the need for a structured conceiving system arises principally as a result of the need to manage complexity. Individual steps should therefore be such that they uniquely contain easily-grasped concepts on the one hand, and do not invoke unattainable leaps of the intellect on the other.

So emerges the idea of a continuum—a set of steps, small and so arranged as to provide a contiguous route from issues to well-formulated design concepts for solutions.

Creative Entropy

Templates are intended to direct the effort, not to inhibit creativity. Stimulating creativity within the template framework is an essential objective of a conceiving system. There is a number of approaches employed in this context; together I have dubbed them as promoting Creative Entropy—see Chapter 3. The term is intended to evoke an intellectual image rather than a mathematical formula, but it requires explanation.

Entropy is a measure of the degree of disorder in a system. Guilbaud (1959) states: "To say that entropy increases spontaneously, in specified circumstances, is simply to say that the physical system in question tends naturally towards states that are more probable, being realizable in a larger number of distinct ways".

Entropy is concerned, then, with variety and possible states. Creative Entropy is the purposeful development of variety and the exploration of possible states, the purpose being to create an information base relevant to some concept-of-interest .

It has long been noted that there is qualitative correspondence between entropy and information, supported by a notable mathematical similarity which de Broglie (1951) suggests is the "most pleasing and most important of the ideas suggested by cybernetics ...". Certainly, the generally accepted view of the relationship between the two measures is that an increase in entropy is analogous to a diminution of information, given suitable statistical models for both.

Creative Entropy, as I define it, is the conscious generation of concepts, variety, connection, data and ideas, using a variety of techniques to provide frameworks and environments to stimulate and direct this essentially creative process of design concept formulation.

Mind-sets. One way to generate concept entropy is to induce intentional mind-sets in the analyst. The template is a high level mind-set. Contained within it is a variety of mind-sets. These mind-sets are self-contained topic areas requiring concentration in which the analyst can roam, generating ideas by brain-storming, idea-writing or cerebral energy. By moving from mind-set to mind-set, a wealth of creative concepts can be stimulated. It is, of course, important to ensure that the sum of such mind-sets is sufficient to cover the necessary range of design issues—that is the rôle of the template. A particularly useful application of mind-set is the necessary and sufficient set.

Necessary and sufficient sets. Survivability may be thought of as comprising three sub-headings:

Avoidance of detection

Self defence

Damage tolerance

Avoidance of detection concerns itself with camouflage, mimicry, covert communications, stealth and the like. Self-defence addresses the ability of the system in question to fight off an attack. Damage-tolerance presumes damage and addresses the ability of the system to continue operation.

Together, they form a set which has some of the formalism of a necessary and sufficient set. Why necessary and sufficient?. Avoidance of detection seeks to survive by not being seen. Self-defence presumes avoidance to have failed. Damage-tolerance assumes self-defence to have failed. Together, all three cover the range of feasible situations. Provided the individual sets can be filled, then the composite set is both necessary and sufficient. Similarly the management set is N&S. A mission will continue to be pursued by a system as long as the system remains viable as a system and as long as there are resources to support both the management of viability and of the mission.

Creative tension. Creative tension is realized by identifying objectives in the design, formulating strategies for achieving those objectives and at the same time elaborating the threats to the achievement of those strategies—see Popper (1972). A typical objective might be the improvement of system availability. Creative tension requires attention to the threat to achieving that improvement, which might be political, skill shortages, cost, inaccessibility or a host of other threats. Creative tension prevents narrow focusing on particular aspects of the problem situation which, for improved availability, might have been simply to increase spares in anticipation of failures.

The Concept of a Prime Directive

Central to the idea of conceiving systems is the Prime Directive (PD). The PD is the highest level of abstract, objective statement of SOI purpose. The expression, prime directive, is borrowed from life sciences and is exemplified by *Homo sapiens'* prime directive, "propagation of the species".

Mention was made earlier of the difficulty faced by analysts in trying to functionally decompose high level requirements, a truly reductionist process. If functional decomposition starts too low in the hierarchy or if there is no real understanding of "function" then difficulties and shortcomings ensue. The difficulty facing radar analysts—see Chapter 1—who start decomposition at the "sensor, communications, processing" point (actually not functional at all, but physical decomposition) is that they can never justify "what *kind* of radar". The *Homo sapiens* PD above is ideal; starting at that point allows the following approach, by comparison with the radar decomposition.

> Humans evolved physically and socially. Social evolution, behavioural evolution during one lifetime, required minimal birth-imprinting. Human children were therefore born helpless and were protected and educated socially within the family circle. Their helplessness necessitated shelter by night so *Homo sapiens* operated principally by day. Optical sensors consequently evolved to be most sensitive in the green part of the visual spectrum, where greatest solar light energy falls by day

Returning to the radar case, were the radar analysts to work from an equivalent prime directive for their radar, stating what the ultimate objective of their radar was to be, rather than from a set of pseudo-functions, then they would learn what *kind* of radar sensor was needed rather than simply that one was to exist.

The prime directive is the point to which all design concepts should be traceable. Clearly its formulation is of considerable importance. The PD is not synonymous with SSM's root definition which seeks to describe a system. The PD presumes a general need and describes the need at the highest possible level of abstraction. A PD must be abstract. It should, therefore, comprise a phrase containing only one verb, in the infinitive. In that one phrase, only the highest principles should be included.

Perhaps the best way to understand PDs is to observe some. We have seen the archetypal PD for *Homo sapiens*. The Royal Air Force has a prime directive (my term, not theirs) for the air defence of the United Kingdom: "To neutralize enemy air incursions into the UK Air Defence Region". This is an excellent PD. It expresses succinctly and precisely the raison d'être, the limits of action and the sphere of activity of the Air Defence forces. It does not over-specify; "neutralize" is vague yet entirely sufficient for purpose and there is no hint of solution in the PD's wording. These, then, are the features that characterize a good PD:

Highest level of abstraction

Ultimate purpose

Sphere of endeavour

Solution transparency

Semantic analysis. Semantic analysis is straightforward; each word in a statement (the PD in this instance) is examined and expanded as far as it can be to extract all meaning, stated and implied, that it might contain.

On first association, semantic analysis may seem boring and pedantic. Experience suggests considerable value, however. A group engaged in semantic analysis come to form a comprehensive, consensus view concerning the statement. Where the process is applied to a document, progress—at first apparently slow—rapidly accelerates as prior ideas that have been understood contribute to fuller understanding of later ideas.

I have developed my own style of semantic analysis for the application under consideration; an example follows, using the RAF air defence PD as start-point. The PD is, again, "To neutralize enemy air incursions into the UK Air Defence Region".

"To neutralize ...	"To eliminate the threat from ...
... enemy ...	... those declared by government to be hostile who ...
... air incursions ...	... enter by air without permission ...
... into the UK ADR ...	... into the designated airspace legally defined and internationally promulgated as sovereign UK air space"
Implied means:	*Use of U.K. air defence assets*

The semantic analysis thus comprises three parts: the PD, the analysis expanded as a continuous sentence, and statement of implied meaning - where such exists. The semantic analysis expands the understanding but without impairing the characteristics presented in the box above.

Strategy and threat. The formulation of a sound PD is necessary, essential even, but not sufficient. Consider the case of *Homo sapiens*; he shares his prime directive with every other biological entity on the planet. The PD alone lacks discriminatory power. That power is developed by identifying both a threat to achieving the PD and a strategy for overcoming that threat (an instance of creative tension in operation)

- The Prime Directive of a system is the highest level statement of its ultimate purpose. The Prime Directive pervades all aspects of the system's development, evolution, performance, behaviour, effectiveness, eventual senility and demise.

- The Prime Directive of homo sapiens sapiens is generally taken as :-

  "To propagate the species"

  This directive requires procreation, nurturing and the social development of the following generation such that they can continue the process. The Prime Directive drives our social behaviour, our instincts, even our human form

- The Prime Directive "To Propagate the species" is shared by every living organism on the planet - as such, it is a poor discriminator

---

Figure 10.3 Prime directives

Using *Homo sapiens* as an example again, the strategy adopted by our forebears in meeting the prime directive of propagation of the species could be described at great length and it certainly had many variations, but it probably included the following:

- The formation of family groups and aggregations of such groups into clans or villages.
- The nuclear family related to a wider family, often matriarchal owing both to the greater longevity of the hardier females and to their continuous presence within the family unit.
- Around the family groups, the males hunted in co-operation, while the females and young children gathered food.
- Families and clans banded together for strength, sheltering in caves and constructions by night and in inclement weather to protect the young, the infirm and the old.

Threats could similarly be elaborated, but might be addressed very briefly as follows. Threats arose from a variety of sources: competing groups of *Homo sapiens*; disease; weather effects on food supplies; carnivores; internal competition amongst aggressive, ambitious younger males, and so.

The *Homo sapiens sapiens* pattern suggests how to tackle the problem. Having established a threat to the achievement of the PD in some depth, various strategies can be conceived for an SOI and tried out against it, until a robust, high-level strategy, or set of strategy options is developed. These will give purpose and direction to the design concepts. This TRIAD concept (Prime Directive/threat to its achievement/strategy to overcome the threat) was introduced in Chapter 6 as the basis for developing robust structure models (see Figure 10.4).

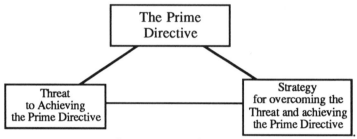

Figure 10.4 The TRIAD

Figure 10.5 illustrates how prime directives, threats and strategies are related in diverse situations.

- How the Prime Directive is to be achieved in the presence of the threat

- Unless the female Praying Mantis bites off the male's head, copulation is inhibited. This bizarre process ensures the male's body becomes a food supply to foster the female and hence their joint offspring. This is a strategem.

- Consider the strategy pursued by a university in its quest to advance understanding. The threat? Lack of funds and resources; diminution of value placed by society on understanding (cf knowledge)

- University strategy must include:-

  - Revalue understanding - via the media and by example

  - Foster current sources and find new sources of funds, from among those who need to understand

  - Development of (valuable?) understanding through research

Figure 10.5 The statement of strategy

Behaviour. An aspect of system seldom discussed is behaviour. The Soviet air defence system that shot down the Korean airliner in recent years certainly exhibited behaviour—fierce territorial imperative. Systems generally exhibit character; it is developed within the design concept by the management structure, the speed of response, by the information presented to the operators, and of course by the behaviour of the operators themselves. If the system is viewed as a single entity, humans and machines together, then behaviour is attributable to the whole. If we look at the two elements separately, then each element enables behaviour on the part of the other.

SUMMARY

The chapter has presented important, fundamental concepts of conceiving systems which act as a bridge between those who simply enquire into problems without a drive to find solutions, and those who drive towards solutions without perhaps enquiring as much as they should. The components of a conceiving system are presented as follows:

- Middle-out design, using a set of templates such that the exploration of concepts and the generation of data and information is structured and directed, rather than haphazard and capricious
- Creative Entropy, a device for generating a diverse information base from which to develop solution concepts
- Necessary & sufficient sets, a means of introducing formality into the information generation, to promote complete coverage of subject matter
- Prime Directive, the concept that any conceived system should be directed towards one overriding objective
- The Triad of Prime Directive, strategy for its achievement, and threat to its achievement as a means of generating useful information

Chapter 10.2
Conceiving Systems— The Seven-step Continuum

To hit upon a right conception is a difficult step. But when the step is made, the facts assume a different aspect from what they had before. That done, they are seen from a different viewpoint, and the catching of this viewpoint is a special mental operation requiring special mental endowments and habits of thought. Before this new state of affairs occurs, facts are seen as detached, separate, lawless: afterwards as possessing innumerable new relationships never before seen.

Whewell. *Philosophy of Discovery.* 1861

ATTRIBUTES OF A GOOD METHODOLOGY

The following attributes are appropriate to a good methodology:

- Applies to any system
- Simple to use
- Comprehensive
- Creative and innovative
- For individual and team use
- Supported by tools and methods
- Delivers—proven in practice

The Seven-step Continuum (SSC) offers a procedure for developing robust design concepts which satisfies the criteria listed above.

DEVELOPING THE CONTINUUM

The SSC has been developed over a number of years. It has been tried in use in industry, used by engineers and students, evolving in the process; its progress may be described as action research

User populations were originally design engineers, but more latterly the SSC has been used with non-engineer students in academia. The students were mixed-sex, mixed-ethnic-origin, mixed-interest groups concerned with the study of systems and management. Their surprisingly ready grasp of the methods and approach was inspiring.

It is concerning to note that industry presently has little opportunity to apply conceiving systems in the real world. Generally, the conception of a system is the responsibility of a customer organization while its design and development falls to a contractor. Thus in UK defence, for example, the Ministry of Defence (MOD) Operational Requirements branches, populated principally by operator/users, detail the requirements for new systems, while MOD Procurement Executive branches let contracts for the study and design and development of those systems. This division might be counter-productive, but in the absence of an accepted conceiving system, it is the present, wide-spread practice. It is, in my view, one of the major, if not the principal, cause of dissatisfaction with procured systems.

The Outline Procedure for Conceiving Systems

The plan is to conceive the human system(s) first, i.e. to ignore the technology and to concentrate on conceiving the organization, processes and procedures before introducing technology, which can then be seen as essentially supporting, enhancing human productivity and performance. This is not the only strategy possible—many pundits advocate re-organizing the human activity system so as to "take advantage of the technology", by which they mean that the people-system should be bent to meet the needs of the technology-system. There are often seductive reasons for pursuing this approach, for it promises much; it delivers little, however, because the people-system rebels against its new rôle as "machine-minder", or slave to the Wurlitzer, or whatever expression is in vogue. Such approaches also overlook the obvious; every job, no matter how trivial, has its "wrinkles", or particular methods. People are very good at finding these ways; designers of complex systems are not. Hence, bending men to the machine can prove ineffective.

Other strategic elements buried in the outline procedure given in Chapter 10.1 include:

* Purpose as a prime motivator
* *Absolute* measures of effectiveness; comparative measures always produce a result, even where a valid design solution does not exist from amongst the options on offer
* Capacity-before-performance. The contention is that requisite capacities and rates set limits on performance and drive costs
* Performance-before-effectiveness. The contention is that Performance is fundamental, while availability and Survivability are bastions of effectiveness which cannot be

established until performance is identified. "Adding" availability and survivability, may of course reduce performance—that phenomenon is accommodated in the SSC

- Develop human system capability first, then support with technology to enhance productivity
- Essential sequence. There is a natural sequence of steps, such that some cannot be started until others are completed, at least in part. This does not mean that iteration cannot take place; on the contrary, iteration is desirable, but only after an initial traversing of the basic steps to provide a sensible basis

The Seven Steps at Level Zero

The SSC suggests, perhaps, that the seven steps themselves form a continuum. That is not quite accurate. The seven steps form a progression from soft to hard, from issue to solution (if there is one), but each step is quite large - too large to be termed a continuum. Each step could be viewed as a set of lesser steps, and each of those decomposed further. The SSC does not operate in quite that formal, reductionist manner, either. Instead the steps are "magnified", revealing more and more detail with increasing magnification. This differs from reductionism in that "smaller" ideas become visible at higher magnification, and are not necessarily simple decompositions from the higher level.

First, the SSC at the highest level, level zero:

1 Understand the issues
2 Establish the need
3 Develop process and structure
4 Estimate capacities
5 Develop performance
6 Develop effectiveness
7 Assess the potential solution

The Seven-step Continuum—Level 1

- The steps clearly move from issue to design concept—the intention is to find a solution, the goal is to attain a result, even where the result is that no sensible solution exists even at concept level
- Steps are taken in sequence, starting at step 1
- There being no established consensus on what constitutes a design concept, steps 5, 6 and 7 develop successive degrees of robustness in the concept. It is, for some purposes, feasible to stop at step 3 or step 4, having become satisfied with the level of understanding for a particular design concept. For others,

stopping at step 5 will satisfy. The full seven steps will provide a well justified, traceable design concept where one exists

- The steps do not, essentially, presuppose a System of Interest (SOI) with objectives; in the real world, it is common for systems to be loosely prescribed by customers without apparent, or at least declared, objectives or with the declared objectives quite different from the real objectives—which have to be inferred

- The SOI is the complete system and *at all times* includes the people and their machines; even when it is necessary to distinguish between, for example, the contained (human) decision forming system and the decision support system which may (but need not) be technologically based, measures of effectiveness will continue to regard the system as one

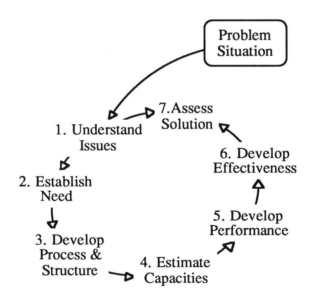

Figure 10.6 The Seven-step Continuum as a cycle

- The SOI is *always* considered as a fully open system, influenced by parent and sibling systems, but it is not those systems. The influences on the SOI are experienced through its many interfaces and the environment

- Some of the steps require understanding, technique and method which may not presently be available either in an acceptable form, or in a form for which there is consensus approval. Nonetheless, it is possible to delineate and describe the characteristics of such needs; indeed, it is useful and important so to do, in order to direct attention to the shortfall in tools and techniques

The seven steps may be presented graphically, as shown in Figure 10.6. The figure shows that the final step, "assess the solution", examines solution and the issue together. It is also implicit in the figure that the problem situation has been identified and explored before this process of developing solution concepts. The SSC connects to the next process in the chain from issues to resolutions as shown in Figure 10.7.

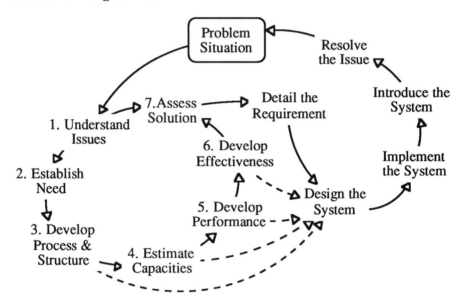

Figure 10.7 The SSC's contribution to design

The Seven Steps at Level One

The first level of resolution is shown on pages 230 and 231 respectively, starting with steps 1 to 3, and followed by steps 4 to 7. The titles of the steps are largely self-explanatory;   content is expanded below:

• The USH Systems Principles are encapsulated in the process model. The Principle of Reactions is evident in step 1, with the identification of contained sibling systems and, if necessary, the concurrent introduction of complementary systems alongside the SOI. This is a most important point It is a departure from conventional thinking, in that it assumes: (a) that the introduction of the SOI will disturb the existing fabric of interacting systems such that their combined responses are likely to be quite unpredictable; (b) that a disturbed fabric will, in its turn, impact upon the fledgling SOI, rendering any fixed part of its design subject to instant obsolescence; and (c) that a set of complementary systems may be introduced to neutralize or manage such disturbance—see Chapter 12

- The Principle of Connected Variety and the Principle of Cohesion are evident in Step 3 with the concern for interflows and intraflows (between siblings and sub-systems respectively—to promote stability), and in the clustering of related activities into functional sub-systems
- The Principle of Cyclic Progression would usefully be observed during the processes of synthesis and assessment, to anticipate any tendency to undue dominance in any of the Siblings or subsystems
- The Generic Reference Model is evident in the reqirement template, the solution template, and particularly Step 4/2, where its use encourages completeness
- Steps 1 to 4 require no particular engineering skills, and are open to participation by users, customers, scientists, psychologists and engineers alike. Tools can be brought to bear during these steps to organize, cluster and link information, ideas and relationships into conceptual structure and architecture, both functional and physical
- Steps 5 and 6 may require some specialist design support
- Step 7, like steps 1 to 4, requires no special engineering skill, and presents the opportunity for full participation by interested parties
- Together, the steps can now be seen as a continuum, encouraging and guiding in terms of tasks that have to be done logically and in sequence, but without any prescription about method that might limit or unduly direct creativity

Note in Figures 10.8 and 10.9 the use of a restricted set of action words at the beginning of each task; typical action words and their meanings follow:

Understand	Gain an in-depth knowledge of all facets
Bound	Describe the limits of the system
Identify	Generate or discover, describe, categorize
Postulate	Propose, put forward
Elaborate	Amplify, expand, decompose
Develop	Create, expand, detail
Estimate	Calculate numerically, approximately
Conceive	Create, generate the idea
Appreciate	Survey and gain an understanding
Enhance	Add features, capability

Formulate	Develop justifiable, traceable rules
Cluster	Group according to formulated rules
Predict	Forecast from model or parametric analysis
Synthesize	Aggregate parts into a whole
Map	Transfer viewpoints
Compare	Model options

Some restriction on the range and meaning of action words is a useful adjunct to the formality of the metasystem process; it militates against misunderstanding without at the same time introducing a set of jargon terms that would deter the non-specialist or newcomer.

Note in the figure at the end of this section that the need (or requirement) template is set up as the output of step 2. The need template is a hinge-pin of the SSC, directing earlier work and setting the stage for the the solution template of Step 4, which provides a similar hinge-pin for the remainder of the design concept formulation process going as far as is needed.

CONCLUSION

The Seven-step Continuum fills a yawning gap between issues and their resolutions. It is the current practice to perform "instant design" on some of the most difficult and complex parts of a system. Aircraft have their size, weight, crew complement, power and configuration decided within days of deciding that a new aircraft is needed. Organizations re-organize themselves along lines provided by an external consultant after a day's consultation when only they have the essential understanding. Manufacturers introduce automated production lines because "information technology is obviously going to help". And so on.

In particular, there is a convention, particularly in larger organizations, that users say what they need, managers decide what the solution should look like, procurers get from the market place what they *think* the manager described and what he *thought* the user needed. Not only is this tenuous chain of information extremely fragile, but results can take so long that the users' needs have changed.

The Seven-step Continuum brings all the parties together, particularly including the user, to overcome misunderstanding and to produce a creative concept in which all have participated and hence to which all are committed. By incorporating sensible strategies and system principles, the result will be the creation of robust systems, *much faster and cheaper*, and *much more likely to resolve the original issue*.

As figure 10.7 illustrates, the Seven-step Continuum draws upon previous chapters for its method and technique. This can be seen more clearly in the following two pages, where each of the steps is elaborated into a fuller process model (see Chapter 6).

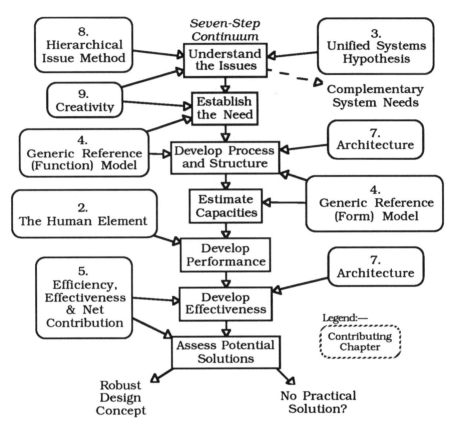

Figure 10.7 Seven-step Continuum—contributing chapters

The following diagram, spread over two pages, is continuous from figure 10.8a to 10.8b; a flow-line is connected from activity 3/5 to activities 4/1, 4/2 and 4/3.

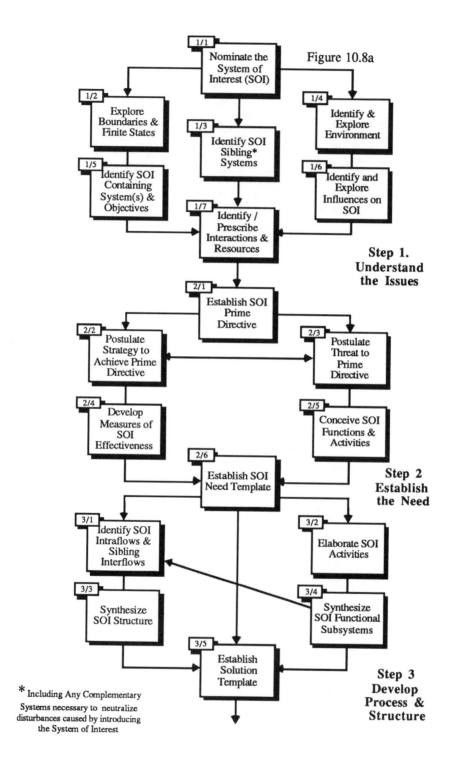

Figure 10.8a

1/1 Nominate the System of Interest (SOI)

1/2 Explore Boundaries & Finite States

1/3 Identify SOI Sibling* Systems

1/4 Identify & Explore Environment

1/5 Identify SOI Containing System(s) & Objectives

1/6 Identify and Explore Influences on SOI

1/7 Identify / Prescribe Interactions & Resources

**Step 1.
Understand
the Issues**

2/1 Establish SOI Prime Directive

2/2 Postulate Strategy to Achieve Prime Directive

2/3 Postulate Threat to Prime Directive

2/4 Develop Measures of SOI Effectiveness

2/5 Conceive SOI Functions & Activities

2/6 Establish SOI Need Template

**Step 2
Establish
the Need**

3/1 Identify SOI Intraflows & Sibling Interflows

3/2 Elaborate SOI Activities

3/3 Synthesize SOI Structure

3/4 Synthesize SOI Functional Subsystems

3/5 Establish Solution Template

**Step 3
Develop
Process &
Structure**

* Including Any Complementary Systems necessary to neutralize disturbances caused by introducing the System of Interest

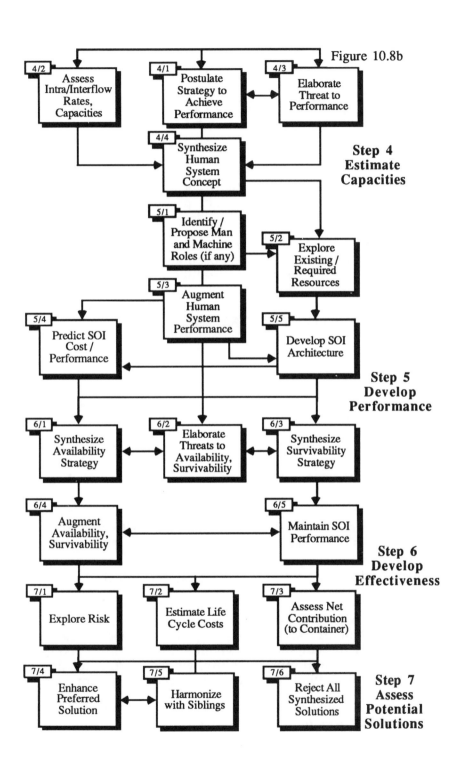

Figure 10.8b

4/2 Assess Intra/Interflow Rates, Capacities	**4/1** Postulate Strategy to Achieve Performance	**4/3** Elaborate Threat to Performance

4/4 Synthesize Human System Concept

Step 4 Estimate Capacities

5/1 Identify / Propose Man and Machine Roles (if any)

5/2 Explore Existing / Required Resources

5/3 Augment Human System Performance

5/4 Predict SOI Cost / Performance

5/5 Develop SOI Architecture

Step 5 Develop Performance

6/1 Synthesize Availability Strategy

6/2 Elaborate Threats to Availability, Survivability

6/3 Synthesize Survivability Strategy

6/4 Augment Availability, Survivability

6/5 Maintain SOI Performance

Step 6 Develop Effectiveness

7/1 Explore Risk

7/2 Estimate Life Cycle Costs

7/3 Assess Net Contribution (to Container)

7/4 Enhance Preferred Solution

7/5 Harmonize with Siblings

7/6 Reject All Synthesized Solutions

Step 7 Assess Potential Solutions

Chapter 10.3
Conceiving Cases

Example is always more efficacious than precept.
Samuel Johnson, 1709-1784

The Seven-step Continuum (SSC) can be tested as a useful approach by employing it against real-world problems. As an example, consider the company change management system which emerged as a potential solution to the first issue case study in Chapter 8.2. The case study which follows will go through steps 2 and 3 in the SSC only, since the first step has been addressed and the last four steps are too detailed to serve as a useful example.

THE SEVEN-STEP PROGRESS

Establish the Need

A change management system stirs different emotions in different breasts. To expand understanding of the projected system further, employ stakeholder analysis from Chapter 9. Stakeholders and their objectives include:

- *Company directors.* Increased throughput. Reduced operating costs. Reduced inventory
- *Company managers.* Reassignments to new tasks. Identification of new skills. management of recruiting. Training needs
- *Employees.* Job security. Job satisfaction. Better wages and conditions
- *Shareholders.* Improved return on capital employed

Using interpretive structural modelling (Chapter 9), these various stakeholders' objectives can be structured as Shown in Figure 10.9. The intent structure shows a dichotomous viewpoint; clearly, the corporate and the employee viewpoints do not entirely concur—or do they? From the intent structure, we may formulate the Prime Directive (or mission) of the change management system as follows:

To improve company performance in the market place while giving employees greater job satisfaction.

Implicit in the Prime Directive is an understanding that fulfilled, well-trained employees will contribute to improved company performance. (Interestingly, while many employers seem even today to question the contribution of training to company performance, few would suggest that poorly-trained employees would perform well. The accepted negative thought does not seem to lead to the expected positive action.) Explicit, and taken from Chapter 8.2, is the concern with marketplace, referring both to company performance and to attracting and retaining employees. The intent structure also shows that identification of new skills (as dictated by market needs) and reassignment of employees to new tasks consistent with the market need are pervasive or systemic objectives. Lastly, reassignments and recruiting management are pivotal within the objectives hierarchy.

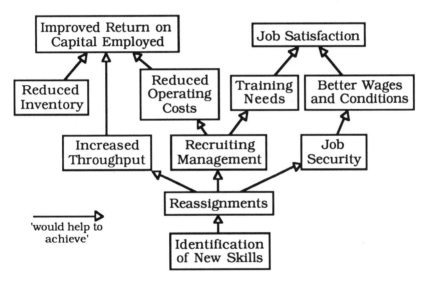

Figure 10.9 Change management system intent structure

Identifying Change Management System Components

To identify components of the system, we may employ the Generic Reference (Function) Model of Chapter 4, as shown in the table. Each functional unit is conceived to satisfy the appropriate component of the model. So, the market research unit is needed to collect and analyse market information in support of mission management. The company performance unit is needed to establish company data and to observe change as it occurs. "Change goals" refers to the setting of mission objectives, since the essential mission is change management. The change planning unit formulates strategy and plans. "Change operations" undertakes the hands-on control, under the eye of the change manager, who is responsible for synergy within viability management—he or she must establish communications and co-ordinate change activities across the company. "Change organization" is the structure within which that communication and co-ordination will take place. A change steering and review panel is needed to ensure that the change management system itself evolves and continues to perform. Such a panel might include external experts and consultants. The change management system, essentially human in nature, may none-the-less need some facilities—processors, software, communications, meeting rooms, stationery—which is provided, and updated periodically, by the change system facilities unit. A separate unit, change facilities purchasing, may be needed to acquire special facilities under resource management where change training may also reside.

Table 10.1 Generic Reference (Function) Model—change management sub-system generation

Mission Management	Viability Management	Resource Management
Market research unit	Change manager	Change facilities Purchasing
Company performance unit	Change organization	
Change goals	Change steering and review panel	Change training
Change planning unit	Change facilities management	
Change operations		

Using the GRM as a guide results in a seeming proliferation of functional sub-systems; each is justifiable however, which is the strength of the approach. (Where Table 10.1 has been left blank, the assumption is that the change management system will either not require a specific sub-system, or that it will make use of common company facilities.)

These various sub-systems may be structured into a functional architecture using the N^2 Chart, as in Figure 10.10. The sub-systems were entered into the original N^2 chart in alphabetical order, clustered, links added to enhance structure, and reclustered. (Sub-system titles are truncated by the computer tool used in this example. The clustering is slightly sub-optimal, but pragmatic.)

Market Research	1	A 1			
Performance Unit	2	1 B 1			
Ch.Steering Panel	3	1 C 1 1			
Ch. Goals	4	1 D 1			1
Ch.Manager	5	1 1 F 1			
Ch. Organization	6	1 H 1			
Ch.Training	7	1 J 1			
Ch.Operations	8	1 K 1			
Ch.Facilities	9	1 I 1			
Ch. Fac.Purchasin	10	1 G 1			
Ch. Planning	11	1		1 E	

Figure 10.10 Change management system—clustered N^2 chart

From the simple N^2 chart of Figure 10.10, a system interaction diagram may be drawn up, as in Figure 10.11.

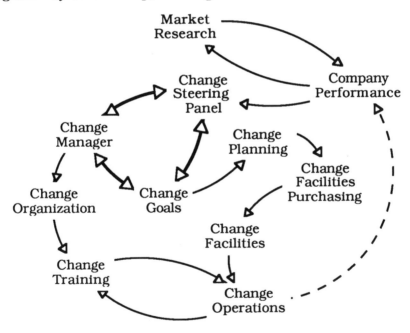

Figure 10.11 System interaction diagram—change management system

The change management system shows the functionally-bound block from the N^2 chart connected by heavier lines, and an implicit feedback as a dotted line from "change operations" to "company performance".

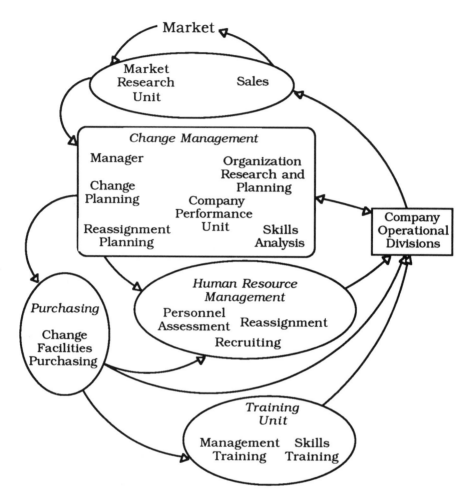

Figure 10.12 Outline change management system design concept

By this stage. we have completed most of step 3, although the full need template has outstanding elements which will be left to the reader to complete. Still outstanding, too, is the establishment of a solution template. Typical solution templates were presented in Chapter 5.1.

Step 4 in the SSC invokes the estimation of capacities. To undertake this task necessitates knowledge of the specific situation, company, contemporary skills, market state and many more. None of these is inherently difficult, but each is detailed and inappropriate to this example. To illustrate the point, however, consider the model shown in Figure 10.13. It is driven by the market and the organization's need to respond to it. Sensibly, a plan would be hinged about the acquisition and analysis of marketing and company data, perhaps on a monthly basis. This periodicity in turn invokes a calculable amount of work each month and hence the capacity required of that part of the interacting systems can be established.

Similarly, there is a need to overcome the natural resistance to change within the company, and its inertia must be balanced against the rate of change essential to catch up with the market. Suppose the organization had eight major sections. One strategy would be to train each section within the company for one week at a time on an eight-weekly cycle, say, returning to the first when the last had been completed—a sort of Forth Bridge painting enterprise, with no end. This strategy would be broken down into a set of activities—see Chapter 6—and the amount of work to be achieved in each eight-week cycle would be assessed. Each section would receive different information, pertaining to the following eight weeks, during each retraining session, and the set of data would include objectives, targets, goals, progress, obstacles, etc.

Note that the interacting system diagram, Figure 10.13, represents a systems model—it is not an information systems diagram, nor an organizational diagram, nor yet an influence diagram. It can be used as a common high-level basis for all of these and more however. Note, too, the avoidance of organograms, those "wiring" diagrams frequently used to show who works for whom. In the opinion of many, they should be banned as unhelpful, since they lack any indication of how work—or anything else—is to be achieved. The systems interaction diagram shows the essential flow of interactions and substance between systems that will make the overall system respond to the external market place. Note, too, that the use of continuous loops in the design development process obviates the need to weight and score the supposed relative merits of various departments—all are seen as members of the one team.

SUMMARY

This chapter has illustrated some of the more unusual aspects of design concept evolution. Several linked techniques have been employed which are valuable, but the SSC is not essentially based on any particular techniques or tools. It is a framework for developing system design concepts from issues, and any methods which achieve tasks within the framework are valuable.

The SSC has been formed by action research, and it is a living framework in the sense that its design is not finalized and fixed— rather it is a skeleton, upon which may be hung at appropriate points new or different tasks, while others may be removed as not relevant to a particular project. In this way the SSC can continue to evolve.

Chapter 11
Classic Systems Engineering

O descend as dove or
A furious papa or a mild engineer, but descend
W. H. Auden, 1907-1973

INTRODUCTION

The Objectives

The perceived objectives of systems engineering vary according to perspective. At the left of Figure 11.1 is the viewpoint which might be taken by a manufacturing company, i.e. that the purpose of systems engineering is to reduce risk, but that in so doing, its cost must be less than the expected loss to revenue which would otherwise accrue, where 'expected loss' might be the product of risk

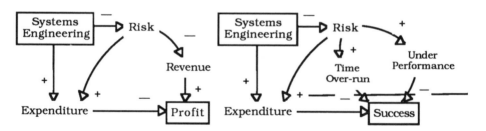

Figure 11.1 Systems engineering objectives—viewpoints

(as a probability) with potential revenue loss. A procuring organization might see things more along the lines of the right hand diagram. For example, a systems group procuring sub-systems for a North Sea oil drilling rig might be more concerned with meeting the very brief window of opportunity which arises each year during which the rig can be launched and towed out to position. To them success might mean more than simply short-term profit. Yet a third view can be taken, and is not expressed in either diagram. This is the view that some tasks are so complex that, without the disciplines imposed by systems engineering, there would be no prospect of achieving the task at any price.

System Life-span—the Seven Ages of System

A system may be thought of as having seven "ages" by analogy with the seven ages of Man. The Seven Ages of System are shown in Figure 11.2, with a new system in the centre supplanting its predecessor only to be replaced in its turn by the system at the right. The figure offers an interesting insight. If a succeeding system is to be ready in time, it is necessary to anticipate the demise of the current system in sufficient time to develop its replacement. This notion presents a self-fulfilling prophecy—the new system will succeed because it is available, even if, in the event, the original system has survived and is in full vigour.

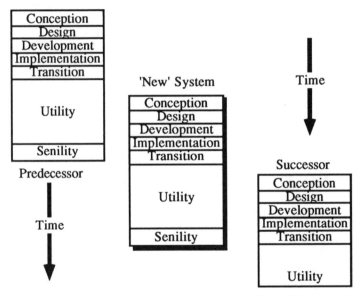

Figure 11.2 The seven ages of system. Reproduced by permission of the Institution of Electrical Engineers

A second insight from Figure 11.2 concerns the need to transfer information between replaced and successor systems. Smooth transition from one to the other dictates that information be accumulated and stored in such a way that it may be extracted and transferred with ease. This is not generally considered in the design of systems. In general, we consider the problem of replacement in singularly few of our systems—witness the problems being literally set in concrete by deep pile-driving of buildings in London, for which there is no known way of replacement.

Transition is also evident in the figure as important—it is, perhaps, the point of stepping from the sinking ship to the life-raft. It is all the more surprising, then, to find curt attention paid to transition in most system designs, which concentrate instead on perceiving the future system in its flowing prime of utility.

System Life cycle

Systems vary in their effectiveness and cost of ownership throughout their lives, as shown in Figure 11.3. Ages of system are mapped on to the axes, as shown; note the x-axis is "cost per unit time". Following the thick arrow, costs rise as the system emerges from development into implementation and into operational usage. Transition—hopefully—sees a gradual fall-off in operating costs as infant mortalities disappear, systematic faults are ironed out and users[1] become familiar. Gradually the system transitions to the top left-hand part of the graph, the age of utility, where it is most effective and costs least to own. From there it is all downhill towards senility and eventual replacement. What causes the demise? We design technological systems with certain fixed features, the value and currency of which erodes with time. Some are shown in the Figure; for example, our system interacts with many others in operation, and these others are continually changing. Our system may have a limited capacity for expansion and change, which becomes used up—hence the onset of senility.

THE ROLE OF SYSTEMS ENGINEERING

The systems engineer or practitioner creates systems in a structured, ordered way. Not all of the activities involved in creating systems are "systems engineering", however. Some are well-understood, conventional engineering activities, responding to clear requirements and often pursued by engineers and technicians trained in conventional, singular disciplines. These are not the work of the systems practitioner; instead, these are defined here as being the province of the project engineer whose purpose is to satisfy a specified requirement.

The systems practitioner, on the other hand, is concerned essentially with the conception and design of two types of system: the application system, to be delivered to a customer; and the engineering system required to produce that application system.

---

[1] Note the implication, general to classic systems engineering, that the users receive the system—they are not, themselves, in the system

Systems engineering as a discipline seeks to provide application systems to customers and users which meet their needs and which can be operated and maintained effectively throughout their intended life. Systems engineering is a whole-system, whole-life, multi-disciplined activity.

The systems practitioner develops, often from an uncertain or "fuzzy" requirement, a model of the application system as it will exist in the future. This model is used to guide subsequent design, development and implementation decisions. The systems practitioner:

- Develops a potential overall design solution
- Partitions it into a mutually-consistent, complete set of sub-systems
- Specifies each sub-system, together with all the consequent intra-connections between the sub-systems that partitioning generates

The sub-systems are developed and integrated into the final application system. The systems practitioner must continually resolve issues which arise during the process of implementing the application system. This is done by reference to the model.

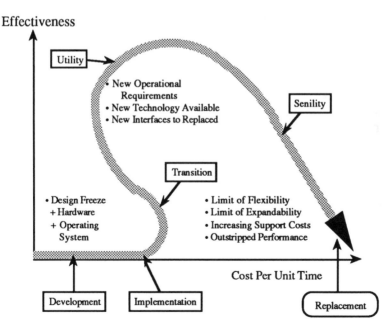

Figure 11.3 The developed system's life cycle. Reproduced by permission of the Institution of Electrical Engineers

SYSTEM PARTITIONING

The partitioning process, vital to the success of the eventual application system, is seen as a core activity, one which may need continual revision throughout the development process and beyond. Partitioning generates the need for:

- Interfaces
- Relationships
- Connections
- Communications
- Protocols
- Control

Partitioning generates the need to manage:

- Flows, particularly of data and information, between sub-systems
- The emergent properties of the system

To achieve requisite operational availability, for example, the reliability and maintainability of the sub-systems formed by partitioning must combine to ensure that the availability target is met. Similarly, if there is a requirement for survivability, partitioning must be such as to achieve that emergent property.
    Partitioning also responds to other major influences; it seeks to provide practical, economic ways in which the application or engineering system might be realized. Partitioning must:

- Recognize the rôle and availability of suitable technology
- Recognize the creating organization's abilities
- Examine the suitability of existing sub-systems
- Consider costs and time scales
- Allow for the customer-organization's ability to maintain that technology
- Consider constraints of installation, the process of integration and test, and many more

In particular, partitioning ascribes some system functions to the end-user, so creating the most difficult of all interfaces, that between man and machine. In selecting those tasks within the overall system most appropriate to the human operators, the systems practitioner has to consider the end-user's skill, training and environment under which operation will occur. An end user under stress, or wearing special clothing, for example, may not respond or be as nimble as otherwise.

Systems engineers and practitioners practise in all these areas and many more beside. The systems practitioner is thus concerned both with the design of the application system and with the design of the engineering system required to implement it.

Note that project engineers contribute to the system design and partitioning process, using their specialist knowledge of particular engineering disciplines. Note also that, while systems practitioners may design the application and engineering systems, project engineers develop and implement those systems. (N.B. An individual may switch between systems and project engineering rôles while working on projects.)

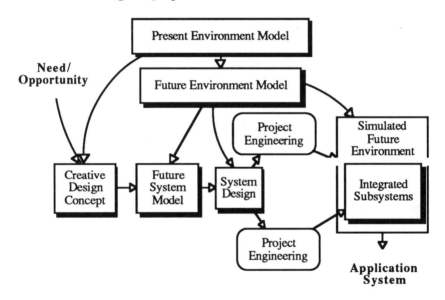

Figure 11.4 Systems engineering perspective

Figure 11.4 shows the creation of an application system, in response to a need or opportunity. Systems engineering is concerned initially with developing models and designs of the future application system, and with the future environment in which the application system will perform, including future changes.

Project engineers:

- Develop, construct and integrate the parts of the application system

- Develop, construct and integrate a simulated environment for its evaluation
- Develop, construct and integrate an environment for its construction (the Engineering System)

Figure 11.4 brings these activities together in the box at the right hand side as activities for project engineering.
Systems practitioners:

- Resolve any system-relevant issues arising during project engineering
- Resolve any system-relevant issues arising during the test and integration processes
- Use their models of the future system and future operational environment as references

System-relevant issues are those affecting emergent properties of the sub-systems or the overall system, or the partitioning characteristics. The test and integration process is therefore a dual arena for both project engineers and systems practitioners.

TRADITIONAL SYSTEMS ENGINEERING CREATIVITY

The by-now classical principles of creativity are presented below:

Highest level of abstraction
Breadth before depth
Level at a time
Disciplined anarchy
Decomposition before integration
Functional before physical
Tight functional binding
Loose functional coupling
Functional migrates to physical

The principles, collected over the years from a variety of sources—including "doing it wrong"—are worth a closer look:
Highest level of abstraction. This is the cardinal rule when approaching a new problem situation or design concept. It is essential to gain a panoramic view of the situation which removes the confusion of detail. Only by actively and assiduously pursuing

this principle, is it possible for the analyst to see his own prejudice and rise above it.

Breadth before depth and *level at a time.* Similar concepts aimed at successively reducing the level of abstraction in an orderly and coherent fashion. These principles oppose the tendency to concentrate prematurely on parts of the design problem in depth, to the exclusion of other parts and of the overall design. Breadth-before-depth implies covering the whole problem "in the round", while level-at-a-time implies that each level of abstraction/decomposition should be completed before descending to the next. Together, they provide an ethic of orderly progress.

Disciplined anarchy. It is essential to create an environment in which new ideas may flourish, rather than "hit the cutting room floor" before being given a real chance. Ideas are generally the province of the young—in mind if not in body—and are incompatible with strict, authoritarian control. Timescales and budgets have to be met, however, and so the principle of Disciplined Anarchy emerges—set periods when creative juices are encouraged and negative thoughts are banned. Organized brain storming and idea writing are among the many approaches to achieving the objective—see Chapter 9.

Decomposition before integration. This principle, taken with the first, proposes that creativity requires the examination of the component parts of a solution prior to their being grouped and assembled. Without such decomposition, often a major task, it is not possible to see how best to combine the various elements of a solution

Functional before physical This principle proposes that it is essential to be concerned with the purpose of the solution before becoming embroiled in its form.

Tight functional binding and *loose functional coupling.* Both principles have been discussed in Chapter 7.

Functional migrates to physical. This principle is self-evident, but can be overlooked in the heat of concept formulation. Eventually, all the functions are going to be realized in some physical form. The grouping of functions for functions' sake is not the end of the matter; functions become bedfellows for physical reasons, too. The archetypal example is, perhaps, the I/O (input/output) for a processing system: functionally, I and O are at opposite ends of the process; physically, their construction is generally very similar and hence they are often grouped together.

It is interesting to note that the principles of creativity find echoes in other spheres, notably art and music. Discussions with painters in oils and with composers indicate that their approach to composition is very similar, suggesting strongly that creativity in the systems arena is linked to creativity in other spheres. For engineers to resort to such notions is unusual, perhaps, but the nature of systems engineering demands an unusual approach. It is within this context that systems practitioners have developed techniques and methods which can only be described as arcane, or at best *ad hoc.*

SYSTEMS ENGINEERING—PROCESS AND TOOLS

Systems Engineering Process

Systems engineering is a discipline with its particular skills, methods and tools. The Guide to Proper Practice[2] of Systems Engineering at the end of the book identifies a *minimum set* of necessary and sufficient tasks; in view of the wide variety of applications, it is not for the Guide to explain in detail how they might be undertaken. There is, however, a widely accepted procedure for system design, as follows:

- Formulate the requisite emergent properties of the application system as a solution-transparent requirement (i.e. ignore supposed solutions until the requirement has been established, to avoid pre-judgement)
- Identify the functions (activities) of the application system necessary to generate the activity-related emergent properties
- Progressively decompose the functions into sub-functions until they can be realised in practical engineering terms
- Group the sub-functions into realizable physical groups—develop optional system architecture(s) and technologies to generate the remaining application system emergent properties
- Develop measures of application system effectiveness and performance
- Evaluate optional solution architectures, technologies, etc., using these measures and, perhaps, models of potential solutions
- Select the preferred option

A set of tools typical of those which systems practitioners might use to help them undertake the tasks is shown below.

The "Missing Tools"

The need for a systems engineers' toolset can be envisaged by systems engineering phases as shown in Figure 11.5. Having a

---

[2] Developed by John Boarder, of Buckingham College, Patrick Ruthven Moore, of Patrick Moore Associates, and myself.

"shadowboard" is useful—it tells what tools are needed—but is, of course, no substitute for the tools themselves

The "shadowboard" of tools is not evenly filled. Scenario models, software requirements tools, environment simulation, logistic models and many more are in abundance. (Requirements tools generally support functional decomposition, but do not execute the decomposition themselves—that is in the mind of the operator.) RAM/FMECA—Reliability, Availability, Maintainability/Failure Modes, Effects and Criticality Analysis—is undertaken quite comprehensively. On the other hand, the following are not in evidence:

System boundary models
Functional decomposition
Functional to physical mapping
Relationship model
Architecture design tools
System design and engineering framework models
Risk models

Operations Analysis	Requirements Analysis	System Design	Project Engineering	Integration and Test	Installation & Commissioning
Solution feasibility & Performance	Requirements consistency & completeness	Design options, interfaces, tradeoffs & specifications	Configuration, compatibility, interchange	Test environment	Customer acceptance

Scenario Models	System Models			Environment Simulation	
	Relationship Models				
System boundary models	Requirements Tools			Threat Simulation	Acceptance Models
	Human engineering				
	Logistics Models			Sub-system Simulation	
Risk Models	RAM/FMECA				
Functional Decomposition	Networks & Architectures		Configuration management tools		
	System Prototyping		Interface control tools		
	Functional/physical mapping		Data management tools		
System design and engineering framework model					
Cost, planning and scheduling tools and models					

Figure 11.5 The systems' engineers tool-shadowboard

Likely avenues of advance to be found in this book are as follows:

System boundary models.............................Causal loop modelling
Functional decomposition.................The Generic Reference Model
Functional to physical mapping.......N^2 chart and cluster analysis
Relationship models...N^2 chart
Architecture design tools...................N^2 chart and cluster analysis
Frameworks................................Creating and conceiving systems

Risk management ....Process modelling, TRIAD building system

Robert J. Lano

Robert Lano is a software and systems engineer who was specializing in methodologies at the end of the 1970s. Regrettably, like many employees of companies, he seems to have published little in the way of papers or books—see Lano (1979, 1980). His lectures were excellent however. He has shown how, using four essentially simple, hand-operated techniques, it is possible to unravel, understand, redesign and re-integrate complex systems. His insight is concerned with levels of abstraction, viewpoints and architecture. His toolset has found wide use in many companies throughout the western world's industry; this book uses the methods (as I have come to apply them—I have modified their application from, principally, software analysis to general system analysis).

CO-ORDINATION			
Structured Design	N2 Charts	Data State Design	SREM Design (R-Nets)
DEFINES:			
Functions Hierarchy	Interfaces Relationships	Data Files Data Relations	Transactions Data Flows
DOES NOT DEFINE:			
Data Files Interfaces Data Flows Transactions	Hierarchy Data Files Transactions Data Relations	Functions Hierarchy Data flows Interfaces	Hierarchy Interfaces Data Relations Relationships

Figure 11.6 Lano's toolset

The Lano Toolset and the Viewpoints

The four tools introduced by Lano were: N^2 Charts, Data State Design, R-Nets and Structured Analysis. Lano did not invent all of these tools. R-Nets, or Requirement Nets are part of a US programme called SREM, Software Requirements Engineering Methodology, see Alford (1985). The R-Net technique is finding application in Manufacturing Systems Design, (Hughes 1986). Data State Design is said by Lano to have been produced by Peterson of IBM. Lano is credited with bringing them together, however, and for using them together to develop differing viewpoints of the system in question. Structured Analysis is well known and documented, (Ross 1977; Ross and Schoman1977; Gane and Sarson1979). Lano seems to have been responsible for recognizing the true potential of the N^2 chart and, of course, for bringing the tools together in a matched set. The viewpoints, advantages and limitations of the four tools are shown in Figure 11.6 and it can be seen that all four tools had to be used concurrently to address any problem at system level. The tools will be seen in use in this book.

Lano's insight unlocked the door to understanding for many designers and systems engineers; he was seminal and inspirational, but, it seems, singularly unrecognized.

SYSTEMS ENGINEERING—ORGANIZATION AND METHODS

Systems engineering is associated with the engineering of large and/or complex systems. Generally, the size of the tasks invokes the formation of teams to undertake systems engineering and the process of creating a system has to be phased. Individual systems engineers may find themselves associated with less than the whole range of potential activities; that does not diminish their rôle as systems engineers. It is for the organization as a whole to address the full range of systems engineering activities.

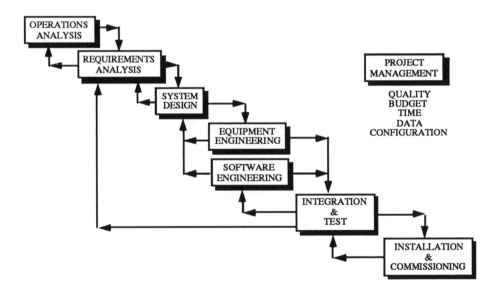

Figure 11.7 Systems engineering phases

The phases employed in the creation of systems also vary, as do the titles ascribed to each phase, but can generally be considered under the following headings (see Figure 11.7) :

- *Operations/requirements analysis*—understanding, agreeing and specifying the customer's requirement and the end-users' needs

- *System design*—designing the application system which will be delivered to the customer to meet the requirement, together with an engineering system to effect the creation of the application system

- *System development/production/manufacture/implementation*

- *System test and integration*—bringing together of the various parts from which the application system is to be formed and establishing that the whole meets the requirement

- *System commissioning*—demonstrating to the customer, often at the site where the system is to operate, that it meets its requirement

Systems engineers have rôles in all these phases and during the subsequent phases when the application system is in operation. Figure 11.7 shows typical phases of an information-based project and their relationships in a so-called "waterfall" diagram, with feedback being invoked as developing work needs to be redone—a not-unusual happening in the best of regulated circles.

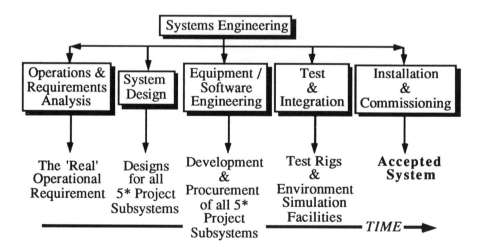

Figure 11.8 Systems engineering—typical project phases

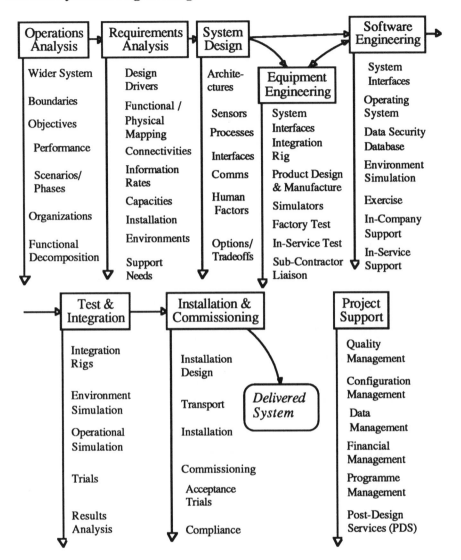

Figure 11.9 Systems engineering activities

System Project Team Structure

Figure 11.8 represents organizational structure. The five project sub-systems referred to are:

- The primary system which the customer wants
- The in-service maintenance system needed to keep it

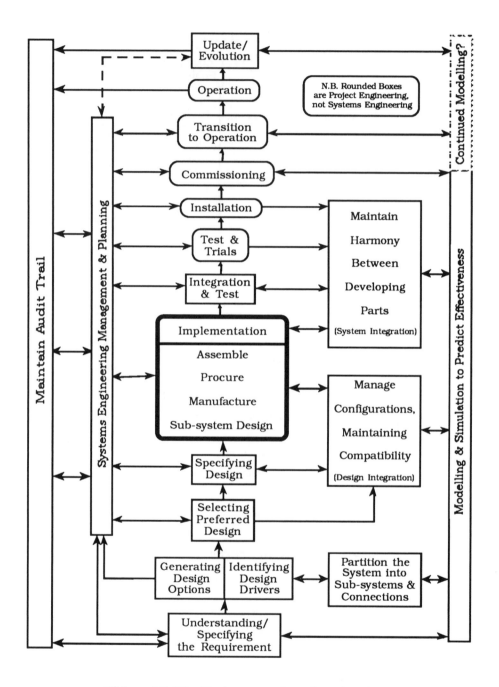

Figure 11.10 Systems engineering structure

operating
- The in-service training system to train users and maintainers
- The in-company engineering system needed to develop it
- The in-company maintenance system needed to keep the engineering system operating

Whether a purchaser of an operational system is aware of it or not, all five sub-systems must be bought for any reasonably complex system—although not necessarily from the same supplier. Thus the purchase of one system generates a plethora of related purchases, not all visible initially to the customer who may develop an optimistic view of likely system cost in consequence.

Systems Engineering Activities

Figure 11.9 shows activities associated with an information technology-based project. Generally, the phases are sequential from left to right, but with two exceptions: equipment and software engineering (project engineering, as opposed to systems engineering) occur at the same time; the right hand column, project support, exists for the duration of the project and is not phased.

An alternative representation is shown at Figure 11.10, after an idea by Mike Smithard of Marconi[3]. The diagram shows activities from concept to in-service update.

Systems Engineering Span

The coverage of systems engineering is potentially almost limitless, since it can, in principle, be applied to almost any system. A typical list of activities with which systems engineers may become involved is as follows:

Mission analysis	Mission system design	System architecture	System requirements	Reliability, availability, maintainability
Man-machine interface	Human-computer interface	Human engineering	System specification	Trade-off analysis
Programming languages	Work breakdown structures	Statements of work	Master schedules	Risk management
Software development planning	Software requirements specification	Failure modes, effects and criticality analysis	Safety management Design to cost	Design reviews and red teaming

---

[3] Mike Smithard introduced this representation into a working party developing National Vocational Qualifications for Systems Engineering in which the author also participated.

Configuration management	Interface control documentation	Programme management	Data management	Quality management
Cost estimation	Electro magnetic compatibility	Integration and test	Test and trials, Trials analysis	Mock-ups and prototypes
Programme evaluation and review technique	Field support	Logistic support analysis	Integrated logistic support	Spares provisioning
Spares provisioning	Design change control	Test and support equipment	Automatic test equipment	Special-to-type support
Software support facilities	Operator training facilities	Configuration identification	Warranty	Modifications and mod. management
Software management	Survivability analysis	Damage tolerance	Maintenance manuals	Operations manuals
Technical publications	Training requirements	Training facilities	Maintenance training	On-the-job training
Life cycle costing	Repair and maintenance philosophies	Etc.	Etc.	Etc.

Work Breakdown

The information presented above is indicative only; it is incomplete and in a form unsuitable for the management of large jobs. For these, some form of work breakdown structure (WBS) is necessary to show all the tasks in sufficient resolution, their mutual relationships and inputs and outputs.

One convenient way to show a WBS is to use Lano's R-Net presentation—see page 130. The R-Net, Figure 11.11, shows the first level of WBS for establishing the basic needs of a systems project. Each box would be further divided progressively until boxes represented tasks that an individual or small team could accomplish; such WBSs can be very large, reaching several thousands of tasks.

Functional Decomposition

The process of functional decomposition has been mentioned several times. This is a difficult topic, nonetheless so because there seems to be little agreement about what constitutes a function in the first place. It is quite possible to use modern decomposition tools as they are intended to be used, but starting from the wrong notion of a function, and so producing rubbish. Figure 11.12 is a simple example of Data State Design (DSD), used for functional decomposition. Note that the Figure is not a flow chart. The ovals contain data, not function, whereas flow-chart boxes predominantly contain process. With DSD, the processes are implied by the arrows. The advantages of DSD is that it maintains the level of abstraction, identifies essential information and progressively decomposes down to data, without regard to physical boundaries or interfaces. In Figure 11.12, the decomposition from level 1 to level 2 is straightforward, but specific and creative. The insertion of a system boundary line identifies data and process internal to the System of Interest, processes which exchange data with other systems and the essential external data. DSD is a useful technique, although it has to be said that it takes some getting used to if you are used to flow-charting; still, the effort is worthwhile.

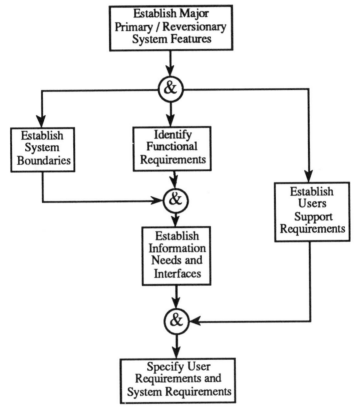

Figure 11.11 Operations and requirements analysis, first level. Reproduced by permission of the Institution of Electrical Engineers

Options and Tradeoffs

Systems practitioners inevitably become embroiled in tradeoffs. The usual method is some form of weighting and scoring, in which a set of design options is entered into a matrix against a set of measures of effectiveness/performance. Each measure is weighted according to perceived importance, each option is scored against each measure, scores are multiplied by weights and aggregated. The highest weighted score wins—see Chapter 5 for effectiveness.

Allocation of Resources to Tasks

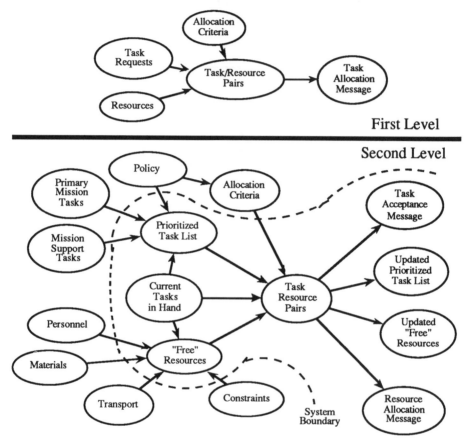

Figure 11.12 Data State Design and functional decomposition.
Reproduced by permission of the Institution of Electrical Engineers

This approach satisfies many participants but is highly suspect. Weighting is highly subjective and viewpoint dependent. Scoring is similarly difficult to do. Aggregated scores may show one solution as marginally better than another, but with no degree of confidence. and so on.

A far better scheme is to rank, as shown in Table 11.1. We find it easy to rank, to say that A is better than B. We find it much less simple to say by *how much* A is better than B, which is what scoring demands[4]. The example is concerned with an operations control centre, and the design choice of how many and of what type the operator displays should be.

Table 11.1 Display system option tradeoff table—Rank Matrix Analysis (RMA). Reproduced by permission of the Institution of Electrical Engineers

| Design Drivers | Sub-Drivers | Display System Options [5] (Example Only) | | | | | |
		1 a	2 a	1 a+ 1 g	1 g	2 g	Row Sums
Utility	Performance	5	4	2	3	1	15
	Fallback	4.5	2	2	4.5	2	15
Availability	Reliability	4	2	3	5	1	15
	Maintainability						
Adaptability	Flexibility	5	4	2	3	1	15
	Expandability						
Interoperability	Communi- cations						
	Protocols						
Usability	Human Factors	5	3	4	2	1	15
	MMI	3	4	5	1	2	15
Safety	Development						
	Operation						
	Maintenance						
	Disposal						
Survivability	Avoidance of Detection						
	Self Defence						
	Damage Tolerance	4.5	3	2	4.5	1	15
Security	Data						
	Physical						
	Rank Sum	31	22	20	23	9	105
	Rank Order	5th	3rd	2nd	4th	1st	

Coefficient of Concordance = 0.5102
Probability of Random Occurrence < 1%

The table contains ranks in rows, always summing to the same value (15 in the example); so, for performance, two full-colour graphics displayed is the first choice. Not all rows are relevant and are not filled in. Columns are summed and the column containing the *least* sum appears to be the winner. To be sure, it is possible to analyse the pattern of numbers to see with what probability they

---

[4] If option A scores 4 and option B scores 8, does this mean that B is twice as good as A? What would "twice as good" mean?

[5] α means an alpha-numeric display, γ means a graphic display which can also show alphas

might simply have occurred randomly (the null hypothesis). In the example, such a probability is less than 1%. This strongly suggests that the complete pattern is not random, and in consequence we may rest assured that the rank order shown in the last row is real—for all the pattern at once. Not only does this show the fifth option as preferred, but it simultaneously confirms the others in rank order.

Table 11.2 Systems/project/quality management specifications

	Systems requirement	Systems design & development	Project control	Quality assurance
Standards for specification of:	Boundaries Objectives Performance User's organization Connectivities Capacities Information exchanges Operational environments Exercise and training RAM/EMC/EMP Functional description Interoperability Security	Architecture Design Support Interfaces ICDs Operating systems Information management applications Integration and test Installation and commissioning Acceptance	Life cycle plans Procurement plans Integration and test Plans Demonstration and acceptance plans Transition-to-use plans	Design quality plans Development quality plans System proving quality plans
Standard Procedures for:	Requirements analysis Bounding systems Functional description Functional decomposition Functional-to-physical mapping RAM analysis	Design Partitioning Test and integration Installation and commissioning Customer support/PDS Estimating Optimization tradeoffs	Planning system design Planning system development Monitoring progress Data management Configuration management Reviewing standards Reviewing procedures	Design audit Development audit Development procedure audit Project control audit Quality plans review Quality audit reviews

I call this process Rank Matrix Analysis (RMA). It is powerful, but many still cling to weighting and scoring because they find it easier to understand/manipulate. In practice, it is sensible to employ both methods in parallel—one to satisfy the group, the other to satisfy the problem—and to compare the results.

Specifications and Procedures

One systematic approach to managing complex projects is to control the process and product of each phase by specification. For example, a specification of system requirements would be one of the principal outputs from a requirements analysis phase. For large or complex projects, such specifications are essential and, of course, where software is concerned the specification process has become big business.

A strategy is essential to organize, correlate and manage specifications effectively, and a sensible strategy is suggested in Figure 11.13:

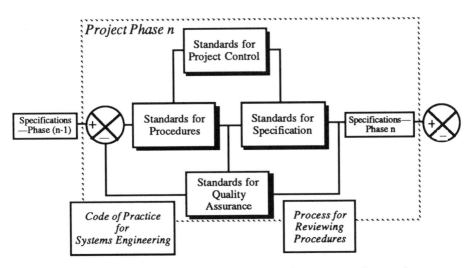

Figure 11.13 Phase specifications and their inter-relationships

Each phase has unique purpose, but standardized approaches and methods are usually appropriate, even essential, to manage and control the flow of work:

- Standards for specifications ensure consistency and completeness
- Standards for procedures guide the systems practitioner as to method, technique, tool, etc., for each of the many

tasks to be undertaken during the phase. For example, a standard procedure might exist for estimating the reliability of a system

- Standards for project control manage the flow of work
- Standards for quality assurance manage the injection and control of quality
- A code of practice for systems engineering provides a reference to what is considered to be the minimum scope and correct practice of systems engineering, and is not necessarily confined to any one phase
- Similarly, the process for reviewing procedures is not restricted to any one phase, but exists instead as a means of preventing standards from becoming organizational strait-jackets

Table 11.2 shows a far-from-exhaustive list of typical standards; note how the standards for procedures contribute to the standards for specification and how one set of standards cross-checks on the performance of another.

The concepts entertained above give natural rise to my notion of creating an integrated systems engineering environment in which creative people, tools, techniques and methods are combined with systematic procedural methods into a comprehensive and high-integrity engineering system—SEAMS.

Systems Engineering Analysis and Management Support Environment (SEAMS)

SEAMS is a notion which could be realized at several quite distinct levels:

- At its simplest, SEAMS could be a paper process model containing a sequenced work breakdown structure and identifying the standards, specifications, tools and methods appropriate to each task
- At the next level of sophistication, the paper process model could be presented as an organized program, with the added advantage that systems practitioners could refer to it easily, progress could be monitored, and particularly that the process model could be a living thing, evolving as experience grew and effectively becoming a "corporate memory", a bank of corporate technique showing "how we go about tackling this type of job". (Increased labour mobility has made dependence on the faithful retainer a thing of the past, rendering a corporate memory essential to many organizations)

- At the highest level of sophistication, SEAMS becomes a fully integrated systems factory, with the systems engineering process controlled by program, practitioners employing computer-assisted tools, data being centrally managed, and so on—see Figure 11.14

SUMMARY

This chapter has presented an overview of the theology and practice of present-day systems engineering. There being no consensus about systems engineering, it is of course open to interpretation. To some, systems engineering is much broader and grander, taking in the full sweep of corporate policy, investment and the like. To others, systems engineering is little more than progress-chasing and trying to make the software work with the hardware.

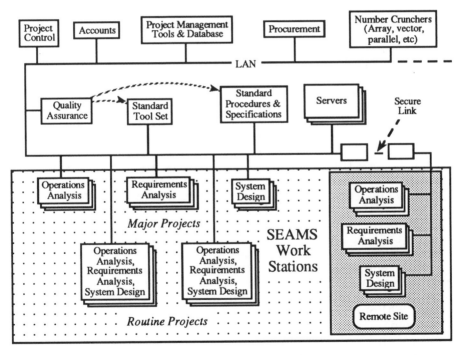

Figure 11.14 A notional full-SEAMS implementation concept

Chapter 12.1
A New Systems
Engineering (NSE)

Nothing more certain than incertainties,
Fortune is full of fresh variety;
Constant is nothing but inconstancy.
The Shepherd's Content,
Richard Barnfield, 1574-1627

SO, WHAT'S WRONG WITH CLASSIC SYSTEMS ENGINEERING?

Attitudes and Understanding

Quite a lot is wrong, really. If you think not, then discuss systems engineering as a discipline with any systems practitioner aged over, say, twenty-eight. Invariably, there are two reactions: too busy to think about such things; a vague dissatisfaction about the lack of theory/lack of success/lack of clarity. Many systems practitioners do not believe that systems engineering is a separate discipline—instead, they prefer to think of it as common sense, although they generally concede that such sense may be far from common.

Further, they may well deny that systems engineering has any special methods or techniques, but is simply an attitude of mind. Such words as 'holistic' will emerge, to encapsulate the 'whole-system' view that most feel intuitively sets systems engineering apart in some degree. They probably would not see systems engineering as strongly related to, or emerging from, Operations Research (or Operational Research, according to taste and country of origin), although every textbook on the subject will show OR as the supposed origin. Textbooks also concentrate heavily on mathematics and optimization, while systems practitioners may find little in either of these to strongly influence their day-to-day activities.

If the run-of-the-mill systems practitioner does not believe in systems engineering, there is indeed a problem. Yet systems engineering has had some spectacular successes. Perhaps the pinnacle of achievement is to be found in the successes in space, with communication satellites, Neil Armstrong and *Voyager*. High-profile mistakes such as the Hubble space telescope can also be seen to have occurred because the simplest of systems engineering practices were not observed—in that case, the failure to integrate and test the complete system prior to launch. (It has to be said that no self-respecting systems engineer would countenance the omission of such a crucial stage in the implementation of such an important one-shot system.)   On the other hand, systems engineering, apparently properly conducted, has been party to some equally spectacular, but distressing, debacles, some in the space business, others notably in aerospace, defence and the stock markets.

Right Approach, Wrong Result?

An interesting aspect of systems engineering is the resistance to it by project supervisors and accountants.   Classic systems engineering strongly emphasizes the initial phases of modelling, research, analysis, whole system design and specification, partitioning, sub-system design and specification and so on.   It contains a careful planning, systematic ethic. Project supervisors, seeing all this preparation and thought, are prone to impatience at the perceived lack of progress towards "cutting metal, punching code".

One major US/NATO tactical communications project was cancelled largely on this account; visiting dignitaries from potential customer countries were dismayed three years into the project to see no hardware but instead to see sophisticated models and simulations of scenarios and future embedded software. The systems engineers working on this international project were proud that they had managed to fend off premature 'metal-bashing' and 'hole-punchery', and at last were doing the systems engineering job properly—full investigation, analysis and planning first. Politics won.

CLOSED SYSTEMS VERSUS OPEN SYSTEMS PHILOSOPHIES

Closed systems Philosophy

Classic systems engineering has developed as a closed systems philosophy. By this, I do not mean that it is not holistic; on the contrary, the approach is to encompass all the systems perceived as relevant (operational, maintenance, training, etc.). Nor do I mean that no account is taken of other systems; interfaces are identified to other systems and are an essential part of classic systems engineering. But interfaces tend to be fixed, once chosen, and the concept of the future system within the interface boundary adapting form and function in response to interchanges across the interfaces is quite alien—unless one counts the notion of incorporating an amount of unused capacity in a system at delivery, "just in case": the idea is admirable, but inadequate, since it seeks to combat the unknown with an arbitrary allowance. A closed systems philosophy exists, too, because of the standard practice of producing a fixed, defined system against a customer's requirement. To systems engineers this may seem wholly admirable, but consider:

- The customer who drew up the requirement may be expert in terms of his or her needs and objectives, without being expert in understanding systems and their (exceedingly complex) interactions
- The requirement addressed a particular situation at a particular time, neither likely to be relevant by the time the system has been implemented and delivered
- The requirement addresses some technologically based solution to a problem which is almost invariably human-centred
- Users involved in specifying the requirement represented their own viewpoint—these users will probably have been replaced by different users with different viewpoints by the time of delivery
- The delivered system changes both the operational environment and the other systems with which it interacts in that environment. In consequence, the new system changes the situation and rules which existed prior to its arrival, generally rendering the original requirement specification *wrong*

The "Engineer's Philosophy"

Against this background, systems practitioners will argue vehemently that they cannot operate if there is no fixed requirement; they cannot design or implement, they cannot deliver against a fluid specification and they certainly cannot operate any other way in a fixed-price contracting environment. Management will support them, so too will the accountants, whose dead hand causes so much "short-termism" in the UK and elsewhere. Yet systems engineering is essentially an open system and the systems it provides for customers are essentially open, too. It is the unfortunate inheritance of systems engineering from conventional hard engineering and from much of classical science that inhibits an open systems attitude.

Amongst soft systems practitioners the term "engineer's philosophy" has emerged. The term embraces the "head-down, slavish adherence to meeting the customer's requirement regardless" attitude which soft practitioners attribute to systems engineers, with some justification. For large-scale and complex systems it is imprudent to meet a customer's requirement blindly, for many reasons:

- Major corporate investment in implementing the customer's requirement may be necessary yet ill-advised. Often the thrill of the competitive chase for a major system contract can blind systems practitioners to the investment risk while at the same time driving down the price and delivery time to beat the competition. Companies can become heavily committed to one or two such systems projects; failure of these can ruin the company concerned.

- The customer may specify requirements poorly—customers do, very regularly—and simply meeting their requirement precisely but blindly may not provide them with what they want or need (often not the same thing). That the company provided the customer with what was specified will be forgotten; that the company produced an unsuccessful system *will* be remembered.

- The customer's requirement may result in a system which will damage the environment, squander scarce resources, endanger populations. In other words, social and ethical questions cannot be ruled out. Engineers generally consider such questions to be dangerous, of course, and to be avoided, but as our systems become larger, more interwoven and complex, the opportunity to avoid consequences diminishes.

Optimization

Classic systems engineering is said to be concerned with optimization. I recently attended a presentation of a concept study into the design of a complex, highly-integrated missile. Each of the several presenters introduced their work: surveillance, tracking, guidance, control, warhead, aerodynamics, propulsion. Each individual had worked hard on his own part and they had then come together, realized that some adjustments were necessary and had "harmonized" the various parts into a missile.

The adjudicators were rightly complimentary about individual performances by the student-designers, but much less so about the overall "system". The missile was too long to fit into transport aircraft or to conceal on the battlefield; it was too expensive; the degree of sophistication needed to achieve its high performance cast doubt on its maintainability; no thought had been given to producing a much cheaper missile and firing salvoes instead of single missiles to achieve the same effect; and so on. The concept study had started in the wrong place; it was no use trying to optimize the parts of the missile and then join them together—that is system integration, not system design. Nor is it any use, at that point of integration, to review the overall result and adjust some of the design parameters—that results in a three-humped camel rather than the hoped-for racehorse.

Open systems Philosophy

Open systems continually interchange energy, substance and information with other systems. They catabolize and anabolize— breakdown and build up—internally, using interflows with other systems to acquire and dispose of energy, substance and information.

All systems are open, saving perhaps the Universe itself. A systems engineering group within a company is an open system: it interchanges people, skills, tools, techniques and ideas with other systems; it can change its size, reduce its entropy and do all the other things that open systems can do that closed systems supposedly cannot.

The systems provided by systems engineers are open systems too. First and foremost they are open to their users to such a degree that users and technology may not be sensibly separable. The combination of user and technology, as a single system, is open to the environment and the sibling systems it contains. The user/technology system will adapt as the sibling interactions and their environment change. And it is principally for this reason that classic systems engineering fails—*it concentrates on producing a fixed technological solution to a continually moving problem.*

Rates of Adaptation

Yet, it has to be said that the concept of adaptation is rather obvious. The dinosaurs died out some 64 million years ago seemingly because the environment underwent a change that was so rapid that they were unable to adapt to it by Darwinian evolution. Simply, environmental rate of change exceeded consequent adaptation rate of change:

For continued system cohesion:
Rate of system adaptation => Rate of change of environment   (12.1)

This simple equation begins to explain why systems engineering has more success in some areas than in others. Communications satellites present a clear requirement in an unchanging environ- ment, whereas a company management information system (MIS) presents a complex, multi-attribute requirement in a constantly changing environment. Treating both as closed systems may work for the satellite, but cannot work for the MIS for long, unless the

technological part can be made to adapt as fast as the human part of
the MIS—something we do not know yet how to do.

What governs the ability to adapt? Variety in a set of interacting
systems enhances their combined ability to adapt, since a change in
environment is likely to favour the characteristics of one of the set,
which will flourish in consequence—the greater the variety, the
greater the chance. A set of interacting systems in which one has
become dominant to the extent of suppressing variety is less likely
to respond to changing environment—the set lacks the essential
nucleus about which to change.

What governs rate of adaptation? In abstract systems terms, the
rate must be limited by:

1 The anabolic and catabolic rates of the interacting set of systems,
  since these set the upper limit to the ability of the whole to adapt
  its function and form in line with the changing need
2 These rates in turn are limited by the variety and capacity of the
  interchange between the systems
3 The strength of the driving force and the mechanism for change.
  In natural systems, for example, propagation is the driving force
  and cumulative selection is the mechanism for change; together
  these constitute natural selection

In pragmatic, everyday terms, these boil down as follows:

1 Responsiveness of investment in, and divestment of, functional
  capabilities and supporting structure/architecture
2 Sources, resources, transport, communications, information
  and infrastructure
3 Threat, competition, initiative, creativity, survivability,
  education & training, endemic change-culture

DESIGNING OPEN SYSTEMS

Carefully-Specified Obsolescence

How can open systems be designed and implemented successfully in
a fixed price environment? The essence of the difficulty facing
systems engineers today is that of providing a fixed solution against
a fixed specification. This is taken to mean that everything must be
specified in ever-increasing detail, so that the supplier can prove it
has been supplied and the customer can be sure it is what was
required. Specification in ever-increasing detail takes longer and
longer, increasing the time delay between emergence of the need and

provision of the solution; the greater the delay, the more obsolescent the system when finally introduced. Hence, I call this phenomenon "carefully-specified obsolescence" and it is in vogue at the time of writing.

Principal amongst the characteristics of open systems are the ability to:

- Adapt to changing environments
- Modify function and structure
- Adapt interflows with other systems
- Adapt intraflows within the system, between its internal partitions
- "Absorb" chunks of negative entropy to use internally (as animals absorb proteins and use it to build themselves) for changes in structure, capability, etc
- Grow and shrink without disrupting system operation
- Replace worn parts without disrupting system operation

If we are to avoid carefully-specified obsolescence, the solution is clear; we must specify the *adaptability* of the system, rather than the simple static features of the system, as at present.

Specifying Adaptability

Specifying adaptability may be easier than it appears. Consider a human activity system (HAS). The individuals are adaptable anyway—we humans are possibly the most adaptable creatures on Earth, it is the way we educate and organize ourselves and our technology that limits our flexibility and adaptability. What can we do to make a group of humans adaptable?

- Add variety—include in the group various skills, ages, characters, capabilities
- Create an organization that constantly reviews itself to see if it could improve its contribution (to its containing system)
- Within that organization create, and continually rearrange, teams which have variety and which compete with each other so that useful variety is differentially rewarded
- Avoid any one team becoming so dominant that team and individual variety are submerged. Dominance tends to be monotonal—it can play only one note, and that is the opposite of adaptability

- Introduce new variety to the team, or new teams, as the environment changes. Dispense with variety and capacity that clearly have no further relevance
- Network with other HASs which offer variety and which complement the HAS of interest. Combine teams across the network. Continually review that networking

If we can operate HASs in such an open manner—and clearly we can, since creative, innovative organizations do—then can we not design technological systems similarly?

At present, we do not. Aircraft, ships, buildings, MISs, defence systems—all are subject to either short lives or periodic refits/overhauls which take them out of service. Such "outages" are extremely expensive, since either reserve capabilities have to be acquired to cover the gap, or the owning organization effectively shuts down for the duration. So intent are procurers on "the fixed price" in an effort to contain initial capital outlay that the consequent greatly-inflated cost-of-ownership goes unnoticed. Manufacturers have a similar axe to grind; if they were to provide open, adaptable systems, their customers would come back much less frequently because systems would last much longer.

So, how to specify technological adaptability. Consider a computer graphic display to be provided as part of an information-decision-action (IDA) system—a system for making decisions in real time, operated by humans with decision support partly from technological devices. We could provide the graphic display in either of two ways:

1 With all the necessary screen formats carefully analysed, designed using the best human factors principles, together with a specification for testing
2 As 1 but with the addition of a screen formatter which enables the future user to adapt existing formats, or create entirely new ones, as the needs of the job, or his/her particular idiosyncrasies dictate

Incorporating the screen formatter from the start costs little more, and perhaps even less since it may simplify development, prototyping, etc.

What can be done for a graphics display can be done for most technological devices. It simply takes a change of perspective—a paradigm shift, to use the jargon. For example, we can design databases for adaptability and we can carefully specify that adaptability. In the future, we must become smarter. We cannot afford to go on replacing one rigid, short-lived system with another. It is expensive, wasteful of resources and gives poor, continually-interrupted performance.

Putting Systems to Work

A NEW SYSTEMS ENGINEERING METHOD

Previous chapters have introduced ideas of openness, structure, architecture, interactions and counteractions, purpose, viability and many more, which will contribute to a new look at systems engineering. This new look is based on the Unified Systems Hypothesis; the objective is to use USH as a theory-base upon which to build a systems engineering structure. since USH addresses any and all systems, such a systems engineering method should be applicable to any system, be it human, economic, technological, or any other.

Design Guidelines

The design guidelines encapsulate the New Systems Engineering are shown in Table 12.1.

Table 12.1—New Systems Engineering guidelines

Step 1	Establish SOI objectives and requirements by reference to containing system(s)
Step 2	Identify (sibling) systems and their interactions to be perturbed by the SOI
Step 3	Conceive complementary systems as new/modified siblings to neutralize unwanted perturbations
Step 4	Design SOI as an open system to complement sibling systems in contributing to containing system(s)' objectives
Step 5	Partition SOI, promoting internal connected variety, avoiding dominance
Step 6	Enhance SOI cohesives, diminish dispersives
Step 7	Interconnect that variety to promote sibling stability, mutual self-reward

---

Step 1. Establish SOI Objectives and Requirements by reference to Containing System(s)

The only tangible value of any system is to be seen in its contribution to its containing system(s)' objectives—see Chapters 1 and 5. Note the potential plurality of containing systems; in the real world it is rare for any System Of Interest (SOI) to have only one containing system—see Chapter 6 for examples. The value of a SOI's contribution is relevant in the context of the similar contributions by its siblings.

Step 2. Identify (Sibling) Systems and their Interactions to be Perturbed by the SOI

Within the containing system(s) are sibling systems with which the putative SOI will interact and which will be disturbed by that new interaction.   They will, in turn, interact with other systems, changing the fabric/environment within the containing system(s) and hence the interactions with the putative SOI.   In complex situation, such interactions and inter-reactions may produce results which are either very difficult to predict, or are *unknowable*.

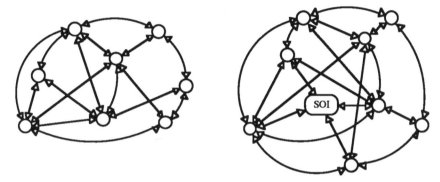

Figure 12.1 Interacting systems re-adjusting to the addition of a new system-of-interest

In Figure 12.1, the set of interacting systems at the left has a new system, the SOI, introduced at the right.   Clearly, there is potential for every system in the set and every interaction to change and, since there is no particular reason to suppose simple, linear and continuous change, predicting the outcome of adding the SOI to the set of interacting siblings may be extremely difficult. These considerations throw the most serious doubt on our ability to formulate sensible system requirement specifications by simply considering a new system.

Step 3. Conceive Complementary Systems as new/ modified Siblings to neutralize Unwanted Perturbations

Figure 12.2 illustrates one purpose and use of complementary systems. (A second purpose will be introduced in Step 7.) At the left is a set of interacting systems, supposedly in equilibrium. At the right a putative SOI is introduced with the objective of changing the status quo. In so doing, it will perturb the equilibrium, not only in the desired way but also in less predictable or even unknowable ways. These unwanted perturbations may be managed by introducing complementary systems as shown which have the net

effect of cancelling out the unwanted effects. Such cancelling can be
complete or simply sufficient to enable control of the interacting set
of systems as they tend towards a new point of equilibrium.

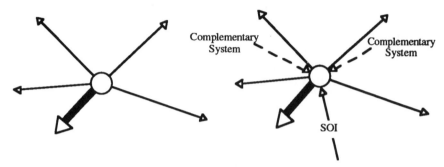

Figure 12.2 Complementary systems neutralizing unwanted
perturbations

Step 4. Design SOI as an Open System to Complement Sbling Systems in contributing to Containing System(s)' Objectives

Designing the SOI invokes many of the classic systems engineering
activities, but always from the outward-looking perspective
appropriate to open systems developed in previous steps —see Figure
12.3. This perspective and the appropriate approach have already
been presented in Chapter 10, as the Seven-step Continuum.

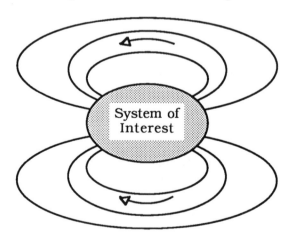

Figure 12.3 The notion of closed-loop design. For a system to persist, or
remain viable, its outputs at right must loop back to its inputs at left,
through a series of cause-and-effect transitions. Only in this way can a
system respond to changes in the external environment and preserve the
resources on which it depends for existence and pursuit of mission

The Generic Reference Model, Chapter 4, provides a basis for confirming completeness of design. The GRM (Function) Model is presented in Figure 12.4 as an open system concept. The design task requires that the designer selects the mission, resource and viability management functional features and realises the GRM (Form) elements of structure, potential and influence so as to achieve the requisite emergent properties of the SOI.

Designing the SOI means establishing its emergent properties, including performance, availability of performance and survival (or durability) of performance, together with the incurred emergent properties (see Chapter 5) such as overall capacity, weight, volume, cost, consumption, dissipation, etc. To complement siblings requires that the emergent properties be established in the context of the set of sibling emergent properties, now including those of the putative SOI. For example, if failure rate were an emergent property of the SOI, it is relevant in the context of the failure rates of all the siblings within the containing system as a set, and in how their combined failure rates contribute to their containing system's objectives.

- Environmental change will occur as soon as the SOI is introduced into its containing system(s) and starts to interact with its siblings
- The rate of adaptation must equal or exceed the rate of environmental change
- System stability is enhanced by connected variety

There is a need, then, to promote connected variety. Dominance is not essentially bad in design; rather it is dominance which excludes variety which makes a system rigid, inflexible and potentially unstable. Remembering Figure 12.1 at Step 2, it is evident that stability, flexibility and dominance will be challenged[1] from the moment of introducing a SOI into its containing system(s).

Step 5. Partition SOI, Promoting Internal Connected Variety, Avoiding Dominance

Partitioning is crucial to the success of any SOI; it determines the sub-systems and their interactions and interfaces, of course; but, much more, it determines the stability, flexibility, responsiveness,

---

[1] Current statistics show that a high proportion of management information systems never pass the introductory phase, for example; those that do are not used to anything like the degree anticipated, the contribution made to company profitability tends to fall woefully short of expectations, and such systems have a short lifetime of only a few years at best.

longevity and the practicability of realizing the putative SOI.   USH
Principles indicate that:

- The seeds of system senility are lack of variety in the SOI, such
  that none of its sub-systems is able to respond to environmental
  change.

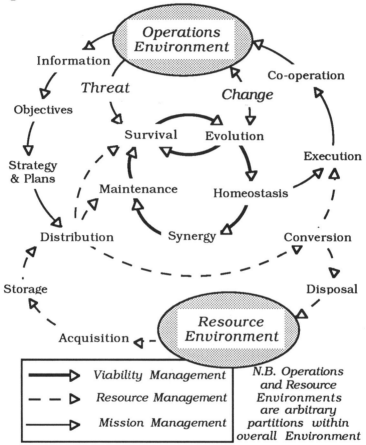

Figure 12.4 The GRM (Function) Model as an open system ccncept.
Mission management is shown as an information-decision-action closed
loop interacting with an external operations environment.   Resource
management similarly draws fresh resources from a resource environment
to which it returns unwanted resources. Resources are deployed within the
System-of-Interest (SOI) in support of mission and viability management.
Viability management maintains the SOI in the face of threat and changing
environment so that the SOI may continue to pursue its mission.   Not
shown are the many links emanating from viability management to control,
co-ordinate, adapt, repair, defend, configure and maintain all the other
features, functions and activities of the SOI

"Promoting variety" invokes employing sub-systems which, although they might have similar functions, are aggregated from different parts, employ different features and skills, should have interfaces which can accommodate much more variety than might be initially perceived, and so on. Some sub-systems may be functionally replicated, while differing in form. It also means a larger number of sub-systems, each perhaps relatively small, rather than a few sub-systems, one or two of which would be large/ dominant, and hence it means more infrastructure within the system. Finally, it means that sub-systems should be viable in their own right, rather than merged to achieve some supposed economy of scale. (These are not the notions of classic systems engineering, where variety is suppressed and dominance encouraged in the interests of cost and simplicity.)

Intra-connection, connection within the system between its partitions, will promote stability; more intra-connection will promote greater stability. Too much stability may be undesirable, since it is another way of describing inertia, or resistance to change. It is part of the designer's art to intra-connect sufficiently, but not too much. Intra-connection must have capacity to match the variety; capacity must exist for the variety of intra-flows individually. Intra-connection requires redundancy, multiple routes for the intra-flows between sub-systems, to accommodate failure or damage. Transitive systems, systems which are so open that they will receive and pass on interflows, greatly enhance system flexibility, stability and survival.

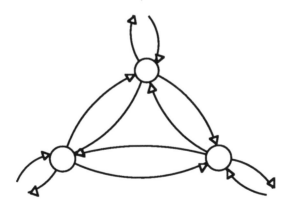

Figure 12.5 Strength of relationship through mutual self-reward

Mutual self-reward is the essence of bonding; any relationship which benefits both parties will tend to be strong and persist. As Figure 12.5 indicates, sub-systems/entities tend to be drawn to each other by mutually self-rewarding relationships—a fact well known to psychologists, negotiators and the like, but equally true for hard systems. Consider a telephone line between two people in which the communication is in one direction only; the recipient never responds to messages in any way. How long would such a communication link persist, there being no reward for the sender? Chains of mutual self-reward can be set up which, like the links in a conventional chain, bind systems together. Authoritative, restrictive relationships tend not to be mutually self-rewarding and require continual reinforcement.

The idea of mutual self-reward works for hard systems too; communications protocols include "handshakes" and error-correcting features so that transmitter and receiver know that what was sent was received correctly or was detected as faulty and corrected or re-transmitted.

Some libraries arrange books using codes which were established by lending books initially without control and placing returned books at one end of a long shelf. Books most frequently lent and returned gradually migrated to that end, whilst less-used books were gradually moved to the other end. By then coding the arrangement of books to reflect their usage, both library and user benefited. A new university campus was laid to lawn, without paths. Students chose routes across the grass suited to their lessons and leisure. Once the pattern of worn grass had established, the paths were laid over the worn strips, so mutually benefiting students and authorities alike—paths went where they were needed, remaining grass was not unnecessarily trampled. These two examples are particularly interesting; the final patterns of books and paths was difficult to predict or may even have been unknowable beforehand. By allowing a period for the patterns to evolve in use, the "designers" encouraged the formation of a robust solution by the system users. This is a particularly valuable approach.

There are many examples of mutually self-rewarding relationships, in all types of system. In biology, symbiosis is mutually self-rewarding, for example. In dealing, commissions provide mutual self-reward. and so on. In general, classic systems engineering does not recognize this system-binding feature.

Step 6. Enhance SOI Cohesives, Diminish Dispersives

System design has progressed to the important point of establishing it firmly, both functionally and structurally. The USH Principle of Cohesion indicates that stable systems exist in a balance of dispersive and cohesive influences. Step 5 discussed one of the cohesive influences, mutual self-reward, and there are many others. For physical systems there may be actual adhesion or cohesion, actions at a distance (such as gravity, electromagnetism, etc) or parts may be joined—in either case, the dispersive influences of forces, corrosives, etc., tend to be obvious. For other systems the influences may be less apparent. What are the cohesive and dispersive influences affecting an ethnic community or a family group, for example? For a close-knit family there is mutual self-reward in belonging, in familiarity, in safety from external threats, from numbers, from well-connected variety, and so on. Dispersive influences include those of the world outside the family, other attractions, knowledge of other, seemingly more attractive or necessary factors which make migration from the close family circle more likely. Even then, the tendency is to migrate from one family to another, or to simultaneously exist within several families at once.

Environmental influences change over time; adaptability is the key to cohesion in the face of changing environment. If a system is intended to persist then it must be adaptable, and a designed system must have adaptability designed into it. Adaptability implies the ability to :

- Modify function and process
- Modify structure
- Utilize changing resources
- Dispose of changing residues

For a system to be adaptable, it needs to sense the environment and respond to change in such a way as to enhance its survivability, perhaps by altering its performance or strategy, perhaps by changing its sources and anabolism or its residues and catabolism. Most significantly, it must be able to respond to change using its internal connected variety so that systems most suited to the changing conditions respond preferentially

For the system we wish to design it is necessary that we identify cohesive and dispersive influences and—carefully, since the reactions may not be readily apparent—enhance the first and/or reduce the second. Why "and/or"? Since the influences are in opposition, it is often in practice much easier to address one *or* the other, and the effect should be less unpredictable than changing both at once.

Step 7. Interconnect that Variety to Promote Sibling Stability, Mutual Self-reward

Step 7 puts it all together. The SOI, together with siblings, complementary systems, variety and intra-connection has to be inter-connected thoroughly into the changing world in which it exists, or will exist in the future. It is at this point in particular that NSE departs from classic systems engineering. The internal variety which has been generated has to be connected through the external environment in closed loops if it is to self-sustain and respond to external influences. Not to so respond is to court obsolescence.

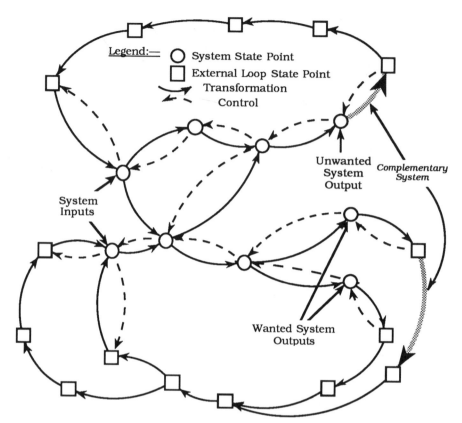

Figure 12.6 Open system design. The system of interest is seen connected in closed loops through the external world. Transformations operate from left to right through the SOI, while controls operate from right to left. As the SOI is progressively de-composed, and variety added, more external closed loops are generated to ensure the SOI's viability. Where loops cannot be established, either the SOI feature is not feasible or an external complementary system is needed to close the loop. The design process is holistic, outward- and inward-looking

Figure 12.6 shows a developing design of an open system. A series of internal states has been established, represented by small circles, each the result of a prior transformation process. These states are regulated by control loops, management, cybernetic or techno-logical, which seek to maintain the state in some degree. The system employs resources entering at the left, where 'resources' may include both wanted and unwanted content. At the right, these two types of output are shown explicitly. Outputs are connected back to inputs through the external environment in causal loops, with states represented by squares, which may invoke considerations some distance beyond that of the immediate System-of-Interest, represented by the small circles above. Successive transformations form loops in one direction; successive controls form loops in the opposite direction. (Only external control loops of direct interest are shown in Figure 12.6). The whole thus forms closed, meshed sets of transformation and control loops with the SOI focused in the centre, but seen in its open context.

The two shaded arrows marked as complementary systems represent the need in such open system design to introduce additional systems in order to neutralise some unwanted effect, or enhance some wanted effect, in conjunction with the SOI. This view complements that of Step 3 above and introduces the second purpose of complementary systems. The USH Principle of Connected Variety, which provoked the concept of complementary systems, has now been addressed. The key concept is one of matching internal variety with external sources and sinks for that variety. complementary systems should interest even the hardest-headed businessman; not only are they essential for sound systems, they also present business opportunities, thus creating an approach that unites systems and business in a (potentially) common cause.

CONCLUSION

The New Systems Engineering introduces an approach, unlike classic systems engineering, based on theory and enabling system designs with clear purpose, which fit into their environments and which contribute, with their siblings, to the objectives of their containing systems. The USH Principles are used throughout. The New Systems Engineering does not negate classic systems engineering—it enhances it, particularly by emphasising the initial and final phases of synthesis—steps 1—4 and steps 6 and 7. Such notions as "top down" are given substance, since the top can be clearly identified with the objectives of the containing systems. Classic systematic disciplines are retained, but with the essential difference that *all* systems, contained, sibling and containing, are treated at *all* times as being open. It *is* possible to design and implement open technological systems to a fixed price by specifying not only their function and form, as at present, but also their adaptability. Systems designed using this approach promise to be flexible, adaptable, reliable, inexpensive to own and long-lived.

The next chapter contains an example of NSE at work.

Chapter 12.2
A Case for New Systems Engineering (NSE)

To Knowledge, Analysis may hold the Key
But Synthesis begets all Creativity
Anon., 1992

NSE DESIGN EXAMPLE

Consider the following simplified example:

A new, fossil-fuel power station is to be introduced to an under-developed region supporting a poor, largely agrarian society. Design a robust power system to contribute maximally to the region and to minimize any undesirable side-effects.

Step 1. Establish SOI Objectives and Requirements by Reference to Containing System(s)

The containing systems will include:

- The regional economy
- The regional society
- The regional ecology
- The regional energy system

The objectives of the economic system might well include an increase in agricultural productivity (through mechanization and cheaper fertilizers), and an increase in industrialization leading to wealth generation and a beneficial change in the balance of imports and exports.

The objectives of the regional society would be to flourish, and to enhance the perceived quality of life by using the increase in electrical power and wealth.

The regional ecology could hardly be said to have objectives, since it is not a purposeful system. However, we may ascribe purpose to it. The "objectives" of the regional ecology are to maintain the variety and balance of flora and fauna, so maintaining the biosphere on which the region is founded.

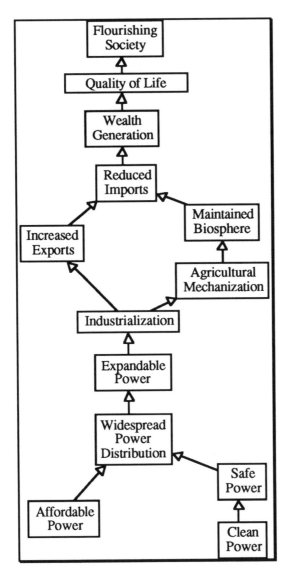

Figure 12.7 Power generation intent structure

The objectives of the regional energy system would be to generate and distribute affordable power for the whole region, safely, cleanly, efficiently, continuously and sufficient to meet the developing need.

Since these are the expectations from the new regional power-generation system, the measure of our system would be in its success in contributing to all these objectives—*not simply those of generating power.*

As Figure 12.7 shows, the objectives can be networked using ISM (Chapter 9), so presenting a structured mission, or Prime Directive, for the new regional power generation system, as follows:

To contribute to a flourishing society with an improved quality of life for all the citizens in the region through the provision of safe, clean, affordable electrical power.

Step 2. Identify (Sibling) Systems and their Interactions to be Perturbed by the SOI

Perturbed systems include almost all of those in the region, social, economic, ecological, transportation, etc. Fossil-fuel for the power station must be mined, causing an increase in population and infrastructure around the mining area(s), while some high-grade fuels may need to be imported. Mining creates an ecological and a visual disturbance. The fossil-fuel will need to be transported over inadequate roads, so a transport system will need to be built, comprising new roads, fuel supplies, fuel dumps, garages, lorries, mechanics, drivers, loading bays, unloading bays, conveyers, chutes, etc., etc. Economic change will be evident in the investment in infrastructure and transportation systems, the training and hire of personnel, their relative affluence and consequent spending on essentials and luxury goods.

Social strain can be foreseen between the new "haves" and the existing "have-nots". The increase in power available within the region will reduce the cost of power, enabling new businesses to form and flourish, shifting the population pattern towards towns and cities for two reasons: increased productivity on the farm will reduce labour needs; jobs will become available in the towns as businesses form, draw together for mutual self-reward and coalesce. All of these represent disturbed sibling systems.

Step 3. Conceive Complementary Systems as New/Modified Siblings to Neutralize Unwanted Perturbations

Complementary systems will be required to:

- Absorb/reuse the waste/effluent/dissipation/spill from mining, transportation, power generation, distribution and utilization.
- Prevent any reduction in ecological variety (which can also be reduced by judicious choice of location for a power station in relation to mining areas and centres of power utilization). This

might include moving species, ring-fencing sensitive areas, submerging infrastructure, etc.

- Manage the move of the regional economy such that increased agricultural mechanization and fertilizer production (objectives) are not impeded by lack of resources, resource wastage or misapplication, and that economic conditions are made and kept suitable for industrialization (objective) to proceed unabated. Pump-priming of small businesses would be a typical feature, together with regional investment schemes, education, training and specialist help.

- Manage the consequent social imbalance and the evolution towards a new social order and equilibrium (objectives). Invest in infrastructure, education, healthcare, job-mobility, transport, housing. Ease restrictions on movement, business, security, foreign travel, etc.

- Lastly, the Principle of Connected Variety suggests that variety, which the above measures are meant to enhance, should be accompanied by connections between that variety. Media promotion is required to report fully and freely on situation and progress from all viewpoints, so that the variety may seek the connections needed for stable change and expansion. Independent radio, TV and newspapers should be encouraged, so that strains in the evolving social fabric become evident while still small and capable of relief.

Step 4. Design SOI as an Open System to Complement Sibling Systems in Contributing to Containing Systems' Objectives

The emergent properties of the SOI include the following:

- Power output, mean, peak, quality needed to satisfy both the immediate and future needs of the area
- Availability of that power, including reliability, ease of maintenance, skill levels to operate and maintain, reserves of fuel, robustness of the transportation system feeding fuel in, and the distribution system feeding power out (a power station is an archetypal open system), risk of major breakdown
- Durability/survivability of that power, in terms of susceptibility to attack by enemies of the benefiting society, its self-defence features if any, its adaptability, the expected lifetime of the powerstation, its replaceability
- The area covered by the station, its feeder roads and distribution networks
- The rate of fuel usage, its quality and availability
- The power dissipated into the biosphere

- Manpower and materials to design, construct, train, operate and maintain
- Etc., etc.

Step 5. Partition SOI, Promoting Internal Connected Variety, Avoiding Dominance.

Figure 12.8 outlines in broad terms a view of an electrical power generation system, with the emphasis on the openness and flow, i.e. the connectivity of the systems with each other and with their siblings, not shown in the picture. Note that, although the power generation system is open, it nonetheless has controls aplenty, particularly aimed at the inflows and outflows to and from siblings, in terms of rates/amounts and qualities. The outflows have been divided into residues (unwanted, polluting and requiring a complementary system to neutralize their effects) and power (wanted). The network of controls generally feed back from right to left as the process feeds forward from left to right.

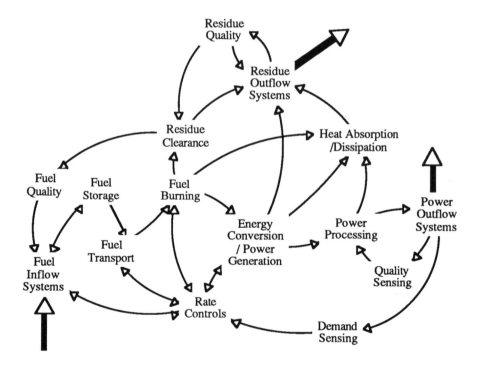

Figure 12.8 Open process and control design concept for conventional power generation

Figure 12.8 does not complete the functional design. It represents only part of the overall SOI; as the Generic Reference (Function) Model shows, the SOI has three basic aspects: mission, viability and resource management. The diagram does not represent a viable system; to make it viable would require every aspect delineated by the GR(F)M to be pursued—this, as they say, is left to the reader! Note in particular, however, that the human resources have not been considered and that the systems need to be maintained and that the whole must evolve/adapt in step with the environment—in this case the environment will include an increasing, but somewhat uncertain demand for electrical energy coupled with a reducing supply of fossil fuel in the future.

Functional design does not tend to reveal variety. By concentrating on function in decomposition, however, openness is maintained and variety can be introduced by reproducing the function using different structures, methods or techniques. The Generic Reference (Form) Model would be used to guide in that respect. Figure 12.9 shows how variety might be introduced in respect of the main task of energy generation. Note how there are no nodes; each power generation path is independent in terms of sources, resources, facilities and outputs. Cross-overs connect the variety, to give stability. Such a system is extremely robust, but involves significant capital outlay. Would it be worth it? In the short term, it would probably be the case that one of the three systems would prove more economical in producing inexpensive power, but that situation need not last. If conditions change unexpectedly, the single-mode system may fail. The best solution, then, would be to design-in all three (or more) systems from the start, to connect them, to provide the bulk of the power from that which is the most economic, but to maintain the operation of the others for use during overhauls, supply shortages, etc. As conditions changed, the burden of power generation could move smoothly and easily between the different modes of supply.

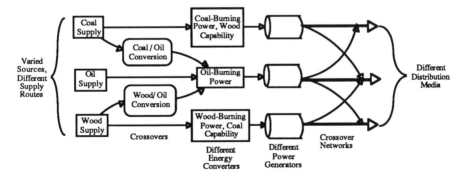

Figure 12.9 Adding variety and connecting that variety—power generation

This approach proffers adaptability too, since the system contains some seeds of evolution; with three different fuel sources, the burden of generation may move between sources as the fuel supply availability and economics shift with time. The conversion capabilities may need development and that may involve research: research would be an investment in adaptability.

The inclusion of wood-burning may appear to be beyond the requirement. Wood-burning systems have a special advantage that they do not add net CO_2 to the atmosphere; burning trees releases the CO_2 absorbed by the trees from the atmosphere in growing (see Szego and Kemp, 1973; Weinberg and Williams, 1990). A forest of suitable softwoods less than 20x20 miles can support the continuous generation of 1000 megawatts of electrical power including all the overheads (Szego and Kemp, 1973): trees are cut for burning and replanted on a cyclic basis such that one complete cycle corresponds to the tree maturation period. The inclusion of a wood-burning capability is therefore a sensible way to prepare for the future within the region, it provides variety in the residue outflow system and it *may* be compatible with the objectives of the regional ecology. Compatibility would require that the regional ecology be undisturbed by the tree-farming needed to sustain the generation of power.

Step 6. Enhance SOI Cohesives, Diminish Dispersives

The simplest method of encouraging cohesion within the system is to promote mutual self-reward: but first, it is necessary to identify cohesive and dispersive influences which would operate within the SOI. Cohesive influences include:

- Perceived good remuneration, including thanks
- High morale, pride, esteem within the community
- Good working conditions
- Comprehensive infrastructure—internal communications, administration, security
- Participation in management and decisions
- Full maintenance—spares, test facilities, skills
- R&D capability, looking to future needs
- Change management system, evolving the SOI in sympathy with the environment

Dispersive influences include:

- Better working conditions and pay elsewhere and accessible to staff

- Lack of perceived change
- Alternative power generation sources offering more attraction within the region—cleaner, safer, less expensive, needing less skill, using more locally-available resources, etc
- Poor performance in primary rôle of generating clean, safe, affordable, continuous power
- Lack of support to maintain, modify and evolve technology within power generation system over time
- Inability to dispose of residues satisfactorily
- Failure of region to flourish, even when supplied with affordable power

Interestingly, nearly all the cohesive and dispersive influences are human issues rather than technological ones—the technology of electrical power generation from fossil fuels is reasonably well-established. Many of the influences will have been addressed if the SOI meets the objectives outlined in step 1 in concert with the complementary siblings nominated in step 3. Disposing of residues, for example, requires a complementary sibling; a suitable system might be found in using the residues to make fertilizers, as aggregate for building, or as raw material for a developing chemical industry. In any of these cases, the concept of complementary systems offers mutual self-reward: both the SOI and the associated industry benefit, the SOI by selling (or even giving away!) the unwanted residue and the receiving industry by having a close, low-cost, indigenous source of raw material. Similar methods of promoting mutual self-reward would be needed to firm-up all the cohesive influences and diminish all the dispersive influences.

Step 7. Interconnect that Variety to Promote Sibling Stability, Mutual Self-reward

Step 5 in particular created variety within the SOI which now has to be connected through closed external causal loops to preserve open system behaviour. Figure 12.10 develops the interconnection theme, and shows some of the variety and how it might be connected. For the new power generations system to promote stability suggests that it should in some way promote the enabling section in each system theme, including the "universal connectors". There would be many ways in which this might be done, including:

- Providing outlets to key enabler in each system theme
- Providing special tariffs for key enablers
- Investing in key enablers, including education, road and rail links, and each of the four universal enablers. Interestingly,

analysis indicated that healthcare was a universal connector like telecommunications because it enabled the population to undertake whatever tasks were presented.

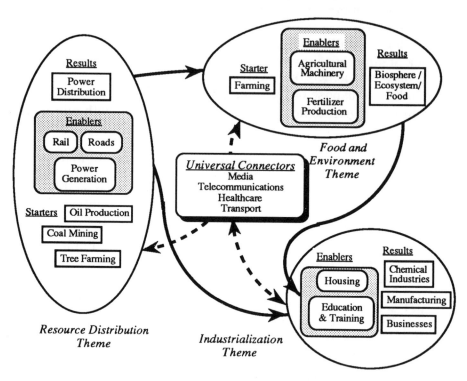

Figure 12.10 Power generation system interaction diagram

A more functional look at mutual self-reward as a basis for connecting the power system into the developing economy and society is offered by causal loop modelling (CLM). As Figure 12.11 shows, power generation effectively stokes-up and drives the causal loops. In some cases, notably those represented by the dotted lines, 'causation' is an over-statement; unless complementary systems are introduced to complete the loops, the hoped-for benefits may not be realized. For example, converting the residue from burning fossil fuel into aggregate for building, aids the development of business and industry which increases the demand for more power. Similarly, wood-burning makes sense only when coupled directly with a tree-farming scheme, which would require agricultural machinery, and so on. It therefore behoves the designers of the power system to consider contributing to those parts of the causal loops that need "pump-priming", so that the original objectives which the power system has to fulfil may indeed be realised.

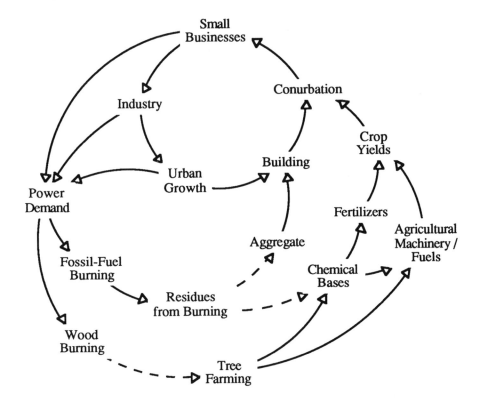

Figure 12.11 Causal loop model showing missing complementary
systems

One difficulty with the rather rosy picture presented in Figure 12.11
is that causation takes time; to go around any of the loops may take
considerable time, and bypasses may arise or side-effects appear,
which may prejudice the whole enterprise. The section of CLM in
Figure 12.12 shows what might be expected to happen if the
mechanization of farming proceeds so rapidly that rural
unemployment causes an early migration to unprepared towns and
cities. This model fits on to Figure 12.11.

Consider also the partial CLM, Figure 12.13, which also fits on to
the original. This model shows how social diseases—infectious
diseases which thrive under crowded conditions, including measles,
rubella, chicken pox and many more—may increase dramatically if
the development of conurbations is not managed and associated
with a similar growth in healthcare. The model also shows how
developing industrial and business wealth may be taxed to fund that
healthcare and the building of infrastructure, housing, schools,
roads, telecommunications, etc. Careful use of taxes and incentives
to slow down and direct rates of development are essential if the

growth cycle shown in the first CLM above is to be maintained; in retrospect, it can now be seen that the first CLM represented a set of nested positive feedback loops which, if not controlled, may accelerate out of control.

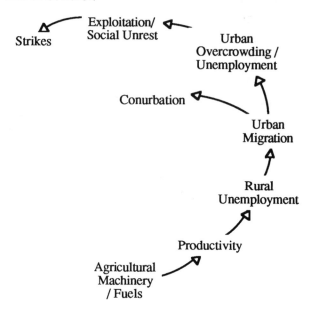

Figure 12.12 CLM additions anticipating system reactions

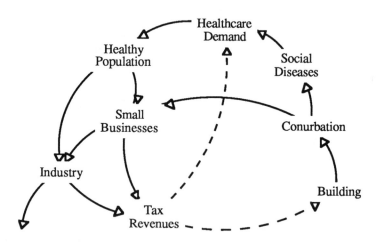

Figure 12.13 CLM additions showing further complementary systems. In the model, taxation has been used as a means of funding the building and healthcare programmes, but also as a means of selectively controlling the rate of change

CONCLUSION

That concludes the brief overview of the New Systems Engineering in action. Much detail has been omitted both for clarity and brevity, but it is hoped that sufficient has been presented for the reader to understand the new approach and to appreciate its strength and integrity. To those familiar with classic systems engineering, it may seem that the NSE is addressing issues beyond its immediate concern. This is a point of view, but it is equally valid to consider the problems generated by the classic approach which, in the situation presented in this case study, might well provide an expensive white elephant. Worse, the classic approach would offer an efficient mono-modal power generation system which might well damage the ecology, economy and social structure it was intended to help. Classic systems engineering has great merit in terms of "getting the job done", but it closes its mind to the real measures of success.

It might be argued, too, that the NSE is much more expensive than the classic approach. I believe it may not necessarily be so. Even if it were more expensive, is it not better to know the real bottom line, so that suppliers and customers are not caught-out as so often at present, by unexpected rises in costs, embarrassing delays, poor quality and systems that are simply not what was wanted? Finally, if suppliers do not employ the NSE, or something similar, customers will; customers become much smarter after they have gone through the trauma of making a bad purchase!

ASSIGNMENT

You are a consultant design-engineer. You have been called in by a client who wishes to restructure part of her manufacturing operation. She wishes to have a flexible, long-lived system which will operate effectively for some two decades. She is CE of an multinational conglomerate operating in the electrical/electronics sector of the market. The manufacturing plant produces high-speed databuses for the avionics, electronics space and information systems industries, and the product range is key to the success of the conglomerate. Unfortunately, the databus market is evolving rapidly with optical processing and connection threatening, and with further technological advancements mooted.

You are required to produce a design concept for a new manufacturing system, using the New Systems Engineering pattern, which will serve the conglomerate in its mission to survive and flourish in a changing, competitive environment.

PART D
Future Vision?

Output

A Human-Centred
Progressive Design/Development
Paradigm

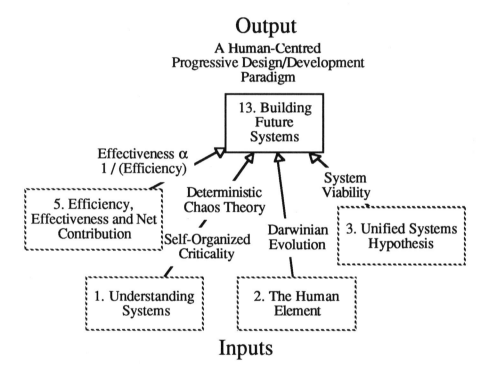

Inputs

Chapter 13
Building Future Systems Naturally

Evolution ... is—a change
from an indefinite, incoherent inhomogeneity,
to a definite coherent heterogeneity.
Herbert Spencer, 1820-1903

ISSUES

The following issues spring to mind when looking at Nature's seeming excellence:

- Why are our man-made systems rigid, short-lived, expensive to maintain and own?
- How come Nature doesn't have all these problems?
- What does Nature do that's so smart?
- Can we hope to emulate Nature?
- Is it a good idea to emulate Nature?
- Are adaptive systems practicable?
- Are generic systems practicable?

NATURE'S APPROACH

Nature has two related approaches in the "design" of animals, depending upon the degree of sophistication in the design. Lower order systems are pre-programmed at delivery, so that their actions are largely determined from the moment of birth. Their behaviour has evolved over many millions of years to be extremely robust. Insect societies, for example, seem to operate extremely successfully without any "managerial" hierarchy, using simple rules which each of the members obeys. Their development, then, in the face of changing environment, is by Darwinian evolution and requires each generation to be succeeded by one with genetic variations favouring survival.

Higher-order systems, such as Man, have relatively limited programming at birth, at least compared with their lifetime potential. This means that they can learn and develop behaviour, adapting throughout their lifetimes. This in turn implies that they can live longer, since they can evolve socially without having to evolve physically. If we could design analogous systems that were, like an infant, relatively bare of information at delivery, but which were able both to learn and to adapt to environment, then our systems would be very much more effective and longer-lived.

MUTUAL SELF-REWARD

Previous chapters have developed the theme of mutual self-reward. Nature perpetuates systems that interoperate to their mutual benefit—self-rewarding relationships, they have been called, see Odum (1971).Typical of such self-reward loops is that between bats and insects, shown in the causal-loop diagram of Figure 13.1. As bats competed for insects, they developed sonar. As insects evolved to survive this aerial predation, some species of moth developed

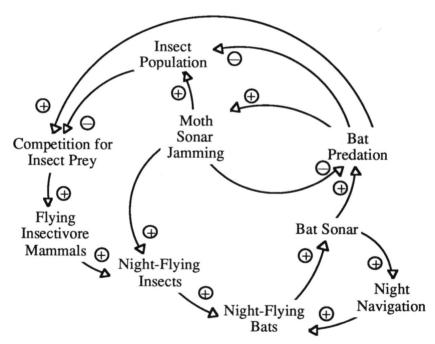

Figure 13.1 Evolutionary self-reward

counter-sonar—jamming signals which convinced the bat to change direction and to miss the intended victim. This ruse in turn is evolving smarter bat sonar, and so on. Self-reward is a powerful stimulus in the animal kingdom and especially in human society. If we can conceive socio-technical systems that self-reward, they promise to be robust.

Note that, although the bats and moths exist in a mutually self-rewarding relationship, there is no regenerative runaway as might be expected from a positive feedback system. For example, neither moths nor bats have evolved a perfect answer to their situation; each is still evolving, each is still limited by the other prey-predator relationships that surround them and with which they have to contend, and each is limited by the physics of their environment. This, after many millions of years of natural selection and evolution.

COMPUTER-BASED SURVIVAL OF THE FITTEST

It is possible to emulate evolution crudely in a computer environment. Figure 13.2 shows a prototype computer tool for evolving structures in a hostile environment. As configured, the diagram might represent an animal such as, say, a tortoise, or an aircraft. (The "creature" is referred to as "sysmorph" out of deference to Richard Dawkins, the zoologist who inspired the idea in his book *The Blind Watchmaker*, and who called his computer bugs Biomorphs.)

"Genes" code for features of the shape; some are structural genes, some behavioural. Structural genes code for shell and processing hierarchy. Behavioural genes code for cooperation, aggression and

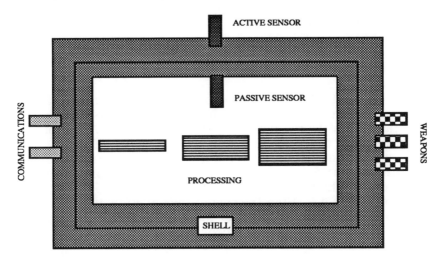

Figure 13.2 A Sysmorph—a computer-generated system shape

stealth, leading to communications, weapons and passive (as opposed to active) sensors respectively.

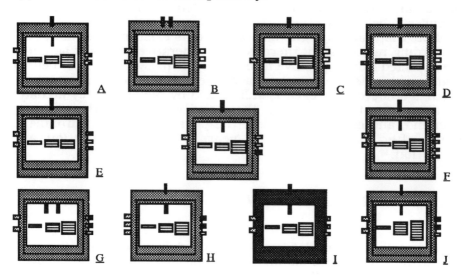

Figure 13.3 A Sysmorph family of offspring. Each offspring varies from the parent in one, and only one, respect

The set of offspring (see Figure 13.3) is subjected to a simulated hostile environment comprising, in the prototype, a set of measures which rate performance, survivability, interoperability, security and of course cost. The best adapted offspring is set up as the parent of the next generation and the process repeated until no further cost-effectiveness benefits can be obtained. The resulting offspring has adapted to the environment.

ON-LINE ADAPTIVE SYSTEMS

Consider Figure 13.4. It shows a design concept for an auto-adaptive system, using ideas much simpler than, but based upon, our understanding of Darwinian evolution. Offspring vary from their parent in some degree which may favour some offspring as the hostile environment changes. The system senses the external environment and generates potential "offspring" system configurations which it tests to see if any is better adapted than the current parent. If it is, then the system reconfigures to the pattern of the offspring. Adaptive systems like this have been prototyped. Such systems can be carefully specified, and delivered against that specification.

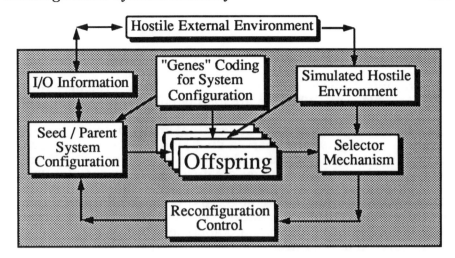

Figure 13.4 Auto-adapting on-line system

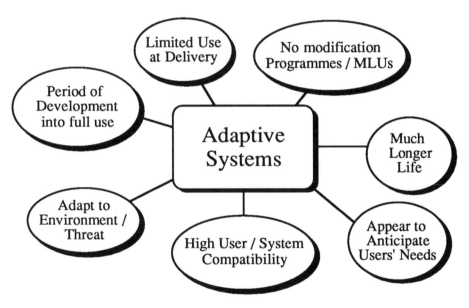

Figure 13.5 Adaptive systems—pros and cons

As Figure 13.5 suggests, adaptive systems have quite different characteristics from those we now produce; some features are beneficial, some less so. For example, they would be of limited use at delivery, like an infant. And, like an infant, it would be some time before they achieved their full potential. Once achieved, however, that potential would persist for much longer.

GENERIC SYSTEMS

An alternative approach would employ generic systems—Nature does, in a big way. While we are fond of pointing to the differences between animal species, it is remarkable how alike many of them are. It has already been observed that many animals have two kidneys, five fingers, one heart, a dual-redundant brain, two lungs, teeth and a tongue, twin nostrils, two eyes, and so on? Clearly a generic model underlies many creatures and, on examination, it seems that there are rather few generic models. How did they arise? Early evolution saw an incredible burst of species variety, much of which has since died out. Nature seems to have evolved its set of generic designs using its standard approach—the severest discipline of all, survival of the fittest.

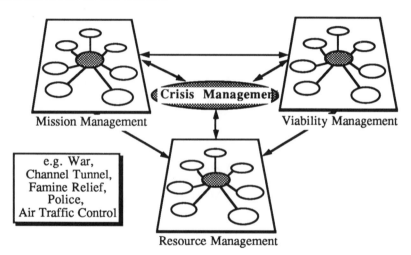

Figure 13.6 A generic command and control system

We can emulate that approach crudely, too. Consider the decision circle of Figure 2.2 It purports to represent the process of group decision forming, starting with "assess situation" and progressively looking at threats and opportunities, constraints, feasible options, and so on. It is possible to take each of the elements in the circle and to build another circle upon it. "Identify threats/opportunities", for instance, can be developed as "balance opposing forces", "project trends", "identify imbalances" (in projected situation) and back to "identify threats/opportunities". The result overall is a generic system for cooperative decision-making and operational control. Situations corresponding to on-line, real-time, reactive decision-making and control abound. In Figure 13.6, each of the management panels has at its core a shaded representation of the decision circle, surrounded by open circles representing further elaboration of each step in the decision process. There are three such panels, from the Generic Reference (Function) Model of Chapter 4, giving an overall generic system.

Figure 13.6 shows three generic systems, mutually interacting to provide one coherent system which can pursue its mission, maintain its viability as a system, and manage its resources. As the panel shows, such a generic template would be appropriate to a wide variety of circumstances.

GENERIC MULTI-SYSTEM ORGANIZATION

Efficiency versus Effectiveness

Figure 13.7 continues the theme of mission, viability and resource management taken from the Generic Reference Model, and presents it as another icon at the top—see Chapter 4. Clearly there are two archetypal ways in which to organize a multi-system system. At left is the conventional company organization, in which mission elements are grouped together, Resource elements are grouped together and so forth. This approach is intended to promote economy of scale. For example, the personnel function for each mission element resides not with the mission element (sales,

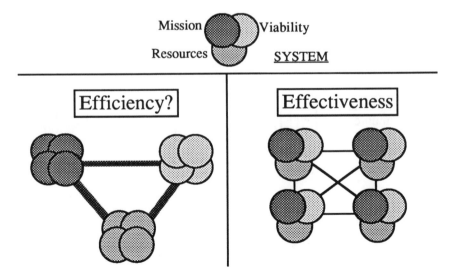

Figure 13.7 Efficiency versus effectiveness

manufacturing, etc.) but is centralized into a personnel department, which then has to be connected to its mission elements. Commonly, insufficient care and investment is put into maintaining such connections, so that not only does the looked-for economy of scale not materialize, but estrangement between units develops.

On the right is the alternative—to maintain fully viable systems, each capable of self perpetuation. This is the strategic business unit, the family of interacting creatures, or whatever. This is Nature's way, too. Gone is the (illusory?) economy of scale, to be replaced perhaps by economy of scope with each system covering less ground and retaining its own independence.

Consider the two paradigms in the event of attack and damage to the system. The left hand approach might seem more efficient, but it is vulnerable since pursuit of economy of scale has developed nodes—singular points which, if not operating, render the whole set of systems non-functional. That on the right is robust and essentially more effective. Why do we always go for the organization on the left?

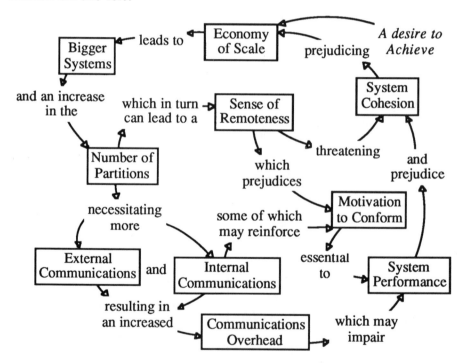

Figure 13.8 Economy of scale. The model suggests that economy of scale has a maximum, beyond which making the system bigger, far from economizing, causes such an increase in communications overheads to maintain consistent behaviour and motivation, that the system is liable to break-up

Economies of Scale

Economy of scale was mentioned above. Figure 13.8 expands on this important theme. Economy of scale seems to be a human intellectual concept; Nature seems to achieve economy through natural selection, which eliminates competitors that waste resources, and promotes competitors that develop energy-efficient strategies—see Chapter 5.

As Figure 13.8 suggests, economy of scale in man-made, man-operated systems presents its own limitations, since it promotes an infrastructure dedicated to its continuance which absorbs resources that might otherwise be used to produce throughput. Psychological feelings of remoteness can arise—we are all familiar with them—which threaten consistent operator/user behaviour, but which can be reduced by constant reinforcement, absorbing more energy internally. Economy of scale is limited; it must be, since infrastructure growth follows an approximate square law, while economy of scale is at best a linear concept. The cost of increasing scale must always eventually outweigh the supposed benefits.

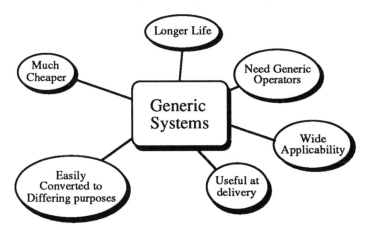

Figure 13.9 Generic systems—pros and cons

Characteristics of Generic Systems

Generic systems, like adaptive systems, have their pros and cons. While they promise to be much cheaper than present approaches because there is less thrown away each time a new system is needed, we should not suppose that a generic system means a generic operator. Most systems depend on the human element to breathe life and purpose into them. So, a system for the Channel Tunnel might be generically identical to one for famine relief in Africa, but would be useful only in the hands of operators skilled in the appropriate domain ... unless. Of course, it might be possible to train generic operators, whose excellence was in making decisions, rather than in their domain.

NATURE'S ECONOMY

Another feature of Nature's designs is her economy—little is wasted and much combined, as Figure 13.10 shows. Evolution must result in economic designs; were it otherwise, organisms would not use

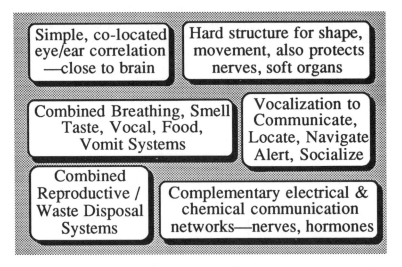

Figure 13.10 Nature's economy—multi-purpose, complementary systems

limited energy sources efficiently and would compete unsuccessfully with those that did. This is not to say that each organism is energy-efficient in the simplistic sense; on the contrary, animals develop a strategy for efficiency, exemplified by the elaborate warning mechanisms used to deter aggression rather than fight. Deterrence also expends energy, but less than combat. Can we learn from Nature in this arena too?

Figure 13.11 presents some simple examples of approaches which a look at Nature suggest might be useful. We have met several of these already. It is no longer considered "lunatic fringe" to examine Nature's example, so perhaps now we can pursue the natural way more systematically.

EVOLVING SOCIO-TECHNICAL SYSTEMS

System Design Paradigms

At present many management information systems fail to satisfy their customers and users. Information Technology (IT), once thought to be an answer looking for a problem, is now more a problem looking for an answer. In particular there is a class of such systems, called information-decision-action systems, in which

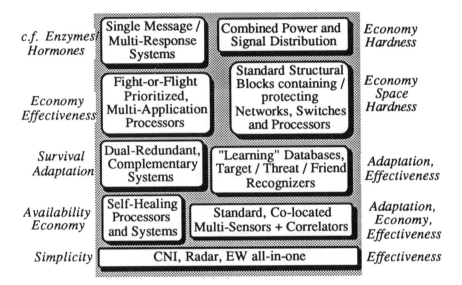

Figure 13.11 Learning from Nature

human operators respond to dynamic situations by making decisions based partly on information collected, organized and presented using IT. Examples of such systems include air traffic management, stock exchange, police incident control, military command and control, power station control and many more.

Such systems are generally designed using a computer-based information handling system, at the heart of which is some form of database. The proposition is that robust decisions are based on sound, up-to-date information and that a database is the way to collect and manage that information. Representations of the stored or incoming data are then made via computer screens.

There are conceptual problems with this almost-universal approach. As we have already seen in Chapter 2, we do not understand how humans make decisions, either individually or in groups, so how can we know what information to present in what form to which people?   Moreover, there is a severe bandwidth problem. We have five senses, and we can make displays which stimulate a few only of those senses.   But we combine the information from our senses, so that we smell fear as well as see it in the eyes and posture and hear it in the voice; we develop one composite picture from all these inputs. Clearly, the combination of our five senses with the processing power of our brains provides a phenomenal performance—one which technology has not even begun to match. Our senses are genetically attuned in certain ways, too; our eyes are designed to detect movement, cannot distinguish colour in fading light, are most sensitive in the green part of the visible spectrum, see colour in certain on/off black and white digit streams and so on. Our senses are, in fact, genetically attuned to interact with other humans in a highly dynamic natural environment, and that is what we still do best.

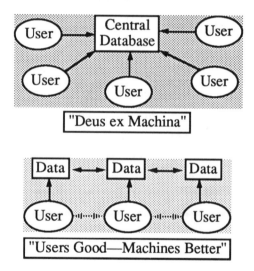

Figure 13.12 Information System Design Paradigms

So, what of the computer database and its displays? They are an interaction blockage.   They lack the variety and bandwidth of humans, and present problems when humans are obliged to communicate through them. Consider Figures 13.12 and 13.13. At the top of Figure 13.12 is the archetypal computer system, with each user employing the machine for tasks and to receive information. The humans are often excluded from person-to-person direct communication and can communicate only via the machine. This presents humans with problems—their senses are under-utilized, the information pathways are slow, and the result is non-adaptive.

It may work in a static environment, but it reduces the humans to machine-minders. Some air traffic systems are of this variety.

The lower diagram in Figure 13.12 shows people communicating with each other directly as well as with their individual machines, which are interconnected. Potentially, this is a great improvement, but again problems can arise in dynamic environments, since the human operators will adapt swiftly to changing circumstances while their machines and their machine interactions will not. The result is that the humans develop their own separate system to respond rapidly to changing situations, and the machines are relegated to supplying background data—not what was intended by the designer or paid for by the customer. Command and control systems often fit this pattern: their environment is constantly changing, while the systems are rarely used "in anger".

There are alternatives to the two paradigms above. There is no job so mundane that a human cannot find a "wrinkle"—a better, simpler, faster, easier way of doing it. This rule applies equally to sweeping the floor and to building a spacecraft. Such wrinkles are not found by sitting gazing at a paper-design, but by undertaking the task personally.

The Accelerated Evolution Approach (AEA)

The same holds for teams of people set to undertake a complex task. As Figure 13.13 shows, it is possible to draw a system with the humans and their interactions as the central theme, and to support individual humans with IT where it is needed to improve productivity. A database is shown, but it is limited so that it does not become a blockage on human interactions.

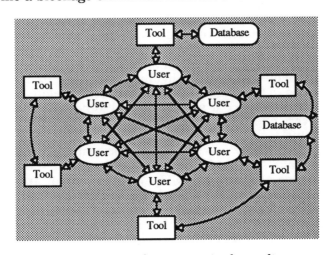

Figure 13.13 A human-centred paradigm

So, how would one evolve a system using this human-centred approach?

Step 1   Eliminate as much technology as possible—create a human system/team of current experts which uses manual methods

Step 2   Give the team time to build its repertoire of individual and group skills, interpersonal relationships, group effectiveness.   Use extra manpower to achieve performance

Step 3   Stress the team—simulated interactions, cooperation with other systems, real drudgery, simultaneous representative variety. Continue until manual team is highly proficient

Step 4   Team identifies sub-teams, bottle-necks, areas for improvement—i.e. the team proposes its own productivity enhancement, individual-by- individual, sub-team-by-sub-team, absolute minimal technology integration

Step 5   Provide the team with its proposed support

Step 6   Repeat steps 2 to 4

Step 7   Resist the temptation to integrate all the technological support features—that's the path to software overruns, project delays and inflexible technological 'solutions'

The approach recognizes that we do not understand how to design such complex information-decision-action systems. Instead, the conditions are established to *evolve* such a system by placing the humans in a harsh environment, obliging them to interact with other systems, real or simulated, and giving them time to develop their job "wrinkles". Time is important; group dynamics are far from instantaneous, and the individuals take time to adapt to each other as well as to the situation—which must, therefore be as real as possible. For preference it should *be* real, otherwise there is a risk of adapting very effectively to the wrong thing.

The evolving team may not be productive or economic initially. Introducing technology as required by the team will reduce bottle-necks, may make some individuals redundant, but should enhance the performance of the team. Step 7 is very important—avoid the temptation to integrate. For a start, the system is already integrated through the humans; for a second, the integration process causes delays and overruns, and for a third the resulting technology blocks human communications and adaptability.

This approach of evolving the solution can be extended to evolve several interacting teams simultaneously, so evolving a robust set of teams, all of them open, interacting, responsive and adaptive.

Advantages of the AEA

The advantages of such an evolutionary approach include the following:

- Conceived and evolved by current experts
- User-effort directed at system performance, not at overcoming technology limitations
- *Guaranteed outcome:*
—evolves from a manual system (=working system)
—degree of evolution controllable (=time/cost controlled)
- Self validating design—user-specified, situation-evolved
- Emergent-property directed—effective, interoperable, flexible, adaptable, damage tolerant (non-nodal)
- Inherent team training
- Avoids "integrate/automate" trap which:
—increases maintenance
—increases cost
—reduces adaptability
—causes near-term obsolescence

CONCLUSION

Conclusions may be summarized as follows:

- Present approach—short-lived, expensive, rigid systems
- Learn from Nature—adapt from generic baseline
- Conceive "higher order" , adaptive systems
- Use genetic methods—evolve surviving systems
- Surviving systems always self-reward
- Generic systems need generic decision-takers, too
- Generic building blocks for adaptive systems offer greater:
  - Efficiency
  - Effectiveness
  - Economy
  - Life/survival

- The Accelerated Evolution Approach offers a guaranteed way to develop complex socio-technical systems, without needing to fully understand the incomprehensibly-complex human interactions inherent in such systems

Glossary of Terms

Closed. Unable to interchange with any other system.

Complementary system. A system with inflows and outflows corresponding to the outflows and inflows of an SOI, respectively.

Contained. A system within a system.

Container/containing. A system containing systems within itself.

Emergent property. A property of a system as a whole which cannot be completely attributed to any particular part of that system.

Entropy. The degree of disorder in a system or set of systems.

Environment. That which mediates the interchange between systems. Total environment is the sum of all such mediations.

Function. A system activity or set of activities which cannot be wholly undertaken by any one part of the system.

Hard. Clearly defined or definable and with evident purpose.

Hierarchy. The levels of organization epitomized by contained and containing systems. Hierarchy is perceived through emergence; interacting systems which display emergent properties *as a set* are contained.

Homeostasis. Maintenance of the status quo. The provision of an environment within a system suitable for the function of its contained systems. The ability of a system to maintain a stable internal environment although the external environment may change.

Method. A set of techniques linked through a process to achieve some purpose.

Mundane. Of an emergent property, that it may be accrued by progressive summation e.g. all-up weight is an emergent property, but its origin is evident, hence mundane.

Open. Interchanging or free to interchange with other systems.

Parent. Containing system

Prime Directive. Ultimate statement of purpose.

Process. A set of sequenced activities to achieve some purpose

Semantic Analysis. Detailed expansion of the Prime Directive to elucidate full meaning

Sibling. System interacting with an SOI within a container

SIF. System in Focus. (syn. SOI)

Soft. Complex, poorly defined, and without clear singular purpose.

SOI. System-of-Interest. The system currently under scrutiny.

Synergy. Co-operation between system parts. Control and co-ordination within a system to produce some external effect.

System. A collection of interrelated entities such that both the collection and the interrelationships together reduce local entropy.

Viability. A system state compatible with continued existence in changing environment.

Aim, Objectives and Activities of Systems Engineering
—Guide to Proper Practice

There is one overriding aim of systems engineering :

To establish and deliver an application system with the emergent properties and through life support facilities required by the customer and satisfying the end-user needs.

The following objectives together satisfy the aim :

A Create, in a structured, ordered manner, an application system with the emergent properties required by the customer

B Create and maintain an engineering system to enable the creation and provision of life cycle support for the application system

C Create and maintain harmony and balance between the developing sub-systems of both the application system and the engineering system such that the intended emergent properties of the application system are realized and their divergence from required values are minimized though life.

The following table presents the guide, with the left hand column providing an activity number, and the right hand column presenting the activities necessary to achieve the objectives. Together, these entries provide the essential systems engineering guide.

Activity number	Systems Engineering Activity
A1	Understand the customer's requirement and the users needs, operational domain, doctrine and environment
A2	• Model the application system in its future environment, including representation of other interacting systems • Adjust the application system model to exhibit the emergent properties required by customers and users

- Adjust the application system model to minimize the effect of undesirable emergent properties

A3 Specify the required emergent properties of the application system

A4 Design an overall application system to meet the requirement

A5
- Model different application system partitioning schemes to identify sub-systems which will benefit sub-system design, development, manufacture, integration, installation, operation, support and eventual replacement
- Select a preferred partitioning scheme that exhibits the requisite emergent properties of the application system

A6 Specify all emergent properties of the preferred application system's sub-systems, interconnections and intra-connections.

B1 Identify and specify the emergent properties of through-life (life cycle) support systems required by the customer/user, including management, logistics, maintenance and training systems

B2 Understand the capabilities, constraints and environment of such support application systems

B3 Design/create such systems as application systems

B4
- Identify those features of the future application system which direct or constrain the needs of the engineering system
- Model the engineering system in its future environment, representing other interacting systems
- Adjust the engineering system model to exhibit the emergent properties required by the creating organization and by its project engineers
- Adjust the engineering system model to minimize the effect of undesirable emergent properties

B5 Specify the requisite engineering system emergent properties

B6 Identify:
- The capabilities of the project engineers, their tools, methods and techniques to create the engineering system
- The constraints imposed by the creating organization, including finance, location and resources

B7 Design an overall engineering system within identified capabilities and constraints

B8   • Model different engineering system partitioning schemes to identify sub-systems which will facilitate sub-system design, development, manufacture, integration, installation, operation, support and eventual replacement

• Select a preferred engineering system design partitioning scheme that exhibits the requisite emergent properties

B9   Specify all emergent properties of the preferred engineering system's sub-systems, interconnections and intra-connections.

C1   • Record all features of the developing application and engineering systems, their sub-systems, mutual interactions, configurations, intra-connections and inter-connections

• Establish and maintain standards for interfaces, compatibility, communications and data exchanges between sub-systems of the application system and other systems with which it will interact in its containing system

• Establish and maintain standards for interfaces, compatibility, configurations, communications and data exchanges between sub-systems of the engineering system and other systems with which it will interact in the creating organization

C2   Record decisions, changes to requirement and specifications, and the circumstances, environment, contemporary knowledge and bases in which they were made

C3   Re-partition and re-specify sub-systems to accommodate unavoidable deviations which would otherwise result in unacceptable changes in application system emergent properties

C4   • Monitor divergence between the application system's operating parameters and its design criteria

• Design to minimize such divergence within the constraints of the Containing system

C5   Anticipate the need for replacement application systems or sub-systems

References and Bibliography

Ackoff, R. L. (1981) *Creating the Corporate Future*, John Wiley, New York.

Ackoff, R.L. & Emery, F.E. (1972) *On Purposeful Systems*, Aldine-Atherton, Chicago.

Alford, M. (1985) SREM at the Age of Eight; the Distributed Computing Design System, *Computer*, **18**(4) 36-46.

Angyal, A. (1941), A Logic of Systems, *Foundations for a Science of Personality*, Harvard University Press, pp. 243-61.

Arthur, Brian W. (1990) Positive Feedbacks in the Economy, *Scientific American*, **262**(2).

Ashby, W. R. (1956) *Introduction to Cybernetics*, Ch. 11, pp. 202-18, John Wiley, London.

Bak, P. & Chen, K, (1991) Self-Organized Criticality, *Scientific American*, **264**(1).

Beer, S. (1984) The Viable System Model: its provenance, development, methodology and pathology, *Journal of the Operational Research Society*, **35**, 7-26.

Beer, S. (1985) *Diagnosing the System for Organizations*, Oxford University Press.

Bird, D. F. (1987) International Standards in Military Communication, *Advances in Command, Control & Communications Systems*. Peter Peregrinus Ltd, London.

Boulding, K. E. (1956) General Systems Theory: the Skeleton of Science, *Management Science*, 197-208.

Boulding, K. E. (1982) Review of Systems Thinking, Systems Practice, *Journal of Applied Systems Analysis*, **9.**

Briggs, I. M. (1990) *Introduction to Type*, Consulting Psychologists Press , Palo Alto, CA.

Broglie, L. de (Ed) (1951) La cybernétique, théorie du signal et de l'information, *Editions de la Revue, d'Optique*, Paris.

Bronowski, J. (1973) *The Ascent of Man*, BBC Publications, London,

Burrell, G. (1983) Systems Thinking, Systems Practice: A Review, *Journal of Applied Systems Analysis*, **10**, 121-126.

Checkland, P. B. (1971) A Systems Map of the Universe, *Journal of Systems Engineering*, **1**(2).

Checkland, P. B. (1972) Towards a Systems-Based Method for Real World Problem Solving, *Systems Behaviour*, Harper and Row.

Checkland, P. B. (1981) *Systems Thinking, Systems Practice*, John Wiley, Chichester.

Churchman, C. W. (1968) *The Systems Approach*, Dell Publishing Co.

Churchman, C. W., Ackoff, R., & Arnoff, E. (1967) *Introduction to Operations Research*, John Wiley and Sons Inc, New York.

Cohen, M. S. (1988) When the Worst Case is Best: Mental Models, Uncertainty and Decision Aids, *Science of Command and Control*, AFCEA International Press, Washington, DC.

Coyle, R. G., (1977) *Management System Dynamics*, John Wiley, Chichester.

Dawkins, R. (1986) *The Blind Watchmaker*, Longmans, London.

Delbecq, A L, et al, (1975) *Group Techniques for Program Planning*, Scott, Foresman & Company, Glenview, IL.

DeMarco, T. (1978) *Structured Analysis and System Specification*, Yourdon.

Duncan, D.A. & Rouvray, D. H. (1989) Microclusters, *Scientific American*, **261**(6).

Emery, F. E. & Trist, E.L. (1960) Socio-technical systems, *Management Science Models and Techniques* **2** , 83-97.

Emery, F. E. & Trist, E.L. (1965) The Causal Texture of Organizational Environments, *Human Relations*, **18**, 21-32.

Forrester, J. W. (1961) *Industrial Dynamics*, MIT Press, Cambridge MA.

Forrester, J. W. (1972) Understanding the Counter-intuitive Behaviour of Systems, *Systems Behaviour*, Paul Chapman Publishing.

French, W. L. & Bell, C. H. Jnr. (1990) *Organization Development*, Prentice-Hall International.

Gane, C. & Sarson, T. (1979) *Structured Systems Analysis: Tools and Techniques*, Prentice Hall, Englewood Cliffs, N.J.

Gilbaud, G. T. (1959) *What is Cybernetics?*, Willaim Heineman Ltd., London.

Hall, A. D. (1962) *A Methodology for Systems Engineering*, Princeton N. J., Van Norstrand.

Hall, A. D. (1989) *Metasystems Methodology*, Pergamon Press, Oxford.

Hitch, C. (1955) *An Appreciation of Systems Analysis*, The RAND Corporation, 699; 8-18; 55; 1-25.

Hitchins, D. K. (1986) Managing Systems Creation, *IEE Proceedings* Pt. A, **133**(6) , London.

Jackson, M.A. (1975) *Principles of Program Design*, Academic Press.

Janes, F. R. (1988) Interpretive Structural Modelling: a Methodology for Structuring Complex Issues, *Trans. Inst Measurement and Control*, **10**,(3), London.

Jenkins, G. M. (1972) The Systems Approach, *Systems Behaviour*, Open University Press, Milton Keynes.

Jones J. & Wilson W. (1987) *An Incomplete Education*, Unwin Hyman Ltd, London.

Jordan, N. (1960) *Some Thinking about "System"*, The RAND Corporation, 1960, pp. 2166:1—31.

Jordan N. (1968) *Themes in Speculative Psychology*, Tavistock, London.

Kast, F. E. & Rosenzweig, J. E. (1972) The Modern View: a Systems Approach, *Systems Behaviour*, pp. 44-58 Open University Press, Milton Keynes.

Klein, Gary A. (1989) Recognition-Primed Decisions, *Advances in Man-Machine Research*, **5**, JAI Press.

Koehler, W. (1970,) *Gestalt Psychology*, Liveright.

Koehler, W. (1938) *The Place of Values in the World of Fact*, Liveright.

Kremyanskiy, V. I. (1960) Certain Peculiarities of Organisms as a "System" from the point of view of Physics, Cybernetics and Biology, *General Systems*, **5**, 221-230, Society for General Systems Research.

Kuhn T. S. (1962) *The Structure of Scientific Revolution*, University of Chicago Press.

Lammers, G. H. (1987) C^3 Effectiveness Studies, *Advances in Command, Control and Communications Systems* Peter Peregrinus Ltd ., London.

Lano, R. J. A. (1979) *Techniques for Software and Systems Design*, TRW series on Software Technology, Volume 3, North Holland Publishing Co.,

Lano, R. J. A. (1980) "Operational Concept Formulation", TRW series on Software Technology, unnumbered, North Holland Publishing Co.

Lewin, K. (1949) Frontiers in Group Dynamics: Concept, Method, and Reality in Social Science; Social Equilibria and Change, *Human Relations*, **1**, (1) 5-41.

Lotka, A.J. (1922) Contribution to the Energetics of Evolution, *Proc. Natl. Acad. Sci.*, **8**, 147-155.

Macgill, S. M. (1983,) Cluster Analysis and Q-Analysis, *Int J. Man-Machine Studies*, **20**, 595-604.

Majaro, S. (1988) *The Creative Gap—Managing Ideas for Money*, Longman, London.

MAP, Version 2.1 (1985) General Motors Technical Center, Manufacturing Building, 30300 Mound Rd., Warren, Mi 48090-9040, USA.

Maruyama, M. (1968) Mutual Causality in General Systems, *Positive Feedback*, John H Milsum (Ed), Pergammon Press, Oxford.

Mayk, I. & Rubin, I. (1988) Paradigms for Understanding C3, Anyone?, *Science of Command and Control*, AFCEA International Press, Washington, DC.

Moore, C. M. (1987) *Group Techniques for Idea Building*, Sage Publications, London.

Odum, Howard, T. (1971) *Environment, Power and Society*, Wiley-Interscience, New York.

Operational Policing Review (1990) Joint Consultative Committee, Surbiton, Surrey, KT6 6LP, London.

Popper, K. (1968) *The Logic of Scientific Discovery*, Hutchinson, London.

Popper, K. (1972) *Conjectures and Refutations: the Growth of Scientific Knowledge*, Routledge and Kegan Paul, London.

Richardson, L. F. (1960) *The Statistics of Deadly Quarrels*, Boxwood Press, Pittsburgh, PA.

Richmond B. , Peterson S. & Boyle D. (1990) *STELLA® II User's Guide*, High Performance Systems, Hanover, NH.

Roberts, N. (1983) *Introduction to Computer Simulation, a Systems Dynamics Approach*, Addison-Wesley, ISBN 0-201-06414-6.

Rock, Irvin & Palmer, S. (1990) The Legacy of Gestalt Psychology, *Scientific American*, **263**, (6).

Romme, W. H. & Despain, D. G. (1989) The Yellowstone Fires, *Scientific American*, **261**, (5).

Ross, D. T., 1977, Structured Analysis (SA): A Language for Communicating Ideas, *IEEE Transactions on Software Engineering*, SE—**3**, (1), 16-34.

Ross, D. T., & Schoman, K.E., Jr (1977) Structured Analysis for Requirements Definition, *IEEE Transactions on Software Engineering*, SE-**3**, (1), 6-15.

Rubenstein, E. (1989) Stages of Evolution and their Messengers, *Scientific American*, **260** (6).

Sachs, W.M. (1976) Toward Formal Foundations of Teleological Systems Science, *General Systems*, **xxi** , 145-54.

Simon, H.A. (1955) A Behavioural Model of Rational Choice, *Journal of Economics*, **69**, 99-118.

Szego, G. C. & Kemp, C. (1973) Energy Forests and Fuel Plantations, *Chemtech*, pp 275-285.

Tajfel H. & Fraser C. (Ed) (1978) *Introduction to Social Psychology: An Analysis of Individual Reaction and Response*, Penguin Books, Harmonsworth, U.K.

Vickers, G. (1968,) *Value Systems and Social Process*, Tavistock, London.

Vickers, G. (1983) *Some Implications of Systems Thinking"*, *Systems Behaviour*, Paul Chapman Publishing.

Von Bertalanffy, L. (1950) The Theory of Open Systems in Physics and Biology, *Science*, **III**, 23-9.

Warfield, J. N. (1973) Intent Structures, *IEEE Transactions Systems Man and Cybernetics*, SMC **3**(2), 133-140.

Warfield J. N. (1989) *Societal Systems*, Intersystems Publications, Salinas, CA.

Weinberg, C. J. & Williams, R. H. (1990) Energy from the Sun, *Scientific American*, **263**, (3).

Wells, H.G. (1922) *A Short History of the World*, Penguin Books, Harmondsworth, UK.

Wilson, B. (1984) *Systems: Concepts, methodologies and applications*, John Wiley, Chichester.

Wohl, J. G. (1981) Force Management Decision Requirements for Air Force Tactical Command and Control, *IEEE Trans.*, SMC-**11**(9), 618-39.

INDEX